French Colonialism

France had the second largest empire in the world after Britain, but one with very different origins and purposes. Over more than four centuries, the French empire explained itself in many different ways through many different colonial regimes. Beginning in the early modern period, a vast mercantile empire based on furs and fish in North America and on sugar cultivated by the enslaved in the Caribbean rose and fell. At intervals thereafter, the French seemed to have an empire simply as an attribute of a Great Power, generally in competition with Britain. Relatively few French people ever moved to the empire, even to the settler colony of Algeria. Under the Third Republic, the French construed a "civilizing mission," melding selectively applied principles of democracy and colonial capitalism. Two world wars and two anticolonial wars broke French imperial power as it had previously existed, yet numberless traces of the French empire lived on, both in the former colonies and in today's French Republic. This narrative history recounts the unique course of the French empire, exploring how it made sense to the people who ruled it, lived under it, and fought against it.

Leonard V. Smith is the Frederick B. Artz Professor of History at Oberlin College, Ohio. He has written four previous books, most recently *Sovereignty at the Paris Peace Conference of 1919* (2018).

New Approaches to European History

New Approaches to European History is an important textbook series, which provides concise but authoritative surveys of major themes and problems in European history since the Renaissance. Written at a level and length accessible to advanced school students and undergraduates, each book in the series addresses topics or themes that students of European history encounter daily: the series embraces both some of the more 'traditional' subjects of study and those cultural and social issues to which increasing numbers of school and college courses are devoted. A particular effort is made to consider the wider international implications of the subject under scrutiny.

To aid the student reader, scholarly apparatus and annotation is light, but each work has full supplementary bibliographies and notes for further reading: where appropriate, chronologies, maps, diagrams, and other illustrative material are also provided.

For a complete list of titles published in the series, please see:
www.cambridge.org/newapproaches

French Colonialism

From the Ancien Régime to the Present

Leonard V. Smith

Oberlin College

CAMBRIDGE
UNIVERSITY PRESS

Shaftesbury Road, Cambridge CB2 8EA, United Kingdom

One Liberty Plaza, 20th Floor, New York, NY 10006, USA

477 Williamstown Road, Port Melbourne, VIC 3207, Australia

314–321, 3rd Floor, Plot 3, Splendor Forum, Jasola District Centre, New Delhi – 110025, India

103 Penang Road, #05–06/07, Visioncrest Commercial, Singapore 238467

Cambridge University Press is part of Cambridge University Press & Assessment, a department of the University of Cambridge.

We share the University's mission to contribute to society through the pursuit of education, learning and research at the highest international levels of excellence.

www.cambridge.org
Information on this title: www.cambridge.org/9781108836685

DOI: 10.1017/9781108874489

© Leonard V. Smith 2023

This publication is in copyright. Subject to statutory exception and to the provisions of relevant collective licensing agreements, no reproduction of any part may take place without the written permission of Cambridge University Press & Assessment.

First published 2023

A catalogue record for this publication is available from the British Library.

Library of Congress Cataloging-in-Publication Data
Names: Smith, Leonard V., 1957– author.
Title: French colonialism : from the ancien régime to the present / Leonard V. Smith, Oberlin College.
Description: New York : Cambridge University Press, 2023. | Series: New approaches to European history. | Includes bibliographical references and index.
Identifiers: LCCN 2022062072 | ISBN 9781108836685 (hardback) | ISBN 9781108874489 (ebook)
Subjects: LCSH: France – Colonies – History. | Imperialism – France – History. | France – Social life and customs – History. | France – Politics and government – History.
Classification: LCC JV1811 .S58 2023 | DDC 325.344–dc23/eng/20230309
LC record available at https://lccn.loc.gov/2022062072

ISBN 978-1-108-83668-5 Hardback
ISBN 978-1-108-79915-7 Paperback

Cambridge University Press & Assessment has no responsibility for the persistence or accuracy of URLs for external or third-party internet websites referred to in this publication and does not guarantee that any content on such websites is, or will remain, accurate or appropriate.

To the Students of History 282

Contents

Illustrations

Maps

Preface and Acknowledgments

In what nostalgia might describe as the simpler world in which I received my excellent graduate education in the 1980s, "French history" meant the history of European France – full stop. To be sure, doctoral students in my day understood that France at one time had possessed a vast overseas empire, and even that bits and pieces of that empire, oddly enough, remained French today. We certainly understood that a war to retain one colonial domain, Algeria, had brought down the French Fourth Republic in 1958. But many young Ph.Ds. specializing in French history back then finished their degrees with an uncertain knowledge of the basic geography of the French empire. Caribbean history, African history, Southeast Asian history, South Pacific history, and Middle Eastern history were specialized vectors of area studies. The history of the "French empire" was mostly a region-based history of the pre-independence of former French colonies.

One salutary effect of the decline of national history in the study of Europe has been a renewed interest in colonialism, as a crucial if often brutal point of intersection between European states and the world. Historians have long found themselves tempted to write the history of empires as extensions of those states, generally of their baser instincts. Given how many regimes ruled France from the Ancien Régime to the present, with accompanying shifts in colonial policy, some explanation here of the history of the metropole is inevitable. Gary Wilder's term "imperial nation-state" reminds us that empires and states construct each other.[1] But the term does not tell us everything we need to know about the subject of this book. France, like the other European imperial powers, was an empire before it was a nation-state – if we take the latter term to indicate unitary governance across a demarcated geographic space.

---

[1] Gary Wilder, *The French Imperial Nation-State: Negritude and Colonial Humanism between the Two World Wars* (Chicago: University of Chicago Press, 2005).

What follows is not French national history with the empire attached. It is the history of a political configuration not reducible to the metropole that organized power and violence on a world stage across a vast expanse of time. J. P. Daughton once told me he considered writing a history of the French empire to be like writing the history of herding cats, because it operated in so many different registers in so many times and places. Fortunately, I am a cat person, and embraced the task here of putting together a narrative history of French colonial rule. But I do not claim to treat all colonial domains equally or believe that doing so would make for a better book.

I wrote this book with a particular pedagogical purpose. It has a decidedly "political" focus, in that it emphasizes practices and institutions of imperial rule. Resistance to that rule, of course, shaped those practices. But some readers may be struck by the focus on "high politics" – at the expense of social, gender, or cultural history, or for that matter the history of race. No one can understand imperial power without using race and gender as analytical categories. But by design, cultural movements I spend a good bit of time on in the classroom, such as Orientalism and Négritude, receive only passing mention here. This book is short enough, and I hope lively enough, that instructors can use it as a foundational narrative that students can read on their own. Instructors can thus spend precious class time on those aspects of French colonialism most likely to encourage interaction and discussion.

Further, this book emphasizes explanation over either incrimination or defense of the French imperial enterprise. To explain, the saying goes, is not to justify. Simply put, I try here to explain how the French empire made sense in the heads of those who ruled it, lived under it, and fought against it. The brutality of colonial rule is certainly explored here, not so much from a position of moral outrage (however justified) but as a register of political discourse. The moral and ethical issues at stake are glaring enough that students and other readers ought to be able to engage them on their own.

This book owes a great deal to scholars who have done so much to frame the issues examined here. In keeping with the practices of the New Approaches to European History Series, I have kept footnotes to a minimum. But the preface is a good place to acknowledge the contributions of pioneers such as Alice Conklin, who taught me to take republican ideology seriously in the empire. The late Tyler Stovall taught me how to think about French universalism in the empire more broadly. Todd Sheppard showed me how the empire had a "French" history at all, whatever the ethical or moral lessons of that history. Eric Jennings taught me how to look for continuities across seemingly endless varieties of French colonial rule. Frederick Cooper helped me understand the arcane and fascinating legalities of decolonization, particularly in West Africa. Patricia Lorcin showed her fellow graduate students at Columbia in the 1980s just how wrong we were for wondering if French race discourse in Algeria was a somewhat obscure dissertation topic. For more than three decades, Douglas Porch has shown me how much the history of war and warfare matters. Matthew Connelly helped me understand how discursive power in the War of Algerian Independence could constitute real power. This book could not have been written without the work of all these fine historians. Responsibility for any shortcomings in interpreting that work, of course, lies with me.

The closeness and remoteness of French and English, inevitably, leads to choices here that might seem arbitrary. Most of the time, I adopt common English usage, such as Algiers rather than Alger, Pondicherry rather than Pondichéry or today's Puducherry, or New Caledonia rather than Nouvelle Calédonie. But Guyane just seemed to make more sense than French Guiana. Ivorians seem to prefer Côte d'Ivoire to Ivory Coast. I drop diacritical marks with persons known throughout the Anglophone world such as Napoleon, but preserve them for other important figures, such as Aimé Césaire or Ahmed Sékou Touré. Vietnamese diacritical marks are so complex that I have omitted them altogether, to keep the text as simple as possible. I use colonial names in their colonial contexts – Tourane rather than Da Nang and Bône rather than Annaba. I tend not to translate French expressions that seem self-evident, such as "République une et indivisible" or "Arabophile." But I provide the French original in footnotes when any translation seems particularly ambiguous. Colonial language trades in ambiguity, to say the least. This book uses the terms "colonialism" and "imperialism" interchangeably.

In life and scholarship, I have always looked for silver linings in some very menacing clouds. One such silver lining narrowly preceded the cloud – a trip to the Mekong and Red River deltas and the Central Highlands of Vietnam in January 2020, supported by the Luce Initiative in Asian Studies and the Environment at Oberlin College. In significant ways, the coronavirus pandemic that followed shortly thereafter made this book possible. Much of it was written during the spring semester of 2021, when Oberlin turned its academic calendar inside out to "de-densify" the campus, a pandemic neologism if ever there was one. A near lockdown in a northeast Ohio winter, it turns out, can focus the mind wonderfully.

Through it all, I enjoyed the invaluable help of the staff at the Mary Church Terrell Library at Oberlin. I also enjoyed the companionship in isolation of my beloved wife, Ann Sherif. Because of her, I was never lonely. Given the vastness of this subject, I had innumerable questions generously answered by colleagues. Zeinab Abul-Magd helped me distinguish varieties of Arabic, Danielle Terrazas Williams varieties of Spanish, Renee Romano the politics of historical justice, Stéphane Audoin-Rouzeau some of the complexities of Rwanda, Rishad Choudhury the proper nomenclature for the Indian subcontinent, Alice Conklin the terminology of legal and social status. Eric Jennings's breadth of knowledge and his support as a colleague provided critical help at several junctures. Kate Blackmer worked her magic, once again, for the maps. Her cartography was supported by the research fund for the Frederick B. Artz chair, probably the greatest honor of my academic career.

At Cambridge University Press, Michael Watson encouraged me to submit this project to the New Approaches to European History series. Liz Friend-Smith has provided so much help, and so much patience, in my bringing it to completion. Laura Simmons and Santhamurthy Ramamoorthy deserve my heartfelt thanks for seeing this book through production. I could complete my role in production under splendid conditions, as a Fernand Braudel Senior Fellow at the European University Institute in Florence in the spring of 2023.

This book had its origin in the Oberlin classroom, where I began teaching an upper-level colloquium on French imperialism in 2003. A Curriculum Development Fellowship in 2017 helped me develop History 282, the lecture course on which I based this book. I will never be able to thank enough all the students so eager to learn the history of French colonialism alongside me. After more than three decades teaching them, I can still be astonished by the commitment, intelligence, and good nature of Oberlin students. They remain what they were when I first got to know them as an Oberlin student myself in the late 1970s – some of the most interesting people I have ever met.

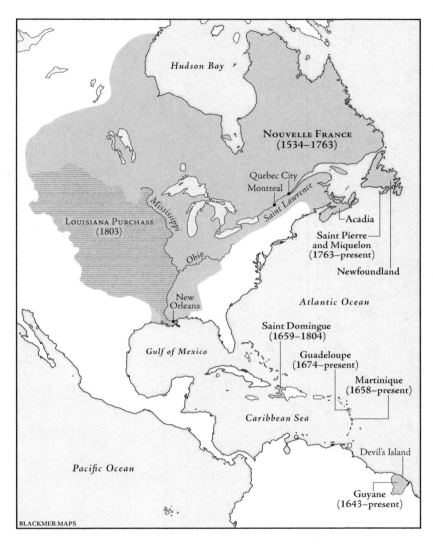

Map 1 The French Empire in the New World (Mercator projection)

Labels visible on the map:

Hudson Bay

NOUVELLE FRANCE
(1534–1763)

Quebec City
Montreal

Saint Lawrence

Acadia

Saint Pierre
and Miquelon
(1763–present)

Newfoundland

LOUISIANA PURCHASE
(1803)

Mississippi

Ohio

New
Orleans

Atlantic Ocean

Saint Domingue
(1659–1804)

Guadeloupe
(1674–present)

Martinique
(1658–present)

Gulf of Mexico

Caribbean Sea

Devil's Island

Pacific Ocean

Guyane
(1643–present)

BLACKMER MAPS

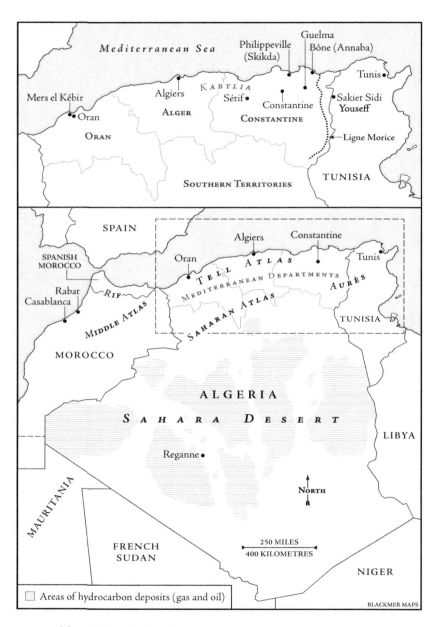

Map 2 French Algeria, 1830–1962

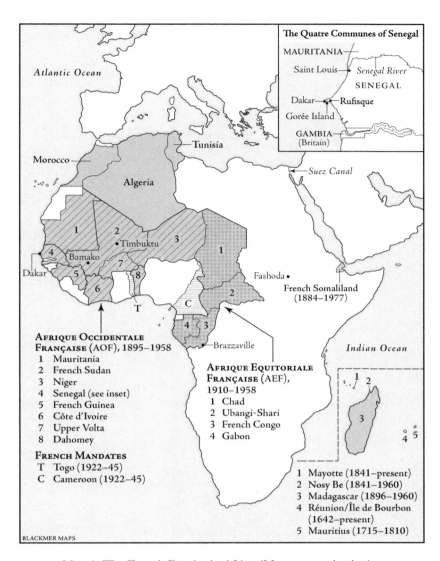

The Quatre Communes of Senegal

MAURITANIA

Saint Louis — Senegal River

SENEGAL

Dakar — Rufisque

Gorée Island

GAMBIA
(Britain)

Atlantic Ocean

Morocco

Tunisia

Suez Canal

Algeria

1   2   3   1

Timbuktu

Bamako

4   7   8   2

Dakar   5

6   T   C   Fashoda

French Somaliland
(1884–1977)

4   3

Brazzaville   Indian Ocean

AFRIQUE OCCIDENTALE
FRANÇAISE (AOF), 1895–1958
1   Mauritania
2   French Sudan
3   Niger
4   Senegal (see inset)
5   French Guinea
6   Côte d'Ivoire
7   Upper Volta
8   Dahomey

FRENCH MANDATES
T   Togo (1922–45)
C   Cameroon (1922–45)

AFRIQUE EQUITORIALE
FRANÇAISE (AEF),
1910–1958
1   Chad
2   Ubangi-Shari
3   French Congo
4   Gabon

1   2

3

4   5

1   Mayotte (1841–present)
2   Nosy Be (1841–1960)
3   Madagascar (1896–1960)
4   Réunion/Île de Bourbon
    (1642–present)
5   Mauritius (1715–1810)

BLACKMER MAPS

Map 3 The French Empire in Africa (Mercator projection)

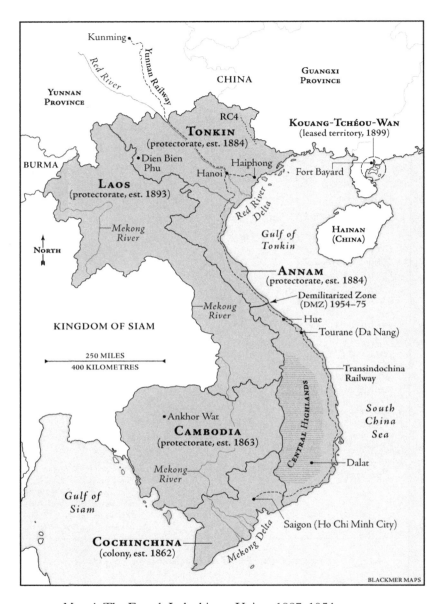

Kunming

Red River

Yunnan Railway

CHINA

GUANGXI
PROVINCE

YUNNAN
PROVINCE

RC4

TONKIN
(protectorate, est. 1884)

KOUANG-TCHÉOU-WAN
(leased territory, 1899)

•Dien Bien
Phu

BURMA

Haiphong
Hanoi•

Fort Bayard

LAOS
(protectorate, est. 1893)

Red River Delta

Mekong
River

Gulf of
Tonkin

HAINAN
(CHINA)

NORTH

ANNAM
(protectorate, est. 1884)

Demilitarized Zone
(DMZ) 1954–75

KINGDOM OF SIAM

Mekong
River

Hue
Tourane (Da Nang)

250 MILES
400 KILOMETRES

Transindochina
Railway

CENTRAL HIGHLANDS

South
China
Sea

•Ankhor Wat

CAMBODIA
(protectorate, est. 1863)

Dalat

Mekong
River

Gulf of
Siam

Saigon (Ho Chi Minh City)

COCHINCHINA
(colony, est. 1862)

Mekong Delta

BLACKMER MAPS

Map 4 The French Indochinese Union, 1887–1954

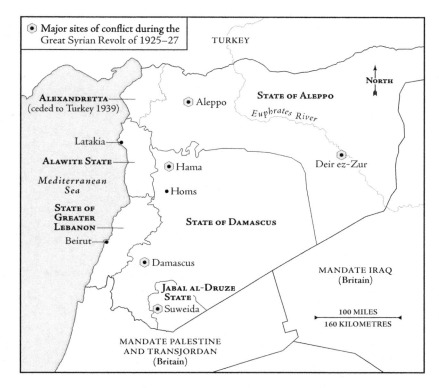

Map 5 French Mandate Syria and Lebanon, 1923–41

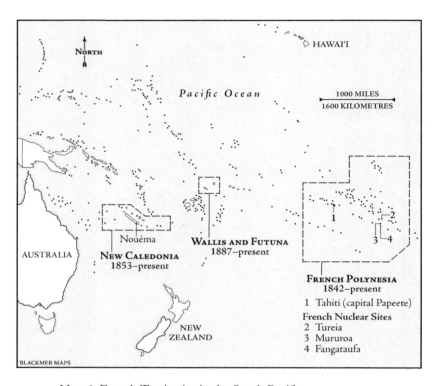

Map 6 French Territories in the South Pacific

Introduction
Why Did France Have an Empire?

The French empire left no more durable a trace than Jean de Brunhoff's 1931 children's classic, *Histoire de Babar, le petit éléphant*. The story originated with the author's wife Cécile, as a bedtime story for their ill son. Cécile concluded that her role in the book was minor enough to exclude herself as co-author.[1] Jean, hitherto a painter and book illustrator, wrote six sequels, his son Laurent twenty-three, the last in 2017. Translations and endless merchandizing made the orphaned elephant an immensely valuable, world-wide phenomenon. Like many children's stories, *Babar* has carried grown-up morals, no doubt several of them. We can read the original story here as a fable of historically specific French imperial objectives and aspirations, and Babar as a generic and highly idealized imperial subject.

The story opens with the birth of Babar in a peaceful forest where the animals either do not consider one another prey or at least eat one another off stage. The baby elephant shows his exceptional abilities early, in his use of a tool, a shell, to play in the sand. An evil hunter disrupts the idyll by murdering Babar's beloved mother. The panicked Babar runs away until he reaches a city. The wonders of human civilization displace his shock and mourning for a time. Babar encounters an inexplicably understanding and generous elderly woman, who instantly understands that he needs clothes to ease his transition to his new surroundings. The now green-suited Babar assimilates to life in the city, up to a point. He eats and exercises with the elderly woman and proves himself a fine student of arithmetic. He ventures about in an automobile purchased for him by his patron. Yet Babar remains a partly assimilated outsider. He charms his patron's dinner guests as an exotic visitor from another world. Most importantly, the more Babar adopts the habits of the city, the more he

---

[1] In Cécile's version, Babar steals money, goes on a shopping spree in the city, and only later is persuaded to return to the forest by his cousins, who understand their proper place in the natural order. See the obituary, *New York Times* (2003). "Cécile de Brunhoff, 99, Creator of Babar," April 8.

realizes his own separateness. He misses the camaraderie of his fellow elephants, and now weeps at the memory of his mother.

A visit to the city by two cousins and their mothers leads Babar to realize his true self. He decides to return to his homeland by automobile, a clothed and forever changed elephant. He regrets leaving the generous elderly woman, the agent of his transformation. During Babar's absence, and fortuitously for him, the sitting king of the forest dies from eating a bad mushroom. The elders decide that the resplendent Babar is the natural choice as successor. Babar's engagement to his cousin Celeste guarantees the stability of the new royal line. The couple marries in a forest-wide celebration. A great many adventures await.

As a fable of French imperial aspirations, *Babar* recounts the evolution of an exceptional colonial subject. He has a natural aptitude for learning above his peers, most of whom will never dig with shells or wear smart green suits. He knows instinctively how to make the most of his encounter with the city. His devotion to his patron is sincere, and he will never forget her generosity. Yet he remains an elephant, with or without the green suit. He knows his destiny lies in extending the differentiated blessings of his own advancement to all the animals in the forest. His kingdom there will be shaped by the superior qualities of its new king. At least through its new monarch, some sort of unspoken contract appears to exist between the kingdom and the city, still the wellspring of civilization. Yet the animal kingdom will never become the city. We assume continued loyalty to the elderly lady and the city she exemplifies. But the exact terms of that loyalty await definition over time. In the real world of the French empire, all this would become known as a colonial policy of association. Imperial domains, the theory went, would square the circle of partly adopting Frenchness alongside French rule, while retaining and developing their own identities.

Association was but one of several conceptual frameworks through which the French made sense of having an empire between the Ancien Régime and the present.[2] This book details the history of those frameworks. As such, it has a "political" focus, defined in a particular sense. It focuses on structures of rule and the operation of those structures. Empires are not nation states, and do not function as such. Nor are they one thing, or even the same thing over time. Empires mean very different things in different times and places. No two empires are alike, and no two empires have the same history. They do not always have clear beginnings, and assuredly do not have clear ends. Important

---

[2] Ancien Régime (Old Regime), used here as a proper noun, refers to early modern France before the Revolution that began in 1789.

vestiges of empire remain today in the French Republic and in many of its former domains.

Empire is not difficult to define in the terminology of political science – asymmetrical contracting that preserves politically significant difference. Some sort of agreement, almost always coercive in nature, joins more powerful and less powerful political entities. An empire has a center, a political and administrative core. The center of the French empire became known as the metropole, meaning the somewhat hexagonally shaped European France. Throughout this book, "metropole" and the "Hexagon," refer to the same thing – European France.[3] The center rules both directly and through intermediaries, colonial officials and local elites. Imperial contracting is subject to constant renegotiation, though the parties remain unequal.

Their many permutations and vicissitudes notwithstanding, empires preserve hierarchies resulting from difference, usually though not necessarily grounded in what today we understand as race. To be sure, hybrid reproductive relationships between colonizer and colonized constantly complicated distinctions based on race. Mixed-race persons would support and contest French imperial rule throughout its history. Structural difference distinguishes empires from expanding nation states. For example, "British India" was by definition "British." But even the most fervent imperialist did not imagine that it would one day become part of the United Kingdom, or even the equal of the United Kingdom within the British Empire. Likewise, "Algérie française" (French Algeria) came to pose an intractable problem for republican France, because the French tried to rule the lands of Algeria as national territory and indigenous Algerians as colonial subjects. This meant treating the minority white and majority Muslim populations in separate and profoundly unequal ways. The tangles of trying to reconcile republicanism and empire constitute a central theme of this book.

In their sweeping survey of the global history of empire, Jane Burbank and Frederick Cooper have reminded us that empire is in fact a more ancient and durable political configuration than the nation-state, which was largely a product of the nineteenth century. They have defined empires as "large political units, expansionist or with a memory of power extended over space, polities that maintain distinction and hierarchies as they incorporate new people."[4] Such a definition points to the dynamic,

---

[3] It bears noting here that "European France" itself was not a static entity. Corsica became definitively French only in 1768, the city of Nice only in 1860. Alsace and Lorraine changed hands at least six times over the period covered by this book.

[4] Jane Burbank and Frederick Cooper, *Empires in World History: Power and the Politics of Difference* (Princeton: Princeton University Press, 2010), 8.

even inherently unstable nature of empires. They must always produce and reproduce the forms of hierarchical difference on which their very existence depends. Empires are always rising or falling, expanding or contracting. Historians often write of them as though they were people, with all-too-human life cycles. Empires are born, thence to grow in strength and size. At a certain point, they get older, weaken, and eventually die. Historians have also often found it convenient to tell stories of empire as tragedies – their demise foreseeable through their evils, inherent contradictions, or other fatal flaws. While those who look for tragedy in history will seldom fail to find it, this book will pay more attention to the continued transformation in the form and content of the French empire, and its myriad afterlives after its "fall."

Yet all the preceding begs the question – what is an empire for? To some extent this is a "European" as well as a national question, assuredly not unique to the French case. Why did Europeans have such boundless imperial ambitions? No other civilization in history seems to have considered it necessary to conquer and rule so many peoples so distant from the imperial center. Why did the French, like other Europeans, acquire so many diverse domains with so little to do with one another? As we will see, the French empire comprised a patchwork – colonies ruled directly, protectorates (foreign supervision of governance), trading posts, local empires subsumed into a French empire, and much else. Why were so many domains, such as the Sahara Desert, so economically unprofitable? Unlike the British, Spanish, or Chinese empires, the French empire never attracted large numbers of settlers. Even in Algeria, barely half the white settlers originated in the Hexagon, most of the rest coming from elsewhere in Mediterranean Europe.

There is no single set of answers to these questions. C. Warren Hollister explained the medieval Crusades, the first imperial adventure of Christian Europe, as taking place through a combination of "piety, pugnacity, and greed."[5] While certainly intellectually appealing at a certain level and quite possibly true, we can neither prove nor disprove such a deep, emotion-based explanation. Throughout, I claim that economics provides a necessary but insufficient explanation for the French empire throughout its long history. As we will see, economics does much to explain the mercantile empire of the Ancien Régime in North American and the Caribbean. But the economic rationale for empire became increasingly problematic in the nineteenth and twentieth centuries – a point not lost on the many critics of imperial expansion from many places

[5] C. Warren Hollister, *Medieval Europe: A Short History*, 7th ed. (New York: McGraw Hill, 1994), 188.

on the domestic political spectrum. More often than not, an economic rationale followed rather than preceded imperial conquest.

What follows is a history of explanations on the part of the French for having an empire, and the asymmetrical contracting that preceded and followed from those explanations. I present a history of the changing dynamics of the French empire as a political construct. All of the lands and peoples explored here had a "French" history – much as Gaul had a "Roman" history, or, for that matter, as Vichy France had a "German" history. From its first ventures, French imperial power based itself on violence and the threat of violence, typically racialized. What follows never contends otherwise. The French empire became the French empire through complicated dynamics of oppression, resistance, and asymmetrical mutual accommodation. These dynamics existed in numerous registers – affairs of state, labor, the environment, gender, and many others. If colonial rule is emphasized here over resistance to that rule, the reason lies in a necessity to understand the precise object of resistance.

Since the imperial power that made and enforced the contracting of empire was based in the Hexagon, the political vicissitudes of European France from the Ancien Régime to the Fifth Republic matter here. Over the centuries, what the French wanted an empire for roughly tracks changes in the way they were governed. Yet the history of the French empire is not the history of the Hexagon with its empire attached for the sake of inclusivity. This book considers from a political perspective what quite a few years ago Frederick Cooper and Ann L. Stoler called for, treating the metropole and the imperial domains as "a single analytical field."[6] From this point of view, France and the French empire created each other. A full explanation of empire, just why the French wanted one, and why so many of the peoples over whom the French ruled found it so difficult to let go of France, may be a permanently receding horizon. It is nevertheless the purpose of this book to chase that horizon.

[6] Frederick Cooper and Ann L. Stoler, "Introduction: Tensions of Empire: Colonial Control and Visions of Rule," *American Ethnologist*, 16, No. 4 (1989): 609.

1   The Rise and Fall of the Mercantilist Empire

Unfortunately for historians, the Native American and African peoples alongside whom the French built their mercantile empire did not keep extensive written records. At the time, their societies left their marks on history mostly through oral tradition and through traces found much later by archeologists. The French, in contrast, wrote and published profusely throughout the history of their empire. One early French imperialist, a Sieur François Delbée, wrote an account of a slaving expedition to West Africa published in 1671.[1] Much of the account is a travelogue, of places and peoples seen. But Delbée included a detailed record of the African notables with whom he treated. We know only Delbée's version of the story. But even from this perspective, what impresses readers today is not the power of this early imperialist expedition, but its fragility.

In 1669, the semi-private Compagnie des Indes Occidentales (West India Company) sent two ships to the West African kingdom of Ardres (in today's Benin) to establish a base for commence, meaning primarily the trade in enslaved persons. The French sought to enter a well-established market. Commerce along what the Europeans would call the "Slave Coast" began with the Portuguese in the 1550s. Dutch traders began to supplant the Portuguese early in the next century. The French, in turn, sought to supplant the Dutch. Galloping demand in Europe for cane sugar drove French expansion in the Caribbean. French settlers first arrived in Guadeloupe in 1625, and King Louis XIV claimed Martinique in 1658. Most importantly, by mid-century, the French had begun to wrest part of the island of Hispaniola (today Haiti and the Dominican Republic) from the Spanish, to establish what would become their colony of Saint-Domingue. Earlier European incursions had brought along European germs, which resulted in the death of much of the

---

[1] Sieur [François] d'Elbée, *Relation de ce qui s'est passé dans les Isles & Terre-Ferme de l'Amerique, pendant la derniere guerre avec l'Angleterre, & depuis en execution du Traitté de Breda, avec un journal* [spelling and accent marks of original] (Paris: Clozier, 1671). Unless otherwise noted, cited translations throughout are my own.

6

indigenous population. Like the competing Portuguese, Spanish, and English empires, the French empire needed labor accustomed to European disease pools. Europeans found that labor by enslaving Africans.

Scholars of Africa do not altogether agree on just what to call the polity of Ardres (also known at the time as Allada, Adra, Adara, and several other similar names), though the most common term is "kingdom." Like many similar entities, Ardres ruled itself through a dynamic matrix of kinship networks rather than through a bureaucratized state. Toussaint Louverture, later a leader of the French Revolution in Saint-Domingue, descended from one such network, according to his son. Ardres had a tributary relationship to the Oyo Empire, financed primarily through the slave trade. Generally speaking, West African rulers cared less than European rulers about fixed boundaries and more about control over resources, goods and particularly people. West African societies had many gradations of servitude, rather more than Europe. As a rule, persons bound to specific households could not be bought or sold. But those who in one way or another had run afoul of royal or elite power could become chattels, to be sold to foreigners.

Delbée arrived on the African continent in 1670 not as a conqueror, but as a salesman, almost a supplicant. Certainly, he treated the sovereign with the respect he would have paid any European monarch. The king of Ardres maintained an elaborate court etiquette, in which the visitors were first received by retainers and only some days later admitted to the royal presence. Once admitted, Delbée met a skilled and experienced negotiator. They spoke Portuguese, understood by them both. The king clearly wanted to conclude a transaction. But first he complained that while he had been informed that "France was such a great kingdom and filled with rare items," the visitors had brought with them "only things similar to what the Dutch had been bringing for quite a while." Delbée promised better in the future, now that the French understood the royal tastes. The king responded with a detailed shopping list for future offerings, including a French-style sword, fabric, lace, and two pairs of shoes, one of velvet, the other presumably of leather, but scarlet. The sovereign had also established a tax regime for the slave trade, involving the payment of the price of fifty enslaved persons for each ship permitted to dock. In addition, he required that the French "pay" two enslaved persons to his son for the right to take on fresh water for their departure. The king also required that the building to be established for trade with the French not become a French fort.

Delbée, for his part, maintained what today we might code as an anthropologist's interest in the inhabitants of Ardres, including those forced to become his cargo. He was particularly interested in their religious objects (*fétisches*), though posited that only the influence of *marabouts* (Muslim holy men) prevented them from becoming Christians. Delbée provided a detailed account of how the enslaved became such – whether prisoners of war, persons paid as tribute, persons born of the enslaved, debtors, or persons convicted of crimes. He spared himself a moment of compassion for the Africans forced aboard his ship, "taken with melancholy to see their homeland disappear before their eyes, some of whom had already fallen ill with sadness." One wife of the king, referred to as the *princesse*, annoyed that her husband had deprived her of some of the goods brought by the foreigners, took it upon herself to sell eight competing wives into enslavement. Delbée felt "such compassion" for all the female captives on his ship that he separated them from the enslaved men. He recounted with pride that not one woman died during the passage across the Atlantic. He did not report what the crew demanded in exchange.

Nothing distracted Delbée from the task at hand, in this land where commerce consisted of only "men and food" (*hommes et vivres*). Along the way to the Caribbean, his ship stopped at the small French enclave in Cayenne, on the South American coast. There they took on supplies and left off the sick, who they supposed would die before they reached their destination of Martinique. In all, of the 433 enslaved persons who boarded at the port at Offra, some 100 died en route. Delbée's ship took on sugar and tobacco in Martinique and returned to France after a voyage of ten months and twenty days.

Delbée's story, and the untold stories of the captives he carried across the Atlantic, was repeated thousands of times through the early modern period. These stories illustrate, among other things, some of the contours of the French mercantile empire. This version of empire intertwined politics and economics perhaps to a greater degree than any subsequent version. The mercantile empire had a specific economic purpose – the enrichment of the kingdom of France. This empire gave rise to many different kinds of power relationships. The king of Andres and certainly not the French held power on this piece of the African coast in 1670. As we will see, the French crown and its agents wielded little more power in its vast claimed domains in North America.

Later, the mercantile empire in the Caribbean gave rise to a veritable laboratory of imperial domination. There, the plantation system extracted what Marxists call the surplus value of labor to a degree seldom seen before or since. It made fortunes for a handful of French. Yet the mercantile empire was never as imposing as it looked on a map. French domains in North America remained lightly held in most places, to say the least. Even in the Caribbean, where the French empire was strongest, the French Revolution precipitated the largest and most successful revolt of enslaved persons in world history. The defeat of Napoleon and the shifting world economy would reduce the French mercantile empire to a relative triviality. France would enter the nineteenth century a minor imperial power.

1.1   Absolute Monarchy, Mercantilism, and Empire

The French built an empire during the Ancien Régime under the direction of the crown. Underpinning this empire lay an elaborate ideological foundation for monarchy as absolute, personal rule. The king of France (Salic law forbidding sovereign queens since the early Middle Ages) ruled as the anointed of God. The king, indeed, had accountability only to God. Divine law prohibited him from doing anything that would imperil the souls of his subjects. But natural law gave him otherwise absolute power on Earth. "Nature" commonly meant what the monarch wanted it to mean. The king alone gave law to the kingdom, at least in theory. "It is he who makes law for the subject," wrote sixteenth-century theorist Jean Bodin, "abrogates laws already made, and amends absolute law." This aspirational absolutism assumed more concrete forms in the seventeenth and eighteenth centuries. The crown largely co-opted the institutional Catholic Church, religious home to the vast majority of the king's subjects. Bishop Jacques Bénigne Bossuet became something of a house theoretician to the most illustrious of the absolute monarchs, Louis XIV (reigned 1642–1715). The king, Bossuet wrote, "was absolute with respect to constraint, there being no power capable of forcing the sovereign, who in this sense is independent of human authority."

Day in and day out, absolute monarchy sought to create its own reality through performance. Indeed, an enormous part of the sovereign's working day involved court ritual, from the *levée*, an elaborate ceremony around the king getting out of bed attended by up to 100 courtiers, to the time he went to bed, when the *levée* was run in reverse. The crown had managed to turn the ceremonial enactment of the most mundane daily tasks into marks of immense social prestige, such as holding the sleeve of the king as he dressed. The king always had to look the part, with wigs, vests, culottes, and shoes made by some of the most skilled artisans in Europe. Louis XIV built the magnificent palace of Versailles as a theater for performing absolutism. Musicians, artists, actors, writers, all paid constant tribute to the glory of the crown. Royal patronage in the form of decorations and offices fell only upon aristocrats who maintained secondary residences at Versailles, sometimes at ruinous expense to themselves.

The theater of absolutism worked hard to conceal a very different reality, a kingdom profoundly shaped by the ancient Society of Orders and the medieval history of the monarchy itself. The realities of absolutism, in turn, shaped the development of the mercantile empire. Centuries of tradition and law had it that "those who fight," the nobility, did not need to contribute financially to the kingdom because of their military service. "Those who pray," the clergy, likewise contributed spiritually rather than monetarily. This left most of the burden of royal finance on the Third Estate, "those who work," who, politically speaking, comprised adult male Christians. Consequently, the nobility and the clergy controlled immense wealth, and enjoyed a social and political legitimacy that they did not owe to the crown.

Moreover, the writ of the king did not even mean the same thing throughout the kingdom. Over the course of the Middle Ages, the French monarchy expanded its domains slowly, almost like an amoeba, from its original domains in the Paris region, the Île de France. France became an empire well before it became a unitary state. Unlike an amoeba, the monarchy did not completely digest what it absorbed. Separate bodies of law and numerous internal trade barriers persisted throughout the kingdom. No fewer than thirteen domains had preserved their regional assemblies, or *Parlements*. These were both judicial and legislative bodies. The most powerful of them, the Paris *Parlement*, had jurisdiction over only about one-third of the kingdom. *Parlements* registered or approved royal edicts, including those concerning loans and taxation. The king could always overrule a *Parlement* through a *lit de justice*, a simple, binding declaration of the king's capacity as lawgiver. But the *lit de justice* remained a blunt instrument, and kings had to spend carefully the political capital required to use it.

Long-standing customary law had prohibited slavery in the French kingdom proper, as a barbaric practice more suited to Muslims than the realm of the most Christian of kings. Masters in the empire would often bring enslaved persons with them to the Hexagon as domestic servants. While this never amounted to a large number of people, the enslaved proved quite visible because of their physical proximity to power. What was the status of the enslaved once in Europe? A 1719 royal edict required registration of all enslaved persons with the Admiralty. Masters who did not do so were subject to the manumission of their servants by the crown. A 1738 decree sought to tighten the regulation of the enslaved brought to the Hexagon and made appropriated persons the property of the crown rather than free. But neither edict was registered by the *Parlements*, nor did the crown see to their enforcement by the *lit de justice*. The matter remained in a kind of legal limbo until the French Revolution.

The French absolute monarchy, like its counterparts in Spain or Austria, ruled with structural financial weaknesses. It could not tax the wealthiest orders in society, and the emerging state bureaucracy had to compete with powerful regional elites. The needs of early modern monarchy for money scarcely knew limits. Of course, the splendor of the crown cost a fortune. But under the Ancien Régime, war and preparing for war constituted by far the most expensive activities of state. "I have loved war too much," lamented King Louis XIV on his deathbed. Few princes, and none ruling large kingdoms, could rely on the personal property of the sovereign. The kings of France could push the burden of finance on to the Third Estate only up to a point. Barring a rationalization of state power that would not happen until the French Revolution, the only alternative involved finding new sources of revenue. Such were the financial problems to which the mercantile empire sought solutions.

All the Great Power monarchies pursued imperial adventures in the early modern period, for many of the same reasons. Most European rulers considered international politics and economics to be a single, zero-sum game. One monarchy could grow stronger only if its rivals grew weaker. All relied on religion for legitimacy and sent missionaries abroad, along with soldiers and merchants. All considered imperial rivalries as overseas projections of rivalries in Europe. Generations of French monarchs feared Habsburg encirclement, through the complex web of relationships between the Austrian Habsburgs (who ruled parts of the Low Countries until 1795) and the Spanish Habsburgs, who until the early nineteenth century ruled the world's largest maritime empire. Rivals to the French at sea included the Portuguese, the Dutch (from both the Dutch Republic and the Austrian Netherlands), the Spanish, and the English.

Mercantilism was more a set of practices than an actual economic theory. These practices sought to increase state revenue through taxing commodities either unavailable or scarce in Europe. Further, a structural trade surplus would enable the kingdom to accumulate precious specie – gold and silver. Most practitioners of mercantilism considered the world supply of specie to be fixed, so that competition for precious metals, commodities, geopolitical power, and colonies tracked one another closely. Mercantilism sought to turn the crown and state-sponsored merchants into profit centers. Conquered lands theoretically became part of the royal domain, though the crown subcontracted many actual functions of state.

Like other monarchies, the French crown preferred to operate through semi-private ventures, royally granted monopolies encouraged with substantial state investment. The crown would then tax goods exported from the colonies. Much of the private capital came from investors with close connections to the state, such as tax farmers (privatized revenue collectors) and managers of the ever-increasing state debt. For investors, colonial ventures held the prospect of considerable profits at considerable risk.

Some indigenous people could make fortunes from mercantile capitalism, such as a Tamil man named Nayiniyappa in Pondicherry in the early eighteenth century. But then as later, the vicissitudes of local colonial politics could break as well as make such individuals. Nayiniyappa fell out with a former French governor, who allegedly in collaboration with the Jesuits had Nayiniyappa flogged and sent to the prison where he died. However, his son Guruvappa, who unlike his father converted to Catholicism, revived the family fortunes sufficiently by 1740 to acquire a knighthood from the French crown. The turbulence of mercantile capitalism and colonial intrigue was never for the faint of heart.

1.2   Furs and Fish in North America

Mercantilism and geopolitics came to operate at cross-purposes in the French empire in North America. Geopolitics called for expansion on a scale that mercantilism could never really support. During what Europeans would call the Age of Exploration, the French tried to circumvent Spanish and Portuguese domination of most of the Atlantic by finding alternative routes to the supposedly unbounded riches of Asia. In 1524, King Francis I commissioned Italian explorer Giovanni da Verrazzano to explore the North American coast in search of such a route. In royally subsidized voyages in 1534 and 1535–6, Jacques Cartier explored what Europeans would call the Saint Lawrence River, as far as today's Montreal. Cartier returned to France only with a handful of indigenous captives and some furs, along with a clearer sense of geography.

The geopolitical stakes in the Western Hemisphere only grew greater with time as European monarchies vied for influence around the world. Over the course of the sixteenth century, the Spanish crown acquired an immense windfall of silver and gold bullion from Mexico, as well as Central and South America. In North America, the English established permanent colonies in Jamestown, Virginia in 1607, and at Plymouth, Massachusetts, in 1620. The French would find their sphere of influence at about the same time in a vast if somewhat theoretical imperial domain that they would call Nouvelle France, or New France.

Alongside competitors such as Holland and England, France would also seek to secure a path to East Asia by way of the Indian Ocean and the Indian subcontinent. France would acquire islands east of Madagascar such as the Île de Bourbon (today Réunion, claimed in 1642), and there would make a brief and unsuccessful effort to diversify its supply of enslaved persons for the Caribbean. It acquired the Île de France (today Mauritius), when the Dutch abandoned it in 1715. Imperial entrepreneurs such as François Martin, Jean-François Dupliex, and

Charles Joseph Patissier de Busy would establish and govern a variety of trading posts along the coasts of today's India. The wealthiest and best known of these was Pondicherry, established in 1674, followed by colonies in Chandannagar (*c.* 1696), Yanon (1723), Mané (1724), and Karikal (1739). As in North America, the French crown made considerable claims to the hinterlands of these trading posts.

In Nouvelle France, furs and fish constituted the main commodities in the mercantilist economy. Fishing along the coast of Newfoundland and Acadia (part of today's Nova Scotia) did not require permanent European settlement. Hardy seamen from Normandy, Brittany, and the Basque country had operated there since at least the sixteenth century. After taking in immense hauls, they could either return immediately with the fish preserved in salt or could dry the fish in the spring and summer and return to France before winter. Furs, notably from the North American beaver, required a permanent European presence, if only for trade with the indigenous people who did much of the actual hunting. Demand in Europe remained high, thanks in part to the cool temperatures of the "Little Ice Age" of the seventeenth century. Europeans were hunting their own beaver population to practical extinction. Yet furs would remain a luxury item rather than a staple commodity, not in themselves the stuff from which France could build a great empire. The fur trade also drew English and Dutch competitors.

A barrier to the expansion of the fur trade, indeed to the imperial enterprise itself, was the reluctance of the French to move to their own empire – a trait they would exhibit throughout their history. Publicists such as Samuel de Champlain (1567–1635) tried hard to persuade the French to emigrate to Nouvelle France. He published at least seven volumes detailing his explorations and life in the New World. Champlain certainly condescended to the indigenous people, whom he called according to common parlance *sauvages*, though the term meant more "wild" or "untamed" than "savage," with its connotations of unbridled brutality. He condemned the widespread indigenous practice of torturing captives, forgetting that in the Hexagon the crown would still draw and quarter those found guilty of exceptional crimes. Champlain understood the complicated politics of the Algonquin, Iroquois, and others, and learned some of their languages. Above all, he considered the indigenous people with whom he could transact business. "I assure you," he wrote, "that many of them have excellent judgment, and respond very well to any question that one puts to them."

Champlain understood that the success of Nouvelle France required settlers, and agriculture as well as trade. Toward that end, in 1608 he founded Quebec City at a strategic location on the Saint Lawrence River.

But of the twenty-eight men who spent the first winter there, only eight remained alive the following spring. Champlain returned as governor of Nouvelle France in 1633, to find a settler population of seventy-seven people in the city. Enticing settlers to such a hostile land required money, which Champlain sought and at intervals received from the crown and the private companies. Theoretically, the crown owned all land in Nouvelle France, and subcontracted proprietorship through feudal grants administered by charter companies. Peasants faced a panoply of theoretical seigneurial dues, parallel to those incurred in the Hexagon. However lightly and haphazardly applied in Nouvelle France, the transplant of seigneurialism did not encourage rural people to brave the perils of emigration. Champlain's efforts met with only very limited and gradual success.

A 1721 description of the European population of Nouvelle France as "a handful of bandits and whores (*putains*)" was less than accurate. But French settlement, in Canada or elsewhere, could never quite shake the widespread prejudice that the people who moved there had run out of options elsewhere. The crown did its best to counteract this impression. Probably the best-known effort to attract immigrants involved the *filles du roi* (daughters or wards of the king), some 800 young and presumably fertile women who came to Nouvelle France from 1663 to 1673. The crown had sponsored them in hopes of making the settler population self-sustaining. This and other efforts proved partly successful, as the settler population of Nouvelle France increased from some 3,000 people in 1663 to some 70,000 a century later. Most of these lived in a narrow corridor of some 300 km along the Saint Lawrence River joining Quebec City and Montreal. In comparison, the English colonies on the Atlantic coast had attracted at least 250,000 settlers by 1783. French settlement left a small footprint on a vast land.

The French Catholic Church would partner with the crown in seventeenth-century Canada, as elsewhere. Indeed, the Compagnie des Cents Associés de la Nouvelle France (Company of the One-Hundred Associates of New France), founded under the auspices of Cardinal Richelieu, envisaged in its royal charter the creation of "a new Jerusalem, blessed by God and made up of citizens destined for heaven." Richelieu opened this company only to Catholics, as a way to counteract the influence in the New World of merchants from La Rochelle, the epicenter of French Protestantism. Catholic missionaries came particularly from the Jesuits, but also from other orders. Missionaries would both make converts among the indigenous and provide a religious infrastructure for future settlers. In Nouvelle France, Jesuits advocated the education of settlers and indigenous alike. Catholicism offered at least theoretical spiritual equality to indigenous people who converted. In addition, the Catholic Church became a major landowner in Nouvelle France, exercising proprietorship over one-quarter of all seigneurial land.

Throughout the history of French colonialism, assigning territories a certain color on a map did not in itself signify effective rule. Indigenous people far outnumbered the French in Nouvelle France throughout the eighteenth century. Had these Native Canadians been more united, they could have dispatched the French had they chosen to do so. That they did not spoke to the appeal of European goods offered for exchange, notably European weaponry, that indigenous people could use against one another in chronic warfare. The French could prove useful allies. Champlain recounted that Innu chief Anadabijou in Acadia in 1603 sent a message of alliance through him to the king of France: "His Majesty should people their land and make war on their enemies and there was no nation in the world to which they wished more good than the French." In Nouvelle France as elsewhere, indigenous peoples and Europeans could make use of each other for their own purposes.

Also present from the beginning in Nouvelle France were hybridized populations. The *coureurs de bois* (runners of the woods) were genetically French, at least the first generation. But their connections to the indigenous population, in language, commerce, and often conjugal relations meant they had far more liberty of maneuver than other settlers, who at times could barely leave French forts. The *coureurs* served as intermediaries in the fur trade, but seldom took orders from the French authorities. Later in the seventeenth century, the crown tried to effect a system of licensing, and to replace the *coureurs* with the more official *voyageurs* (literally voyagers). Most were indentured servants, and likewise took indigenous mates. With limited success, missionaries tried to forge a francophone indigenous elite. *Coureurs* and *voyageurs* proved at least as likely to embrace indigenous beliefs as indigenous peoples to embrace Christianity. Frequently, both combined old and new beliefs in unorthodox ways.

French exploration and the resulting territorial claims radicalized over the course of the seventeenth century. René-Robert LaSalle remained fixated on the idea that a water route to Asia existed through North America. He established Fort Fontenac in 1673, where Lake Ontario meets the Saint-Lawrence River. From there, LaSalle explored the Great Lakes to the Ohio River, then down the Mississippi River. Here as later, France sought imperial expansion on the cheap. The crown gave LaSalle a monopoly over the fur trade in the lands he explored, but no subventions. This meant that LaSalle had to finance his exploration by debt and trade with Native Americans. Nevertheless, in 1682, he claimed the entire Mississippi Basin for King Louis XIV, and named the vast territories therein Louisiana (see Illustration 1.1). Colonial entrepreneurs

Illustration 1.1 René Robert LaSalle claims the Louisiana Territories, April 1682 (1883 print).
Source: United States Library of Congress (public domain), Digital ID cph3a18168//hdl.loc.gov.loc.pnp/cph.3a18168).

such as LaSalle always made enemies as well as friends. In the wake of a failed, quixotic scheme to take Mexico from Spain in 1687, LaSalle's own troops murdered him in today's east Texas.

Inevitably, an empire so lightly held would prove fragile, indeed somewhat theoretical. Imperial contracting in North America was not between ruler and ruled so much as between equals. Or perhaps more accurately, the indigenous peoples in North America tolerated or even welcomed imperial contracting because they saw advantages in doing so. The French mercantile empire in North America fell not because of native resistance, but because of the vicissitudes of European politics. Nouvelle France became an increasingly contested imperial space from late in the seventeenth century. Certainly, British traders, many willing to settle permanently, were drawn to the fishing and fur trades, backed by the increasingly powerful Royal Navy. As the number of settlers in the English Thirteen Colonies grew rapidly over the course of the eighteenth century, they sought more and more land over which France claimed sovereignty. Both the French and the English formed and manipulated alliances with indigenous peoples. Not for the first or last time, waves of European expansion crashed against each other, here in Canada.

In the end, France would barter away what Voltaire contemptuously referred to as its "few acres of snow" (*quelques arpents de neige*) in its North American empire in order to extend or simply preserve its influence on the European continent. After the war of the Spanish Succession of 1701–14, a branch of the Bourbon family continued to sit on the Spanish throne. But as part of the Treaty of Utrecht (1715), France ceded to Great Britain its claims to the drainage basin of Hudson Bay, Newfoundland, and much of Acadia. We can properly consider the Seven Years War of 1754–63 a "world war" over mercantile empire. While its roots lay in the balance of power in Europe, its battlefields included North America, South America, the Caribbean, West Africa, the Indian subcontinent, and oceans around the globe. The outcome of the war would determine British predominance in South Asia. In North America in 1754, a young George Washington commanding colonial militia helped inaugurate what Americans still call the French and Indian War by ambushing French forces in today's western Pennsylvania.

Cartographically speaking, the Seven Years War proved a disaster for France. The French presence in India was reduced to Pondicherry and several smaller settlements. Most of Nouvelle France came under British occupation during the war and remained British thereafter. "I am like the public," wrote Voltaire, "I love peace more than Canada, and I believe France can be happy without Quebec." In the Treaty of Paris (1763) and subsequent agreements, France ceded the Louisiana territories east of the Mississippi River to Britain and the territories west (as well as the fast-growing port city of New Orleans) to Spain.[2]

Nevertheless, the French left traces in North America. In one of the early afterthoughts of empire, France retained some fishing rights in the Gulf of Saint Lawrence, and two small fishing islands, Saint-Pierre and Miquelon. These remain French national territory today. France also left behind settler colonies in Louisiana and Quebec, where succeeding generations worked hard to preserve their Francophone identities in the Anglophone seas around them. Dialects survived, parallel to dialects of Spanish left behind in Chile, Argentina, and Cuba. Some 4,000 refugees from Acadia who settled in Louisiana came to be called Cajuns, known today particularly for their cuisine and their idiosyncratic dialect. Settlers in Quebec proved fruitful and multiplied. Francophones comprise over three-quarters of the present population of Quebec. Their language, Québécois, owes much to the language of Champlain, and today is usually subtitled on French television. Francophone settlements in North America would find their destiny beyond the formal French empire. In the meantime, French imperial attention turned to a region of far greater economic significance than North America had ever been: the Caribbean.

1.3   The Slave Empire and the Plantation System

Imperial contracting under mercantilism operated at both ends of a spectrum of power. As we saw, French traders, merchants, and farmers in North America were at best political equals to the indigenous peoples among whom they settled. The slave system in the Caribbean operated at the other end of the spectrum. The sugar, coffee, and indigo plantations showed mercantilism at its most vicious as well as its most profitable. As Delbée's narrative illustrated, European slave traders and African rulers collaborated to turn people into chattels. Plantations came to constitute laboratories of domination, ruled overtly by terror. Only in World War II would Europeans perpetrate cruelties upon each other with the intensity or the scale of their treatment of Africans in the mercantile empires of the Western Hemisphere. Yet terror in the Caribbean, as in other times and places, proved a tactic of weakness rather than strength. The complexities of plantation society revealed its vulnerabilities as well as its brittleness. In the end, the French empire in the Caribbean would prove a house of cards, which would ultimately collapse as the authority structure ruling over it began to fracture beginning in 1789.

---

[2] France would reclaim the cessions to Spain under Napoleon, the lands that would become the Louisiana Purchase of 1803.

Sugar processed from cane would transform the French empire as profoundly as bullion had earlier transformed the Spanish empire. Cane sugar apparently originated in Southeast Asia as early as the eighth century CE and gradually made its way to Europe through trade with the Islamic world. Before the seventeenth century, Europeans considered it an exotic item, more likely to be used as medicine than as food. Christopher Columbus brought cane to the island of Hispaniola on his second voyage in 1493. By the middle of the sixteenth century, Portuguese, Spanish, and English plantations were all growing sugar for export. The more sugar arrived in Europe, the more Europeans wanted to consume. Coffee, cultivated in Africa since at least the fifteenth century, likewise reached Europe through trade with Muslims. By the late-seventeenth century, coffee became the popular social stimulant in Europe that it remains today. Peruvians had used the rich blue dyes made possible by indigo since at least 4000 BCE, and the ancient Greeks knew it as a luxury product. Europeans discovered that coffee and indigo could grow in the Caribbean.

Europeans partitioned the Caribbean in the seventeenth century largely according to their own geopolitics. Bullion from Latin America had to pass through the Caribbean on the way to Spain. No pirate could resist such an opportunity, and no rival monarchy could resist collaborating with pirates in exchange for a share of the proceeds. Semipermanent but largely unorganized settlements on Caribbean islands followed. In 1635, the French unofficially seized Martinique and Guadeloupe, on the arc of islands joining Puerto Rico and South America. In 1643, the French founded a small settlement in Cayenne, which would evolve into their colony of Guyane.

Late in the sixteenth century, the Spanish had undertaken some settler agriculture in Hispaniola. But as they became drawn to the riches of the bullion colonies on the continent, Hispaniola became a backwater. This opened the door to French settlement, particularly as a base for the operations of the *flibustiers* (one French word for pirates). Earlier Spanish settlement had left behind pigs and cattle that became feral. *Boucaniers* (buccaneers in English) hunted these animals and sold their meat to all manner of sailors and soldiers passing through. In the Peace of Rijswijk (1697), the Spanish recognized de facto the French presence on the Hispaniola, which subsequently became divided between the Spanish colony of Santo Domingo and the French colony of Saint-Domingue.

As cane sugar became a staple commodity in European diets in the eighteenth century, its production transformed the Caribbean. Making sugar combined agriculture and industry. Indeed, some historians mark large-scale sugar production in the New World in the sixteenth century rather than textile production in England in the eighteenth century as the proper beginning of the Industrial Revolution. Sugar cane was not planted in plowed furrows, rather in deep, individually dug holes. Fields needed irrigation, weeding, and harvesting by hand. Then machines powered by animals or people crushed the cane to extract the juice. This would be boiled to extract molasses, then further refined for brown and white sugar. Rum is distilled from molasses or cane juice. All these processes required many skilled as well as unskilled workers.

Sugar production also required considerable capital investment, here through the Compagnie des Indes Occidentales (West Indies Company), founded in 1664 by the first minister of the crown, Jean-Baptiste Colbert. Private and public capital remained practically indistinguishable, not for the last time in the history of the French empire. This company lasted only for about ten years, at which point the crown directly administered the sale of monopolies and privileges that along with land constituted the company's property.

Saint-Domingue became by good measure the Golden Goose of the French mercantile empire – indeed a rare episode in the economic history of imperialism when the French temporarily outmaneuvered the British. At one point, Saint-Domingue produced some 40 percent of all sugar consumed by Europeans and 60 percent of all coffee. Whole cities on the French Atlantic coast, such as Nantes, Bordeaux, and La Rochelle, depended on transatlantic trade. While these cities maintained links with French colonialism in Africa long after the loss of Saint Domingue and the abolition of slavery, they never again attained the prominence in the national economy that they had enjoyed in the eighteenth century. By the French Revolution, Saint-Domingue had become one of the most valuable pieces of real estate on earth.

The modest Spanish agricultural production in Santo Domingo had generally relied on indigenous labor, people known as Caribs. However, this population largely perished over the course of the seventeenth century, because of European diseases such as smallpox, whooping cough, and the measles. To be fair, this biological genocide was unintentional, given that no one at the time had a scientifically sound concept of where disease came from. But to remedy the resulting labor shortage, Europeans turned to partnerships with African rulers to send masses of enslaved persons to the New World. Centuries of trade had provided long exposure, and thus resistance, to European diseases. But the enslaved brought their own diseases – notably parasite-borne malaria. While malaria killed Caribs, Africans, and Europeans alike, it exacerbated the labor shortage in mosquito-infested sugar fields. Demand for sugar, disease, and enslavement all fed off one another.

The scale and horrors of the Atlantic slave trade are well known. The trade accelerated over the course of the eighteenth century. Saint-Domingue alone imported some 2,000 enslaved persons per year between 1700 and 1725. This doubled by about 1750 and doubled again, to some 8,000 per year, by 1775. By 1777, Saint-Domingue imported some 22,000 enslaved persons per year. This number peaked in about 1790 (that is, after the French Revolution began) with 48,000 persons per year. Roughly one-sixth (16.7 percent) of the captives died during the Middle Passage across the Atlantic, actually fewer than the roughly 23 percent who died on Delbée's voyage in 1671. Once in the Caribbean, some 5–10 percent of enslaved persons died per year from disease, malnutrition, or physical abuse. So finely honed was the machinery of enslavement that planters found importing more enslaved persons cheaper than tending to the survival of those already there. High child mortality, coupled with probable abortions and infanticide, meant that the enslaved population could not grow proportional to the increasing need for labor. In all, some 500,000 enslaved persons lived in Saint-Domingue when the French Revolution began, the majority born in Africa.

At the top of the racial pyramid in Saint-Domingue stood a population of some 30,000 whites (including wives and children). A small percentage of these comprised planters, who lived on some 3,000 plantations of various sizes. The remainder became known as *petits blancs* (literally small whites), a largely landless population of shopkeepers, artisans, and day laborers. Manumission of the enslaved for various reasons, particularly of a child born of a white man and an enslaved woman, helped create a population of some 25,000 free people by 1789 known as the *gens de couleur* (literally persons of color). While discriminated against socially and politically, many *gens de couleur* found economic success, more so than many *petits blancs*. Quite a few owned enslaved persons themselves. The *gens de couleur* would prove a pivotal population once the power structure of the plantation began to fracture after 1789. There was also a small number of free blacks, such as Toussaint Louverture, who apparently did not have any white forebears. By the French Revolution, the enslaved population outnumbered the free population by at least 9:1.

The planter may have been master of his plantation, but the king was master in everyone's plantation, or so the theory went. Absolute monarchy was aspirational as well as performative, nowhere more so than in the regulation of slavery in the empire. The very foundations of Ancien Régime society lay in differentiated rule over differentiated persons. Enslaved persons, legally speaking, were simply another variety of subject of the king. Further to define that subject, the crown issued a collection of royal edicts known as the Code Noir (Black Code) in 1685, further refined in 1723 and 1724. Certainly, the code existed to support the institution of slavery as essential to the prosperity of the empire. The king's magistrates followed the French flag almost everywhere, to protect and adjudicate the interests of the colonizers. A complex legal tradition treated the enslaved like household furniture, valuable as cultural as well as economic accoutrements. The attachment of the enslaved was to the owner rather than the land (Article 44). Also like furniture, the law considered the enslaved to function ideally as sets, here meaning as families. They could marry subject to their masters' permission, any children of such unions becoming the property of the master of the mother (Article 12). The code forbade masters from separating families created through marriage if the same master owned the spouses and the young children (Article 47).

Unlike furniture, however, the enslaved were living creatures presumed to have rebellious instincts. The Code Noir prescribed hideous punishments, though not wholly beyond eighteenth-century norms. As per Article 38, escapees for one month or more would have their ears cut off and one shoulder branded with the royal insignia of the *fleur de lys*. Second offenders would have their hamstrings cut (thereby permanently reducing their capacity for work) and would receive a branding on the other shoulder. Death awaited three-time offenders. Likewise, striking a master or his family, if it drew blood (Article 33), was a capital offense. At the discretion of their masters, slaves could be enchained and beaten with rods and cords (Article 42).

But if the enslaved constituted private property, the code circumscribed rights over that property in non-trivial ways. The point was not so much humanitarianism as articulating the sovereignty of the crown. In the empire as in the Hexagon, Catholicism and the crown supported each other. The enslaved had souls, and thus had to be baptized and receive Catholic religious instruction (Article 2). Indeed, religious orders established themselves in the Caribbean, there to cultivate an enslaved religious identity rooted in submission. Article 22 prescribed weekly food rations, including precise amounts of cassava flour and salted beef or fish. Article 25 required masters to provide each enslaved person two outfits per year, or the equivalent in cloth.

The crown took an avid interest in the most intimate matters of the slave system. Free men who fathered children with enslaved women were subject to a fine of the value of 2,000 pounds of sugar (Article 2), a draconian punishment indeed given the widespread nature of the offense. If the man was the master and married, the woman and the children would be taken from him. An unmarried white man would be compelled to marry the enslaved woman, and the children manumitted and made legitimate. Article 42 authorized beating, but masters could not under normal circumstances "administer torture, nor mutilate any limb" (*membre*), on pain of confiscation of the enslaved body by the crown. Article 23 required masters to care for the enslaved in case of old age or sickness, even incurable illness.

But actually enforcing the Code Noir as written would have required a complex, highly intrusive, bureaucratized state unknown to colonial governance in the eighteenth century. The mere existence of some 25,000 *gens de couleur*, to say nothing of an unknown but surely substantial population of enslaved persons with white fathers, indicates that few planters took provisions forbidding such unions very seriously. The handful of royal officials in the colonies had to work through local elites. The stated right of the enslaved to complain to the royal authorities about illegal treatment remained theoretical. Like most systems of physical oppression, the plantation system implicated the oppressed. *Commandeurs*, an elite of enslaved persons, handled a good bit of the day-to-day enforcement of the master's wishes. Ominously for them given what followed, planters armed *commandeurs* and gave them more or less complete freedom of movement. *Gens de couleur* constituted a majority of the *maréchaussée*, a professionalized constabulary charged with hunting down the enslaved who had escaped.

Terror enables a small population to rule a large one, rooted in a simple message: There is no limit to the violence to which the rulers will resort to dominate the ruled. Like that of the absolute monarch, the power of the master was in part about public performance, typically in front of assembled companies of the enslaved. Masters sometimes inflicted punishments themselves, but more often left matters to experienced subordinates, some enslaved themselves. The recipient of the punishment had a vital part to play in the performance. One master recommended twenty-five lashes administered over a fifteen-minute period, "interrupted at intervals to hear the cause which the unfortunates always plead in their defense," the entire sordid exercise to be repeated two or three times as necessary. Potentially dangerous irritants such as salt, lemon, or hot peppers could be rubbed into the open wounds. On a daily basis, masters performed their power over the bodies of enslaved women. Few masters in the colonies, whatever their marital status, denied themselves enslaved mistresses. While such relationships could include complicated emotional components, the least horrific of them involved women who were the legal property of men who, practically speaking, could do what they liked with them.

At the end of the day, however, the plantation system resembled absolute monarchy in that it could never exercise all the power it claimed to posess. Saint-Domingue was roughly the size of the state of Maryland. With a 9:1 ratio of enslaved to free persons, the problem of *marronage* (the escape of enslaved persons) proved simply unsolvable. Much of Saint-Domingue not under cultivation was mountainous and forested. Coffee plantations needed higher elevations and required fewer laborers. These worked under less supervision than those enslaved in the sugar fields. Spanish Santo Domingo generally welcomed refugees from Saint-Domingue and had a more relaxed regime of slavery, as well as a tradition of accepting free persons of African origin. Moreover, the enslaved of Saint-Domingue, like the enslaved of other times and places, proved expert at wielding what political scientist James Scott famously called the "weapons of the weak," simple evasion and dissimulation.[3] Traditional healing practices that the enslaved brought with them from Africa could produce poison, administered on occasion to the master's livestock or even the master himself. Instilling a fear of poisoning, far in excess of its actual incidence, constituted a tactic of counter-terror.

In its way, the French mercantile empire in the Caribbean would prove as brittle as the empire of Nouvelle France. The Comte de Mirabeau, an early leader of the French Revolution, wrote that the planters in the Caribbean were "sleeping at the foot of Vesuvius." The institutionalized violence underpinning the plantation system could "work" only so long as it induced despair. Whether a slave revolt would have eventually overthrown the plantation system in the absence of the French Revolution, of course, is not knowable. What is knowable, however, is that the Revolution initiated the fracturing of the whole system of power relations on which the plantation system rested. Once the enslaved saw the possibility of changing their situation, they did so.

1.4   From Saint-Domingue to Haiti

Practically speaking, everyone in the Caribbean in 1789 had their own grievances against the Ancien Régime. The enslaved had some allies, though none who appeared to be of much immediate use. Most *philosophes* of the Enlightenment disapproved of slavery, though most, such as the Baron de Montesquieu, considered it a practical necessity. Abolitionists gradually grew in numbers. But most, in line with the most important abolitionist organization, the Société des Amis des Noirs (Society of the Friends of the Blacks, founded 1788) advocated a long transition and compensation to owners. Before the Revolution, the *gens*

---

[3] James C. Scott, *Weapons of the Weak: Everyday Forms of Peasant Resistance* (New Haven: Yale University Press, 1985).

de couleur sought not so much to displace white supremacy as to join it, through full civil equality. The *petit blancs* detested the planters for their wealth and the *gens de couleur* and the enslaved for their color. No one hated the enslaved more than the *petits blancs*; no one more avidly supported slavery, which alone stood between them and the bottom of the social hierarchy. Even the planters resented the *exclusif*, that corollary of mercantilism that required them to purchase the accoutrements for their luxurious lifestyle from the Hexagon rather than from English, Dutch, or Spanish traders. Resistance to the *exclusif* sustained lively trades in piracy and smuggling.

The absolute monarchy expired as a process more than as an event. The Estates General, the institutional expression of the Society of Orders, met in the late spring and summer of 1789 to resolve a state bankruptcy, as the crown became unable to raise sufficient new loans. A handful of colonial representatives had inserted themselves into these complicated machinations, to lobby for the interests of the planters. On June 20, the Third Estate separated itself, invited the other orders to join it, and declared itself – and not the crown – the repository of national sovereignty. So began a protracted, often bloody, and decade-long search for stable government. At first, few imagined that France would even attempt to dispense with monarchy. Fewer still foresaw how profoundly the Revolution would transform the mercantile empire in the Caribbean.

On August 26, 1789, the Constituent Assembly made the first of many attempts to put the core principles of the Revolution into a legal document – the Declaration of the Rights of Man and Citizen. Those who made the French Revolution in its many incarnations wanted above all the establishment of one law for all of France, essential to making France a nation-state as well as an empire. Throughout the revolutionary era and long thereafter, opinions would differ as to whether the colonies were "France" or something else. The Declaration never mentioned slavery, nor for that matter the empire. But the planters understood the Declaration well enough to call it "the terror of the colonials." It posed the uncomfortable question of just who the enslaved were. Article 1 proclaimed simply: "Men are born and remain equal in rights." Article 18, on the other hand, established property as "an inviolable and sacred right," of which no one could be deprived without "public necessity" and proper compensation. Were the enslaved "men" or "property"? For the next four and a half years, the French would try to have it both ways.

For the time being, however, the status of the *gens de couleur* posed an immediate problem. As free, they certainly were not property. But the planters, supported by many in the Hexagon with colonial investments, ferociously opposed recognizing them as citizens, and so effacing a line based in color. Subjects of the king could have many colors, simply as one of many varieties of differentiated subjectivity. But what of citizens of the nation? The men who made the French Revolution had no problem excluding women, increasingly so as the Revolution continued. But they fretted a good deal more about whether and according to what criteria to exclude one another. From the first, many in the Constituent Assembly feared that a swift weakening of racial barriers would lead to the nightmare scenario of a slave revolt. Others argued for inclusion of the *gens de couleur* as a source of stability, since doing so would nearly double the number of full citizens in the colony.

Vincent Ogé was a wealthy *personne de couleur* based in Saint-Domingue, and himself a slave owner. He had many connections in Paris, notably with the Société des Amis des Noirs. Ogé, like many in the Société, favored very gradual abolition and compensation to owners. In the meantime, however, he argued for immediate citizen rights for the *gens de couleur*. In October 1790, Ogé returned to Saint-Domingue from Paris to press this demand. Rebuffed by the colonial authorities, he established his own militia of some 250 *gens de couleur*. In February 1791, after the defeat of his militia and his capture, Ogé was executed by being broken on the wheel. This medieval method involved tying him to a wheel, breaking the major bones of his body, and simply leaving him to die. Capital punishment is always about sending a political message. Executing Ogé in this manner meant that the planters would cling to the policy of terror by taking their revenge on the body of an individual who had dared to take up arms against them.

Ogé had many friends in Paris, and so began the first of many attempts of the revolutionaries in the capital to catch up with events in Saint-Domingue. The argument for inclusion gained ground. In May 1791, the Assembly granted full citizenship rights to those *gens de couleur* whose parents had been born free. This displeased everyone in Saint-Domingue. The planters became incandescent at the very idea of citizenship crossing the color line. The *petits blancs*, seeing before them the disappearance of their sole form of privilege, closed ranks with the planters. Even the *gens de couleur*, while emboldened, could not have been satisfied. How many of them would have had both parents born free? Most importantly, the enslaved population quickly became aware of the changes afoot in Paris and the divisions among those who dominated them. As early as July 1789, the same month the Paris crowd stormed the Ancien Régime prison of the Bastille, an unauthorized crowd of enslaved persons assembled in Saint-Pierre, Martinique, on the mere rumor that the king had freed them and that the local authorities were thwarting the royal will.

The slave revolt in Saint-Domingue began in August 1791. Its immediate cause remains somewhat obscure, and to some extent beside the point. A forest fire is still a forest fire, whether started by lightning or a carelessly thrown match. On various sugar plantations in the rich northern plains, bands of the enslaved attacked managers, destroyed equipment, and burned buildings and fields. Things could go badly for the enslaved who sided with their masters. *Commandeurs,* who already had considerable leadership skills of the brutal sort, turned on masters whose will they had enforced literally hours previously. One revolt at Bois-Caïman was preceded by a kind of ceremony at which a speaker cried out: "The god of the white man calls him to commit crimes; our god asks only good works of us. But this god who is so good orders revenge!" Some such rituals involved animal sacrifices and other religious practices brought from Africa. One rebel was caught with religious objects his captors called "fetishes," alongside pamphlets in French extolling the Declaration of the Rights of Man and Citizen. Other rebels invoked the king as a kind father, his will subverted by the evil planters. But the planters, indeed the entire white population and many of the *gens de couleur,* were astonished and terrified by the extent and sophistication of the uprising, and the level of cooperation among the enslaved from various plantations.

Atrocity stories tend to get better with the telling – which is never to say that atrocities do not happen. No one can deny that the Revolution in Saint-Domingue was bathed in blood from its first days to its last, in what descended into a Hobbesian world of all against all. Stories circulated of carpenters sawn in half, women raped atop the bodies of their dead husbands, and much more. Future radical revolutionary Camille Desmoulins blamed his enemies the abolitionists "if so many plantations have been reduced to ashes, if pregnant women have been eviscerated, if a child carried on the end of pike served as standard of the blacks." Abolitionism, to Desmoulin's way of thinking, simply unleashed African brutality. Of course, those who sustained a plantation system based on bondage and terror should not have been surprised when its methods were turned on them when its victims saw the opportunity to do so.

Whatever the ethics of the matter, the rebellion soon eviscerated the mercantile economy of the French Caribbean and made it ungovernable. The planters certainly understood their predicament. They had already arrived at a no-win situation. "If we do not defeat and destroy the rebel slaves," one wrote, "we will all end up being destroyed by these monsters, and by destroying them we destroy our fortunes. For it is in these slaves that our fortunes exist."

In the meantime, revolutionaries were losing control over the Revolution in the Hexagon. A conservative constitution written in 1791 called for a strong but clearly non-absolute monarchy. But in June, King Louis XVI attempted to escape his own kingdom, in the hope of returning to an absolute throne supported by foreign and émigré armies. While his subjects thwarted this foolish plan, Louis put the National Assembly in a difficult position. The revolutionaries probably could not live with the king, but the 1791 Constitution certainly could not live without him. In Paris, both Left and Right came to pursue a strategy of war with foreign monarchies – the Left to consolidate the Revolution, the Right to annihilate it in defeat. By April 1792, France was at war, and by summer it faced a combination of internal chaos and foreign invasion. On August 10, 1792, the Paris crowd overthrew the monarchy and declared France a republic. Republics, as we will see, accommodate politically significant differences all the time. But they seldom do so comfortably.

The situation in the Caribbean became more complicated still as Britain and Spain eyed the prospect of seizing the Golden Goose of the French empire. Over the course of 1792 and 1793, a virtual bidding war ensued for the allegiance of the one population capable of deciding the situation, the formerly enslaved. To be sure, the British had not a great deal to offer this population, given their own commitment to slavery in the Caribbean. But many planters and not a few slave-holding *gens des couleur* welcomed British intervention, particularly in the cities. The British would eventually land some 20,000 troops plus some 6,000 German mercenaries, making them a substantial military presence on the island. Further, the powerful Royal Navy could disrupt or assist attempts to support the planters as it chose. For its part, the Spanish crown in 1793 ordered officials in Santo Domingo to offer the formerly enslaved of Saint-Domingue freedom and land in exchange for helping Spain reconquer all of Hispaniola.

From the summer of 1791 to Haitian independence in 1804, the authorities in Paris worked to catch up to events in Saint-Domingue that they could not fundamentally control. In the summer of 1792, an unstable French government dispatched Léger Félicité Santhonax as its emissary to "stop" the revolution in the Caribbean. Armed with 6,000 fresh troops and a printing press to disseminate the will of Paris, Santhonax sought to enforce existing policy – the granting of citizenship to the *gens de couleur* and the restoration of the slave system. Such a policy, of course, was too much for the planters and not nearly enough for the self-freed, formerly enslaved. The insurgency continued, with increasing foreign support.

Finally, on August 29, 1793, Santhonax on his own initiative issued a decree in the name of the French Republic, stating flatly that "all the Negroes and mixed-bloods presently in slavery are declared free and

presently enjoy all of the rights attached to the status of French citizen."
This decree had its fine print. Freed persons presently attached to plantations needed to resume their labors, in exchange for a share of the revenues as pay. Former owners, in time, would receive compensation. But
without the explicit approval of Paris, its commissioners had abolished
slavery in order to save the mercantile empire in the Caribbean.

The revolution in Paris continued to radicalize. Power now rested with
a National Convention, elected in the fall of 1792 according to universal
male suffrage. This body had voted to execute King Louis XVI in January 1793. It operated under constant pressure further to radicalize from
the nucleus of the Paris crowd, the *sans culottes*. As the Jacobin political
club became the dominant party, the French began to set limits on their
Revolution. *La République une et indivisible* had to be governed by a single
law, an aspiration since the absolute monarchy. But who would that law
include and exclude?

On February 4, 1794, the Convention abolished slavery in France,
including the empire. It declared all colonial subjects citizens, subject
to the same subordination by gender as in the Hexagon. A small but
revealing episode took place at the Convention, which showed that the
Republic could efface boundaries of race by affirming boundaries of gender. Upon passage of abolition, deputy Pierre-Joseph Cambon revealed
that a woman of color sitting in the gallery "has just felt so keen a joy at
seeing us give liberty to all her brethren that she has fainted." Cambon
insisted that this be noted in the minutes. The deputies put the woman
on display for the rest of the session, seated next to the president and
wiping tears from her eyes. Her publicly performed passivity authorized
and legitimized male equality across the color line.

Meanwhile, there arose in Saint-Domingue the first real anticolonial
hero in the French empire, Toussaint Bréda, better known as Toussaint Louverture.[4] Like many subsequent anticolonial heroes, Toussaint
instrumentalized a hybrid identity. Born enslaved, Toussaint, according
to his son, learned the Arada language of his royal parents. Toussaint
apparently spoke Créole more comfortably than European French, and
had his formidable written correspondence mediated through secretar-
ies. Toussaint's father passed on a devotion to Catholicism, which Toussaint saw as a bond joining Saint-Domingue and the Hexagon. He had
not done badly under the plantation system. Manumitted about 1770 at
about the age of twenty-seven, Toussaint even owned an enslaved person for a time, and operated a small coffee plantation worked by rented
slave labor.

---

[4] Like Napoleon, Toussaint Louverture is commonly referred to by his first name.

Above all, Toussaint would show himself a leader of formidable military and political abilities as the insurgency gathered strength. On August 29, 1793, the same day as the decree from Sonthonax proclaiming abolition, Toussaint, still technically in the service of the king of Spain, issued his own proclamation of a distinct path forward: "I want Liberty and Equality to reign in Saint-Domingue. I work to bring them into existence. Unite yourselves to us, brothers, and fight with us for the same cause." Toussaint was precisely the sort of figure the emancipation decree sought to win over, and he duly changed sides. He brought with him the 4,000 now-experienced soldiers under his command, among them his successor Jean-Jacques Dessalines.

In the Hexagon, the Reign of Terror gave way in the summer of 1794 to a much more conservative republic under the Directory. The new regime recalled Sonthonax to Paris, a nod to the still-powerful colonial interests in the Convention. But the Constitution of the Year III (so named after the revolutionary calendar and promulgated in August 1795) declared that "the French colonies are integral parts of the Republic and shall be subject to the same constitutional law." In other words, formerly enslaved men retained full rights as French citizens.

The situation in Saint-Domingue remained fluid, as British and Spanish forces continued to contest Hispaniola. Traders from the United States made money from all sides. Abolitionist John Adams became president of the United States in 1797, and provided aid to Toussaint, much to the consternation of slave-owning rivals such as Thomas Jefferson. In Saint-Domingue a war of decolonization continued as a civil war. Toussaint had a powerful opponent in a former ally, *personne de couleur* André Rigaud. Largely responsible for the campaign in the southern part of Saint-Domingue, Rigaud came to act increasingly independently of his nominal superior. Rigaud's free birth and mixed-race origins highlighted their personal differences, as did Rigaud's stronger belief in maintaining a racial hierarchy. But not for the last time in anticolonial and postcolonial history, it remained difficult to separate personal and political antagonisms. If the personal was political, the political was personal. Toussaint moved south as he consolidated his victory in the north, and Rigaud fled to France in 1800.

Indeed, Toussaint's position became strong enough for him to issue his own constitution in 1801. That constitution prefigured many issues of postcolonialism generations later. Taking a colony out of the French empire, even partly, was one thing. Taking the political culture of the Hexagon out of the former colony would prove quite another. Essentially, the constitution provided for an approximation of what the British later would call Dominion status. Saint-Domingue would manage its

internal affairs, "subject to particular laws" of its own making (Article 1).
Yet it would remain part of a French empire. It affirmed the end of slavery: "All men are born, live and die there free and French" (Article 3).
Article 5 declared equality under the law, and that "no other distinctions
exist than those of virtues and talents." Article 6 proclaimed Catholicism as the only religion "publicly professed," surely as part of a future
culture war on African religious practice. The constitution established
Toussaint as a powerful governor for the remainder of his life (Article
28). A Central Assembly would vote on laws proposed by the governor,
but the constitution remained vague on what would happen if the two
disagreed (Article 24.)

The most "particular" of the particular laws envisioned the reestablishment of the agricultural economy along highly traditional lines.
Indeed, the constitution reflected Toussaint's extended effort to restore
relations with those planters still on the island and willing to accept the
new regime. Article 15 explicitly referred to the plantation as a family
and its owner or his representative as the father. While workers would
share in the revenues, "any change in domicile on the part of cultivators
brings with it the ruin of farming" (Article 16). Essentially, this meant
that the formerly enslaved would become serfs, no longer chattels but
still bound to the land. Most ominously, so indispensable was agriculture
to the economy that Article 17 appeared to open the door to the import
of new unfree labor, through the still-flourishing slave trade.[5]

By 1801, Napoleon Bonaparte ruled France, initially as first consul,
after 1804 as emperor of the French. He succeeded in "stopping" the
French Revolution by consolidating certain changes and pointedly closing others. In the empire, stopping the revolution meant stabilizing the
mercantile economy through reestablishing slavery. The abolition of
slavery throughout the empire had never been absolute. In the Île de
France (today Mauritius) and Réunion, the planters had done everything they could to thwart abolition in practice. The First Consul made
little effort to conceal his intentions in the Caribbean.

In any event, Bonaparte would never permit Saint-Domingue to write
its own constitution. To him, the colonies were "France," but had to be
governed by a separate law that came from Paris, and Paris alone. The
issue was not just the position of Toussaint under the constitution, but
the fact that the constitution existed at all. Bonaparte had his own plans
for the French domains in the New World. In 1800, the First Consul

---

[5] The constitution charged the governor "to take appropriate measures to encourage and
favor this increase of the labor force." The French reads "encourager et favoriser cette
augmentation des bras."

wrested control over the vast if theoretically held Louisiana territory from Spain. Thereafter he sought to reestablish the French empire in the New World with two poles – one based on New Orleans and the Mississippi River basin, the other in Saint-Domingue. At last, the theory went, mercantile adventures in North American and the Caribbean would join hands. The first step in this project involved reestablishing Paris (and himself) as master of Saint-Domingue.

Bonaparte proposed to decide the matter by force. He had a simple immediate goal, the resumption of full agricultural production in Saint-Domingue under firm control from Paris. In Saint-Domingue as elsewhere, Bonaparte combined force with guile and duplicity. He issued specific instructions on the reestablishment of French rule to General Charles Victor Emmanuel Leclerc before his departure for the Caribbean in October 1801. The first phase would establish French control over strategic sites, notably the cities and the all-important plains housing the sugar plantations. Preferably, they would enlist the help of black leaders such as Toussaint. In the second phase, the French in association with black troops under their command would consolidate their control first over the French part of Hispaniola and then the Spanish. The French would assure the black population early and often of their good intentions. In the third phase, the French would betray their black allies, and would deport their leadership to Europe. Leclerc's instructions specifically marked Toussaint and Dessalines for deportation. Some 7,000 French troops immediately left for the Caribbean, of some 80,000 that France would ultimately commit to the enterprise.

For a time, the Leclerc mission was not unsuccessful. The French skillfully exploited divisions among the formerly enslaved and *gens de couleur*, as the civil war continued alongside the war of decolonization. Even Dessalines would fight alongside Leclerc for a time, against Louverture. Dessalines may even have colluded in the arrest of Louverture, who died in a French prison in the Alps in April 1803. Yet doubts gathered about French intentions. In March 1802, the Treaty of Amiens restored Martinique to French rule, and resulted in the swift reimposition of slavery. A French expedition to Guadeloupe would do the same later that year. The French continued to claim that they would not seek to restore slavery in Saint-Domingue, though few understood just how they could restore a stable mercantile economy in a Caribbean empire partly enslaved and partly free. The people of Saint-Domingue, of all races, drew the necessary conclusions.

As the war intensified in 1802 and 1803, it became more overtly anti-French, as more black and *gens de couleur* units changed sides. On October 7, 1802, Leclerc wrote to Bonaparte that the French were simply outmatched in commitment. After a particular engagement, of 176 prisoners, "173 strangled themselves on the way [to deportation], with the leader of the battalion at the head. These are the men we have to fight." The mountainous terrain of Saint-Domingue lent itself to guerrilla war. "Victors everywhere," a French officer recalled later, "we possessed nothing but our rifles. The enemy held nowhere, and yet never ceased to be master of the country."

The French faced another deadly enemy in mosquito-borne Yellow Fever, which particularly afflicted Europeans. "They will fight well at first," predicted Dessalines, who became the leading figure after the removal of Toussaint, "but soon they will fall sick and drop like flies." By the second half of 1802, only 10,000 white soldiers remained combat ready, nowhere near enough to conquer a territory the size of Maryland. Yellow Fever would eventually claim the lives of the conqueror of Guadeloupe, General Antoine Richepanse, and Leclerc himself. In a letter to Bonaparte written on October 7, just one month before he died, Leclerc wrote: "Since I have been here, I have seen only the spectacle of fires, insurrections, murders of the dead and the dying. My soul has withered, and no joyful idea can ever make me forget these hideous scenes." Leclerc could have said the same of his entire mission.

The military campaign raged on as its own variety of fever. The war in Saint-Domingue came to look like a war of extermination. The Viscount de Rochambeau, son of the Count Rochambeau who had helped George Washington win the Battle of Yorktown in 1781, succeeded Leclerc as commander of the French expedition. He ordered dogs from Cuba specially trained in eating human flesh to hunt the enemies of France (see Illustration 1.2). He staged a public display of his new weapon, in which he had a black prisoner sliced open further to encourage the animals. Yet the formerly enslaved rebels eventually regained the upper hand. In November 1803, Rochambeau, surrounded in the city of Le Cap, negotiated a humiliating surrender in which he and several thousand survivors departed as prisoners on British ships. Unusually, Bonaparte decided to cut his losses in the New World. The would-be conqueror of Spain and Russia relinquished not just Saint-Domingue but sold the French claim to the Louisiana territories to the United States. The Louisiana Purchase of July 1803 would dramatically raise the stakes in the debate over slavery in the young American Republic.

In the meantime, Saint-Domingue would become independent Haiti. The new nation, whose name came from an indigenous term predating slavery, would blaze its own revolutionary path. True independence would become as much cultural as political, necessitating the eradication of Frenchness and whiteness. In a famous meeting of the victors on

Illustration 1.2 Blood hounds attacking a black family in the woods (Saint Domingue, 1805).
Source: Musée Carnavalet, Paris (public domain). Creative Commons Zero (CC∅).

December 31, 1804, a young officer proclaimed to Dessalines that for the Declaration of Independence, they needed "the skin of a white man to serve as parchment, his skull as an inkwell, his blood for ink, and a bayonet for a pen." While the authors did not appear to take the officer literally, the actual Declaration made the point clearly enough: "Let them [the French] tremble when they approach our coast, if not from the memory of those cruelties they perpetrated here, then from the terrible resolution that we will have made to put to death anyone born French whose profane foot soils the land of liberty." Nor was this loose talk. After independence the remaining white settler population – men, women, and children – would be systematically hunted down and killed by the new regime.

The Haitian Constitution of 1805 described the new polity as racially black. As per Article 12, no white man could ever own property in Haiti. Article 12 did away with an entire Ancien Régime racial category, the *gens de couleur*: "Haitians will henceforth be known generically as Blacks." Strictly speaking, the authors of the constitution crafted their document in the name of the sovereign people, as "the faithful voices and interpreters of their will." Haitians defined themselves as citizens, not subjects. The only persons of European descent given access to Haitian citizenship were small numbers of German and Polish immigrants who had fought the French (Article 13). But independent Haiti would call itself not a republic but an empire. It conferred vast powers on the person of Dessalines as emperor, to be known as "His Majesty." The emperor combined functions of head of government and head of state. With no legislative body at all, he "makes, seals, and promulgates the laws." There would be no state recognition of any religion, a nod to African religious practice.

Yet not for the last time in the history of decolonization, even independent Haiti showed many traces of the France it so pointedly claimed to have rejected. The founders chose the term "empire," even though Article 36 barred the empire from making any plan "to disturb the peace and the internal regime of foreign colonies." They understood the international perils, not least from a United States now led by slave owner Thomas Jefferson and the threat posed by the British slave colony of Jamaica. Yet no one could have failed to notice a concentration of personal power parallel to that of the emperor of the French, and the glorification of that power. Some articles came nearly verbatim from the Declaration of Rights of Man and Citizen, such as those declaring equality under the law (Articles 3–4) and the sanctity of property (Article 6). The article declaring the military obedient and forbidding it from making political decisions (General Measures, Article 4) proved no more effective in Haiti than had virtually identical provisions in France.

Independent Haiti would prefigure many of the problems of later decolonized states. Nothing about independence made bitter divisions disappear among those who had led it there. Dessalines's constitution would never really come into effect, as he was assassinated by two of his subordinates in October 1806. In the aftermath, two competing regimes would try to rule from the northern and southern parts of Haiti. The United States would not recognize independent Haiti until 1862, when doing so could no longer be blocked by the southern states. Restoration France agreed to recognize a reunited Haiti in 1825, but only at the price of trade concessions and a gigantic indemnity of 150 million gold francs, to compensate the former planters. Estimates have placed this sum at ten times the value of the $15 million paid by the United States for the Louisiana Purchase. French banks provided loans for the indemnity, setting in place a dysfunctional cycle of financial dependence. Eventually, the loan principle was reduced, and payment proved less than consistent in such a poor and troubled country. But only in 1947 did French banks formally close the books on the indemnity loans.

Nature itself seemed not to favor an independent Haiti. Geological instability and tropical storms proved periodically devastating, as did sustained environmental degradation through deforestation that began in the colonial period. Moreover, the commercial success of French mercantilism in Saint-Domingue would prove fleeting. Sugar cane, coffee, and indigo could all grow in a great many tropical and subtropical places. Sugar beets could even grow in northern climates, and beet sugar came to compete successfully with cane sugar over the course of the nineteenth century. Today, with massive overproduction subsidized by the United States and the European Union, no poor country can make an honest living from sugar, even given sugar-stuffed diets in developed countries.

Nevertheless, the Revolution that turned Saint-Domingue into Haiti had taught a lesson to the world in general and to France in particular. Enslaved people had shown that the slave system was not destiny. The example of Haiti haunted plantation slavery for the rest of its miserable existence in the Western Hemisphere, notably in the American South. Men and women recently in chains had seen off the most feared military power in Europe. Haiti was the first imperial domain to break free of France through anticolonial force, and the last until Vietnam in 1954.

Indeed, French imperialism itself seemed past its prime early in the nineteenth century. The mercantile empire in North America had always been an illusion to some extent, given the fragile French hold on all of its territories. It evaporated over the vicissitudes of European geopolitics.

Saint-Pierre and Miquelon could not confer imperial greatness, at the time or subsequently. After the Napoleonic wars, France would rule only Martinique and Guadeloupe in the Caribbean. In the Indian Ocean, it would rule Réunion, but would lose the Île de France (now returned to its prior name of Mauritius) to the British, because of its strategic port. In South America, France would maintain its small enclave in Guyane, too marginal to become of interest even in the Napoleonic wars. Mercantilism itself fell gradually into disuse and disrepute, as the Industrial Revolution and economic liberalism gained prominence. To become anything but a footnote to history, the French empire would need not just new lands but new foundations.

2 Reinventions of Empire in the Nineteenth Century

Whatever else could have been said of it, the mercantile empire at least had a logical rationale. France had an empire to enrich the crown, the state, and the kingdom – probably in that order. Colonial institutions, from the fragile settlements along the Saint Lawrence River to the organized terror of the slave empire, existed to generate profits. The defeat of Napoleon by 1815 left France with scattered islands and enclaves, none with a compelling economic or political rationale in a changing world. The Hexagon and its empire would remain laboratories of political experimentation through most of the nineteenth century. No fewer than four separate regimes would rule France between 1815 and 1870 – two experiments in constitutional monarchy under the Bourbons and the Orléans, a Second Republic, and a neo-Napoleonic Second Empire. The French would have a good deal of trouble deciding just where sovereignty lay in the Hexagon, whether in a crown, in its citizens, or in some combination of the two.

France would have at least as much trouble determining the contours of sovereignty in its empire, as well as the very purpose of that empire. French colonial policy would prove experimental if not haphazard between 1815 and 1870. The only constants remained a need to restore French greatness in the world and an unfocused search for domestic political legitimacy through foreign conquest. "Colonial penetration" (*pénétration coloniale*)– a gendered and sexualized term repeated for decades by contemporaries and historians – would continue. This period, after all, corresponded with the heyday of French Orientalism, a gendered and sexualized cultural movement if ever there was one. The exotic colonial Other attracted imperialists at most any conceivable register. The imperial impulse, in turn, would penetrate in myriad directions.

France would establish a settler colony in Algeria, for reasons of domestic politics in the Hexagon. In 1848, France would to some ill-defined extent directly assimilate Algeria and the other remaining colonies through annexing them as national territory. Entrepreneurial missionaries and officers would lead expansion in West Africa and Southeast Asia.

Crown and state would cooperate with these entrepreneurs in imperial expansion, as they had under the Ancien Régime. France would experiment in the imperialism of international capitalism in the Suez Canal, and in empire by proxy in Mexico. Yet when the regime of Emperor Napoleon III collapsed in 1870, the whole of the French colonial enterprise still somehow seemed less than the sum of its parts.

2.1   The Conquest of Algeria

From the day their forces first landed on the coast of Algeria on June 14, 1830 to the day of Algerian independence on July 5, 1962, the French of the Hexagon never seemed entirely sure whether they wanted to colonize Algeria or not. Certainly there were zealots, such as the young Adolphe Thiers, who four decades after 1830 would help found the Third Republic. But most of the French needed convincing. From the first, propagandists sought to sell the idea of a French Algeria as the land of limitless possibilities. There, the French could establish a settler colony not dependent on the increasingly disreputable practice of slavery, still legal in the remaining French colonies. Settler Algeria would look to the future, like British Canada, Australia, New Zealand, and South Africa. Further, a settler colony could draw off the "surplus" (meaning poor) population migrating to the cities who might otherwise take to the barricades at times of trouble. Not least, by conquering Algeria, the French could check British control over the Mediterranean by inserting themselves between the British domains of Gibraltar and Malta. Further, propagandists contended, France could harvest the riches of Mediterranean agriculture. This required downplaying the need for expensive irrigation and forgetting early and often that France already had a Mediterranean coast. The conquest of Algeria was never about resources. Only with the discovery of massive hydrocarbon reserves in the mid-1950s would French Algeria acquire a plausible economic rationale.

The immediate cause of the conquest was comically trivial, and not closely related to its real cause. The Regency of Algiers had been a largely independent vassal state under the Ottoman Empire, ruled by a dey (governor) elected for life by an assembly of notables. In 1799, Napoleon's Armée d'Italie had contracted with two Jewish merchants in Algiers for provisions, final payment for which had never been settled. Pierre Deval, a professional French diplomat, met with Hussein Dey on April 29, 1827 in hopes of finally resolving the matter. Discussion became heated, and the dey either struck or brushed Deval with his *éventail*. Whether he struck or brushed Deval and whether an *éventail* is a fan or a flyswatter depends on the account. Either way, the dey refused to apologize for the incident.

The French government responded with a three-year campaign of political, military, and cultural mobilization against what it construed as the quintessential Oriental despot. Propagandists exhumed stories of the long-expired practice of raids on the French Mediterranean coast by corsairs, Muslim pirates who had absconded with some Europeans whom they took into slavery. That Ottoman Algeria held a great many more enslaved persons from sub-Saharan Africa seemed not to matter. The many French supporters of the Greeks in their war of independence against the Ottomans (1821–32) found stories of Ottomans enslaving Europeans appealing. France could portray itself as the liberator from Muslim oppression, a latter-day Crusader mythology. The French navy blockaded the Algerian coast later in 1827 and landed 37,000 soldiers on June 14, 1830. By July 5, the dey had surrendered Algiers, including its citadel, the Casbah.

In fact, the Bourbon monarchy invaded Algeria to address an evolving crisis of legitimacy in the Hexagon. The Bourbons had returned to the throne in 1815, thanks to the foreign armies that definitively crushed Napoleon. Two brothers of the executed King Louis XVI ruled in succession. The crown gave the kingdom a constitution, the *Charte constitutionelle*, as the personal gift of the sovereign to his subjects rather than as a recognition of any rights of their own. The king ruled as both head of state and titular head of government, in cooperation with a Chamber of Peers and a Chamber of Deputies elected by a microscopic franchise comprising only the wealthiest Frenchmen. While surely many French were ready for a more conservative regime after the drama of the Revolution, many also had been raised on the possibilities of liberty, fraternity, and equality. Moreover, the royalist cause was itself divided, between Constitutionalists, willing to consider slow liberalization, and Ultras, who sought nothing less than a return to the absolute monarchy of the Ancien Régime. A quick, effective victory to expand the empire, the theory went, would help the crown and government balance these competing forces.

It was often said that Bourbons learned nothing and forgot nothing. King Charles X (reigned 1824–30) could not learn how monarchy had changed in the new century, because he could not forget the Ancien Régime of his youth. In the nineteenth century, kings could still call themselves the anointed of God, so long as they did not take that claim too seriously. On July 27, 1830, in a highly premature attempt to capitalize on the success of the campaign in Algeria, the king issued the July Ordinances. This ensuing crackdown on the Chamber of Deputies and press freedom antagonized everyone but the most reactionary Ultras. The proclamation ignited the Trois Glorieuses, three days of popular rebellion mostly in Paris beginning July 27. In the wake of the uprising, the Bourbons departed for exile.

Louis Philippe, of the House of Orléans and a distant cousin of Charles X, assumed what he promised would be a more authentic constitutional monarchy. There would be only one Orléans king, who would reign until the Revolution of 1848. What posterity would give the undistinguished name of July Monarchy would maintain strict standards of inclusion to the franchise by property, as well as gender. Probably the most famous expression attached to it was attributed (not entirely accurately) to chief minister François Guizot: "Si vous voulez voter, enrichissez-vous" (If you want to vote, get rich).[1] Louis-Philippe, who took the title *roi des français* (King of the French, as opposed to the Bourbon title King of France), had his own crisis of legitimacy. Many who had risked or given their lives on the streets of Paris had done so for a republic, not another monarchy. Supporters of the Bourbons, who called themselves Legitimists, saw in Louis-Philippe a usurper, who as a young man had fought in the armies of the hated Revolution.

In opposition, Orléanists and liberals had scorned the campaign in Algeria – as one put it, "this onerous legacy of the Restoration." In power, however, the new dynasty understood that imperial domains once taken could never be relinquished lightly or without a loss of prestige. To be sure, Napoleon Bonaparte experienced reverses in the empire, but had compensated for them by military triumphs in Europe. Louis-Philippe would seek to capitalize on reengineered memories of the Napoleonic legacy by deepening the French commitment to Algeria. Images such as Illustration 2.1 sought to deepen such connections, even when they failed to resemble actual combat in either Napoleonic Europe or colonial Algeria. Further, the Orléans king, aged fifty-seven when he came to the throne, had the future of his dynasty to consider. No fewer than four of his sons served in the Armée d'Afrique, the colonial army in Algeria. Louis-Philippe tied the prestige of the House of Orléans to the success of the colonial enterprise there.

Since the invasion of Algeria proceeded from a domestic crisis, the French had no clear idea what they would do with it if they succeeded. In effect, and not for the last time in the history of the French empire, this lack of forethought gave considerable discretion to officers in the field. Most of the time, the military governed French Algeria until the Third Republic. At the outset, the Bourbon commander, Louis-Auguste-Victor,

---

[1] Apparently, the exact quote is: "Enrichissez-vous par le travail et par l'épargne et vous deviendrez électeurs" (Enrich yourselves by work and saving and you will become electors).

Illustration 2.1 The 63rd Infantry Regiment conquers Algeria (depicted in an 1892 print).
Source: Wikipedia Commons (public domain).

Conte de Ghaisnes de Bourmont, declared to local elites that the French had come simply "to drive out the Turks, your tyrants," and that little would change. Eventually, a policy called "restricted occupation" would emerge, in which France would hold the major cities on the coast – Algiers, Oran, and Bône (today Annaba) – along with their immediate hinterlands. The French, the theory went, would rule the rest of the former regency indirectly, through vassal relationships with regional chiefs.

Entrepreneurs in the army, notably General Thomas Robert Bugeaud, who would revolutionize warfare in Algeria and serve as governor-general from 1840 until the Revolution of 1848, advocated a long-term policy of European settlement. The first guidebook for prospective settlers published in 1832 proclaimed: "Africa has always been represented as a beautiful woman whose head is a crown with ears of wheat, a symbol of abundance." Another guide from 1843 affirmed the trope of untapped abundance: "A pass of the plow has never been unfruitful for the colonists, and it always will be thus as long as the plowman is patient and intelligent."

Indeed, settlers would need considerable patience, because the key to Mediterranean agriculture has always been irrigation, which the Romans and their successors understood requires expensive infrastructure. Only the most hopeful could believe that wheat grown in Algeria would actually compete with wheat grown in the fertile and naturally well-watered fields of northern and central France. The French even invented a remarkably resilient if largely inaccurate environmental narrative, which later they would apply throughout the Maghreb. Arabs and Berbers had turned what they called the "granary of Rome" of antiquity into a wasteland because of poor land management, deforestation, and overgrazing. French occupation, the argument went, would restore the natural bounty of Algeria.

Some huddled masses yearning to breathe free did migrate to Algeria, thanks to promises of land and subsidies for transport. Europe would never lack poor people looking for a new start, as well as merchants and speculators who sought to profit from their doing so. But from the 1830s onwards, many settlers came not from the Hexagon but from elsewhere in Mediterranean Europe – Spain, Italy, Malta, Greece, and elsewhere. As of 1839, the European population numbered only about 25,000 people, some 11,000 of them from the Hexagon. Settlement increased substantially in the 1840s. By 1847, Europeans settlers numbered some 109,000, of whom about 47,000 originated in the Hexagon. From the outset, the settler population of Algeria was never one of European French transported to the other side of the Mediterranean. "France" plainly wanted Algeria. The French were not so sure.

Land appropriation began right away. The French immediately claimed the lands held by the dey (the *beylik*) and by the former Turkish authorities. The French then laid claim to the land of anyone who had opposed them, as well as lands held in trust by religious authorities for charitable purposes (*habous* or *ḥubūs*). Eventually, for reasons of "public utility," meaning the extension of colonization, the French would claim more and more of the *melk* (de facto freehold land). The French adopted an increasingly generous interpretation of what constituted "uncultivated" or "waste" land and appropriated it for the colonial state. An 1844 ordinance declared uncultivated lands state property unless the owners, individual or collective, could provide title documents acceptable to the colonial authorities. All expropriations up to that time were considered final, with no compensation beyond any already received. The French also began highly suspect investigations of land titles in general. In one such investigation in the area around Algiers in the mid-1840s, out of 168,000 ha investigated, 95,000 (56.5 per cent) were found to belong to the state, 37,000 (22 percent) to individual Europeans, and only 11,000 (6.5 percent) to indigenous Muslims.[2]

In Algeria as elsewhere, explanations of French imperial expansion followed conquest rather than preceded it. Perhaps the greatest French liberal theorist of the nineteenth century, Alexis de Tocqueville, sought as a young and aspiring politician to make himself a recognized authority on the new colonial venture. He laid out many of the issues of what would become liberal imperialism. Tocqueville wrote two "Letters" (really essays) in 1837 providing his views on Algeria. He admitted in an oblique way that the French blundered into Algeria with no plan. Consequently, in simply displacing Ottoman rule, they had created anarchy. But Tocqueville never suggested that the French leave; quite the reverse. Like many liberal imperialists after him, he believed that for France to reassert itself as a Great Power, it needed a viable empire.

Tocqueville's liberalism had two foundations – a belief in human improvability and a distrust of centralized power. Like many liberals, he did not believe that most humans improved from the same starting point, or equally. Indeed, he argued, "it would be as dangerous as it is absurd to apply the same laws to different beings." In articulating differentiated rule in Algeria, Tocqueville took at face value an already existing stereotypes of Arabs and Kabyles, Muslim like Arabs but mountain and desert people speaking completely distinct Berber languages. Tocqueville affirmed the trope that Arabs, part nomadic and part sedentary,

---

[2] 1 ha (10,000 m^2) equals approximately 2.47 acres.

condemned themselves to perpetual combat. Arab *marabouts* (holy men) were the "mind of the Algerian body," and had to be dispatched directly. Berbers prized their independence more than anything else, he insisted, with the partial exception of sensual pleasures. They could only be seduced, as it would be "easier to conquer them with our luxuries than with our cannons."

To a liberal such as Tocqueville, the key to making Algeria French lay in creating a marketplace of civilizations. He advocated gradual European settlement based on the fanciful claim that because the Arab population "occupies much more land than it can possibly cultivate," they will "sell land readily and cheaply." Settlement would juxtapose European, Arab, and Berber cultures. In time, the indigenous Algerians would see the intrinsic superiority of European ways and adopt them. Tocqueville even made a remarkable prediction: "It is easy to predict a time in the near future when the two races will be intermixed in this way throughout much of the regency." He avoided details, but the unproblematic nature of this union suggested a one-way assimilation. Algerians would become French without "Frenchness" changing in the process.

In the meantime, flesh-and-blood Arabs and Berbers in Algeria had to face intrusive strangers in their midst. Within a few years of the initial invasion, the French presence created the first anticolonial hero since Toussaint, the *marabout* Abdelkader (1808–83). Like Toussaint, Abdelkader combined considerable military and political skills. Abdelkader also had religious gravitas through his Sherifian descent (from the Prophet Mohammed) and excellent Islamic education. As with many anticolonial heroes, Abdelkader's record was more nuanced than his reputation. His strength was in the western part of the former regency, where he sought primacy both over his fellow Arabs and the remaining Ottoman authorities, as well as over those lands under the influence of the king of Morocco. Abdelkader proved more able than Toussaint at triangulating competing imperial interests. Indeed, he made formal treaties with the French – the Treaty of Desmichels in 1834 and the Treaty of Tafna in 1837, which partitioned much of the former regency.

Such arrangements, however, were always literally going to deconstruct – fall apart because of their internal contradictions. Abdelkader had not seen off the Ottomans and his indigenous rivals to share Algeria permanently with the French. Further, as the reputation of the charismatic fighting *marabout* grew, he found it difficult to resist encroaching on lands theoretically ceded to the French. For their part, the French continued to learn that imperial expansion could feed on itself. Migrants in Algeria, in the 1830s as later, tended to cluster in cities, partly for reasons of security. They would not settle the countryside until they felt safe. French conquest thus extended through the Tell, a term of Arabic origin meaning an elevation of the terrain extending to the Atlas Mountains. War between Abdelkader and the French would resume by 1839.

Continued French conquest would require a brutal change in military tactics, led by Bugeaud. Hitherto, French troops had moved much as they had in European warfare, in large, heavy, slow-moving columns, typically with artillery in tow. This left them open to attacks by small and expert groups of Arab and Berber horsemen. The French had focused on conquering territory, their opponents on damaging the enemy. Bugeaud concluded: "We must forget those orchestrated and dramatic battles that civilized peoples fight against one another and realize that unconventional tactics are the soul of this war."

One way to begin was with the recruitment of an organized indigenous force willing to fight for the French. Joseph Vantini, better known by his Muslim name Yusuf, was supposedly kidnapped at the age of seven by corsairs, only to prosper in the service of the dey of Tunis until the discovery of his affair with the dey's daughter. He fled to the French in response and served them as an interpreter. Yusuf later so distinguished himself as a commander that in March 1831 the French authorized him to form the Spahis, indigenous light cavalry. Resplendent in adapted "Arab" uniforms with flowing capes and riding magnificent horses, the Spahis yielded to no one in imperial splendor. One Spahi regiment continues to serve in the French army today, as an armored unit.

Bugeaud called on his troops to become "even more Arab than the Arabs" by appropriating tactics of desert warfare, through what became known as the *razzia*. "In Africa," one colonial soldier wrote, "how do you act against a population whose only link with the land is the pegs of their tents? The only way is to take the grain that feeds them, the flocks that clothe them. For this reason, we make war on silos, war on cattle, the *razzia*." Lightly armed "flying columns" would scout out positions for attack. People not simply killed or executed in the *razzia* could become hostages, to be exchanged for good behavior. The *razzia* effaced any distinction between soldiers and civilians. It should be noted, however, that the French often had local collaborators in such operations. Individuals and whole tribes could use the French to settle personal scores.

The *razzia* reached its nadir in June 1845, when one of Bugeaud's subordinates, Colonel Aimable Pélissier, trapped nearly 1,000 Arabs in a cave in Dahra in the western mountains. Their leader, Ouled Riah, refused French terms of surrender. In response, the French built an enormous fire in front of the cave and asphyxiated the occupants, men, women, and children. Pélissier explained simply: "There are five hundred brigands down there [presumably the men] who will never again butcher Frenchmen." Asked in parliament about what became known as the *enfumade de Dahra* [suffocations of Dahra], Bugeaud responded coolly: "I consider that respect for humanitarian rules will make the war in Algeria go on indefinitely." The French army in Algeria would turn again to this explanation more than a century later. Parisian politicians wanted the war won, but not to be troubled about the methods used to win it. Dahra was not the only *enfumade*, simply the most notorious. Reports of the incident even reached the *New York Post*, before the days of wire services. As one French investigator remarked, forlornly: "We have surpassed in barbarism the barbarians we were coming to civilize."

Once subdued, a given tribe or region would deal with the colonial authorities through administrative successor to the *razzia*, the *Bureau arabe*, or Arab bureau. Run typically by French junior officers with at least some knowledge of Arabic, the *bureaux arabes* would familiarize the local population with relevant regulations and handle some matters of justice. At this grassroots level, the *bureaux* were essential to creating the identity of the *indigène*, a more derogatory term than "indigenous."

At intervals, the *razzia* followed up by enhanced colonial administration subdued resistance. Sometimes, Abdelkader and his supporters could be lured into open battle, such as the Battle of Isly, on August 14, 1844. The French victory earned Bugeaud the noble title of duc d'Isly. Sometimes, the French could substitute mythmaking heroism for victory, as in the Battle of Sidi Brahim, from September 22 to 25, 1845. Abdelkader's forces had killed or immobilized all but about 80 of some 450 French light infantry. These survivors fixed bayonets and charged rather than surrender. Remarkably, some sixteen ultimately returned to the French lines alive. But thereafter, the tide of war began to turn against Abdelkader. He failed to attract much support among the eastern tribes of Algeria. The Treaty of Tangier (1844) between France and Morocco recognized the French presence in Algeria, thereby depriving Abdelkader of his most important ally. He surrendered to the French on December 21, 1847. Like Toussaint before him, he was led to a French prison. Unlike the anticolonial hero of the Caribbean, however, Abdelkader would have a political second act under a new regime in the Hexagon.

In October 1841, Tocqueville wrote his "Essay on Algeria" after an actual visit to the colony. His views on liberal imperialism narrowed considerably. He remained more convinced than ever that the French had to stay in Algeria – if only because if they left, a more vigorous rival (probably the British) would replace them. But his liberalism would apply only to the settler community. Settlers constituted the truly oppressed population, under unaccountable, inflexible, and dogmatic military administration. "I am not surprised at the small number of colonists who come to Algeria," he wrote, "I am astonished that any of them stay." Henceforth, the liberal community would include settlers alone.

Repenting his earlier position, Tocqueville now believed: "The fusion of these two populations is a chimera that people dream of only when they have not been to these places." In the future, Arabs and Berbers could live juxtaposed with Europeans, but would have to be governed wholly separately. The tactics of Bugeaud to maintain order were simply "unfortunate necessities." Europeans, Tocqueville noted accurately enough, had done that much and worse to each other in centuries of warfare. Social evolution had to be given a hand in Algeria. "The Arab element is becoming more and more isolated, and little by little it is dissolving," he wrote, while failing to note the murderous role of colonial warfare in this perceived development. Not for the last time, the open hand of liberal imperialism came to resemble a mailed fist.

2.2   Assimilating the Empire in the Revolution of 1848

The fall of the mercantile empire left the French flag flying in several small, highly dispersed domains, which in 1848 the revolutionary government would annex as national territory. As part of restoring France to the "family of nations" after Napoleon, France regained unambiguous sovereignty over Saint-Pierre and Miquelon, Martinique, Guadeloupe, Réunion, and the enclaves in West Africa. Trade in the Indian Ocean still held enough promise for the French to acquire in 1841 two other islands east of Madagascar – Nosy Be by mild conquest and Mayotte through purchase from the Sultanate of Ndzuwani. The British also returned Pondicherry and the other French settlements in India after the Napoleonic wars. While these domains remained profitable and durable (Pondicherry would join independent India only in 1954), France would never seriously contest British influence on the Indian subcontinent.

Chattel slavery, increasingly considered by the European Great Powers a distasteful practice suited to depraved Muslims, decadent Spanish and Portuguese, and uncouth Americans, continued its slow decline in the French domains. Although France committed itself to ending the slave trade at the Congress of Vienna in 1814–15, quasi-legal and illegal trade continued for some time. Some 482 French ships forcibly deported Africans between 1814 and 1831, some thirty a year on average. Thereafter, a new law imposed criminal sanctions on slave traders. While too profitable to expire entirely, notably in the islands of the Indian Ocean, the French slave trade had largely died out by 1848.

In its remaining Caribbean domains, France sought to blunt the edges of slavery. In 1832, it abolished a special tax for manumission, and outlawed the branding of recaptured escapees in 1833. The state required a census of the enslaved in 1834, an act bitterly resented by the planters, who did not want the state to know the actual size of the population they still held as property. In Martinique, home to some of the more modernized plantations, many of the enslaved were receiving payment for their labor by 1848. Only in remote Guyane did the import of enslaved persons actually thrive, and there for idiosyncratic reasons. In 1820, the crown designated the colony as the reception site for all persons designated contraband, notably from ships seized for engaging in illegal slave trade. Guyane also received enslaved persons awarded as maritime prizes following international arbitration.

Slavery left its shadow elsewhere. The earliest French settlements in Senegambia (today's Senegal and Gambia) dated from 1624, created mostly as a means of organizing the slave trade.[3] By 1750, some 7,500 people lived in the city of St. Louis, some 2,500 on the island of Gorée, near Dakar. As elsewhere in these oldest colonies, relatively relaxed Ancien Régime attitudes toward racial mixing had given rise to a *métis* or mixed-race population. Often born Catholic or converted by missionaries, the *métis* had lower social status than the white settlers, but much higher status than the indigenous masses, who were mostly Muslim, Animist, or some combination. In addition to trading human beings, the French in West Africa traded for ivory and acacia gum, harvested mostly by Africans enslaved to other Africans. But with Saint-Domingue gone and Martinique and Guadeloupe becoming more economically marginal by the year, the French presence in West Africa was going to need a new rationale.

The Revolution of 1848 in France, as elsewhere in Europe, began with a challenge to monarchy in the streets. At least temporarily, the regime departed rather than shed blood or, worse, risk military disloyalty. Idealists inspired by Romanticism took center stage, believing that they could accomplish everything immediately. Mutually contradictory agendas fell apart because of their internal contradictions in a matter of months. Across Europe, new and somewhat reformed monarchical structures stepped back into the vacuum.

On February 22, 1848, the July Monarchy banned a political banquet in Paris, hitherto one of the few semi-legal forms of expression available. Faced with an uprising in the capital, Louis-Philippe fled for England. A provisional government took charge by committee. It comprised a who's who of the opposition, from centrists Alexandre Ledru-Rollin

---

[3] The Treaty of Versailles (1783) effectively partitioned Senegambia into French Senegal and the surrounding British Gambia, around the Gambia River.

and Adolphe Crémieux to the Romantic author Alphonse de Larmartine and the socialist Louis Blanc. The committee even included a "worker," referred to condescendingly at the time and by many a bourgeois historian thereafter only by his first name, Albert (last name Martin). The new regime further affirmed its middle-class credentials by assuming the national debt it inherited from the July Monarchy.

Nevertheless, the revolutionaries also promised *la République démocratique et sociale*, based on social protections as well as political equality. The provisional government committed itself to the reorganization of work, notably through the *Ateliers nationaux*, or national workshops. These proved both insufficiently thought through in advance and very expensive. Not for the last time in French history, a regime forced to choose between pleasing "the people" and appeasing the credit markets would choose the latter. Moreover, any new taxation required to stabilize the markets would fall mostly on the peasantry, as most of the French still lived in the countryside. Rural people benefited relatively little from the social conscience of Paris.

When closing the ateliers in Paris as an austerity measure provoked a new Paris uprising in June 1848, the Republic did what the July Monarchy declined to do – use the army for repression in the streets. Ominously, the leader of the forces of order in Paris was General Louis-Eugène Cavaignac, who had learned his craft in Algeria. Despite the repressive bloodshed, the now Center-Right republic went ahead with presidential elections under universal male suffrage. The rural majority elected a populist, Louis-Napoléon Bonaparte, a self-proclaimed illegitimate nephew of the former emperor. Karl Marx caustically labelled the outcome of the first French Revolution a tragedy, the second a farce.

Establishing a republic in 1848 meant confronting again the dissonance between the commensurability among citizens on which a republic depends and the difference on which empire depends. Article 109 of the November 1848 constitution technically abolished the empire, by proclaiming that all "the territory of Algeria and the colonies is declared French territory." But here, as later, *la république une et indivisible* turned out to have a good bit of divisibility. In vague legalese, the article stipulated that these domains would continue to be governed by "particular laws," until "such time as a special law places them under the regime of the present constitution."[4] However, the new legal regime would have an immediate and profound effect on the empire through the abolition

---

[4] The French reads: "le territoire d'Algérie et des colonies est déclaré territoire français" that "sera régi par des lois particulières jusqu'à qu'une loi spéciale les place sous le régime de la présente constitution."

of slavery and the direct annexation of Algeria and what had become known as the *vieilles colonies* or "old colonies."

The April 27, 1848 decree abolishing slavery condemned it as "an affront to human dignity." Moreover, it constituted a "flagrant violation" of the foundational republican principles of liberty, equality, and fraternity – a clear if unspoken slap at the sister republic in the United States. But in the tradition of the Declaration of Rights of Man and Citizen of 1789, the decree treated the formerly enslaved as both persons and as property. As persons they were free as per Article 1 – but not for two months, to give planters time to get their affairs in order. The decree banned physical punishments in the interim. As property, they were the object of future compensation to their former owners. Article 5 promised that the National Assembly would "regulate the level of the indemnity owed to the colonists." This contradicted the advice of famed abolitionist and new minister of colonies Victor Schœlcher, who argued that the formerly enslaved also deserved compensation. Ultimately, only former owners received compensation, in the form of government bonds or shares in colonial banks.

The French abolished chattel slavery fifteen years after the British (1833) but seventeen years before the United States (1865). With the abolition decree, more than 260,000 enslaved persons in the French empire acquired legal recognition of their freedom (see Illustration 2.2). Abolition occurred mostly peacefully, though the long-term economic marginalization of the sugar colonies continued. Most of the newly freed wanted to become independent farmers, not wage laborers on sugar plantations. While French imports of sugar from the Caribbean fell by a good third between 1848 and 1850, sugar beet production would make up the difference. Between 1843 and 1860, yearly sugar production from beets in France grew from 30,000 metric tons to over 100,000 metric tons. Only in Guyane did the economy actually collapse, as some 20,000 of the former enslaved abandoned their plantations immediately. Senegal had little chattel slavery because it had few plantations. More common was *engagement à temps*, a form of contractual indentured servitude, which the emancipation decree abolished.

But what did this new freedom actually mean? No women of any color received the vote because of the Revolution of 1848 in France. The constitution did not explicitly guarantee the vote to men of color. One planter described the newly freed as "big children, unaware of their rights and duties." Some white politicians recalled the unhappy political experience of independent Haiti, omitting the active role of France in creating that unhappiness. Schœlcher argued for full citizenship: "We cannot make of them half-citizens or quarter-citizens, political hermaphrodites who

Illustration 2.2 Abolishing slavery in Réunion, December 1848.
Source: New York Public Library Digital Collections (no known copyright restrictions), Image ID 5318301.

have neither place, nor rank, nor character in the democratic society gloriously founded by the February revolution." But over the short life of the Second Republic, his colleagues and jurists worked hard to limit the implementation of universal suffrage.

Nevertheless, even this limited opening of the door to equality led to some fine theater for which the "springtime of the peoples" of 1848 came to be known. Article 21 of the November 1848 constitution guaranteed thirteen seats in the National Assembly for representatives from the empire – a visible, but not too visible, presence in a body of 750 seats. Representation of the colonies was not proportional to their populations and did not claim to be. Algeria received three seats, Martinique, Guadeloupe, and Réunion two seats each, Guyane and Senegal one seat each. Martinique elected Schœlcher, who entered the National Assembly flanked by a person formerly enslaved and that person's former master. There was something very 1848 about the old order marching unproblematically alongside the new into the chamber of the sovereign people.

Assimilating the empire in the Revolution of 1848 proved a complicated matter, as the empire continued to mean different things in different places. It seemed easy enough to declare the colonies "national territory," but what about the peoples living there? Even so fervent an abolitionist as Schœlcher believed different people should be governed differently under the law. In Senegal, full annexation applied only to what became known as the Quatre Communes (the Four Communes of Saint-Louis, Dakar, Gorée, and Rufisque). In Senegal and the French settlements in India, the monarchy had bequeathed a legal position to certain Muslims, who could continue to live under Muslim civil law. After 1848, these acquired *citoyenneté dans le statut* (statute citizenship). Muslims born in the Quatre Communes, known legally as *originaires*, could commonly vote and, in theory if not always in practice, enjoy the rights of French citizens.

In Algeria, annexation meant something quite different, with monumental consequences. The territory became "France." But those of non-European descent, that is, the vast majority of Algerians, remained colonized. The republic divided Mediterranean Algeria into three *départements* on the French model, each based in one of the three largest cities – Oran, Algiers, and Constantine. This organization would continue until Algerian independence in 1962. Unlike the Quatre Communes, the *départements* of Algeria constituted a vast space with a large majority of inhabitants pointedly excluded from French citizenship as *indigènes*. The Second Republic would not survive long enough to live with the consequences of this bifurcation of ostensibly democratic rule. But the existence of a large subject population on French national territory so close to the Hexagon would undermine the coherence of French republicanism for more than a century.

The provisional government put forward a new initiative to attract settlers to Algeria through agricultural colonies, the *colonies agricoles*. The brainchild of socialist deputy Pierre Leroux, it drew from the utopian notion that the world could change not through fighting in the streets but through creating ideal communities that would serve as a beacon to a better way forward. Their pre-Marxist socialist origins notwithstanding, the *colonies agricoles* drew support across the political spectrum of the Hexagon. Conservative republicans approved of anything that would get the poor and disaffected away from the barricades and to the other side of the Mediterranean. The Armée d'Afrique approved of almost anything that would draw more European settlers. Even the settlers already in Algeria approved, so long as the colonial state appropriated the land to be settled from Arabs and Berbers, not themselves.

On September 19, 1848, the National Assembly voted the massive sum of 5 million francs to settle some 12,000 new settlers by the end of the year. Each settler was to receive between 2 and 12 ha of land, and within three years a house, livestock, farm equipment, and seed. This would have constituted by a good margin the largest public, non-military investment France had ever made in its empire. The entire scheme very much spoke to the imaginary of 1848, according to which good faith could accomplish everything immediately.

Operational challenges lay ahead for the *colonies agricoles*, to put it mildly. The government had to identify, equip, and transport thousands of people in a short period of time. The transition from urban unemployed to Mediterranean farmer was never going to be easy. The newspaper *Démocratie Pacifique* observed in October 1848: "What up to now has been the profession of these men that we suddenly want to turn into farmers? All or nearly all of them come from the workshops of Paris." In the event, many of the newcomers ended up as agricultural laborers on existing farms. The miracle was not that 4,000 of nearly 14,000 people who migrated to Algeria under this plan returned to Europe, but that 10,000 remained. These remainers deepened the French footprint on this most consequential colony that, legally speaking, had ceased to be a colony at all. The Revolution of 1848 had made the empire more complicated, not less.

2.3   The Empire under the Second Empire

Louis-Napoleon Bonaparte, who after he abolished the republican constitution in 1851 became Napoleon III, *empereur des français*, never really lived up to his somewhat farcical reputation.[5] The founder of the Second Empire remains an enigmatic figure for someone in power for so long (1849–70). Historian Gordon Wright described him as "a man of complex and imaginative temperament, [who] sensed some of the trends of his times and sought, in quite un-Cartesian a fashion, to adapt an old and complex nation to those trends."[6] The Hexagon truly entered the coal- and steel-driven phase of the Industrial Revolution during his reign and experienced a period of sustained economic growth not rivaled until after World War II. Fewer and smaller families capitalized on this prosperity, as French population growth became glacial for nearly a century. This meant that even fewer French than before had any interest in relocating to the empire. Napoleon III's great urban planner, Baron Georges-Eugène Haussmann, redesigned the Paris still recognizable as such today. Even politically, Napoleon III proved more flexible than his namesake, or his own authoritarian beginnings. The second French emperor basically ruled by decree from 1851 to 1859, then began a cautious liberalization that would lay the groundwork for the Third Republic in 1871.

Foreign and colonial policy under the Second Empire constituted two sides of the same coin. "*L'empire c'est la paix*" (the empire means peace) proclaimed the emperor, to distinguish Napoleon III from his aggressively expansionist forebear. In this second incarnation of empire as regime, diffuse policies could fit under a broad umbrella of a modernizing France poised to reemerge in the front rank of Great Powers. As we will see, Napoleon III would develop what young people today might call a "frenemy" relationship with Britain. The two would collaborate in maintaining the balance of power in Europe, notably in the Crimean War of 1853–6. But increasingly, they would compete in imperial expansion. France acquired other friends along the way, at least temporarily. Napoleon III would provide crucial support in the wars leading the unification of Italy after 1859. A fleeting alliance with the Habsburgs would lead to a great imperial misadventure in Mexico.

But throughout the reign of the second Bonaparte, the French never had an effective counterpart to free trade for the British as a single unifying explanation of empire. This lack of direction gave considerable latitude to French imperial entrepreneurs – soldiers, missionaries, the emperor himself, and capitalists. They helped create a French empire larger and more diffuse than ever. All these actors worked in overlapping

---

[5] Napoleon Bonaparte's son, the theoretical emperor Napoleon II, died in 1832.
[6] Gordon Wright, *France in Modern Times*, 5th edition (New York: W.W. Norton, 1995), 137.

ways. Different actors mattered more and less in different places and at different times. Because each actor contributed in unique ways to establishing the contours of the French empire, it makes sense to examine each separately.

2.3.1   The Missionaries' Empire: Africa, the South Pacific, and Southeast Asia

Christians throughout Europe in the nineteenth century heeded the call of the Gospel according to Matthew 28:19 to go forth and teach all nations the road to salvation. The end of the revolutionary era and Romanticism fostered a general religious revival across faiths. Some of the devout would feel compelled to preach overseas, the more remote the lands the better. French priest François Libermann, the converted son of a rabbi, called upon missionaries to "Make yourselves Negroes among the Negroes" (*Faites-vous Nègres parmi les Nègres*), to make Africans peoples of God. At the time, *Nègre*, a highly controversial term today, was more condescending than *Noir* (Black) but probably less condescending than the English "Negro." Whatever his views on racial hierarchies, Libermann sought to convey the seriousness of missionary work. Just as Jesus identified with the most oppressed to bring them to God, so too should those who sought to bring the Word of the Christian God to all corners of the Earth.

Nor did God call only upon men. Anne-Marie Javouhey, who served as a missionary in Senegal, Réunion, and the Caribbean, founded the Sisters of Saint Joseph de Cluny in 1808. She recalled a vision in which a voice told her: "These are the children God is giving you. I am St. Theresa and I will protect your institute." Women would play a critical role in European missions throughout their history, notably as caregivers. Images such as Illustration 2.3, in which indigenous sisters much more resemble their charges than European nuns, show that missionaries as well as photographers could take care to preserve colonial hierarchies.

Missionaries had a complicated relationship to empire everywhere. Many devout Christians had not forgotten the turbulence of the revolutionary era. "Precious cross," wrote Bishop Pierre Pigneau de Behaine not long before his death in 1799, "the French have knocked you down and removed you from their temples. Since they no longer respect you, come to Cochinchina." Most but not all French missionaries were Catholic. The 1802 Concordat with Napoleon did not explicitly cover missions, but the state sometimes provided discreet subsidies. The state, for its part, would prove eager to subcontract to missionaries basic functions such as education and medicine, notably nursing. For their

Illustration 2.3 African nuns caring for the sick at the Hôpital des Soeurs (Catholic Hospital) in Brazzaville, *c.* 1900.
Source: Wikipedia Commons (public domain).

part, missionaries often needed protection only French military power could provide. In the end, however, missionaries would always answer to a higher authority than the French state. While neither Bonaparte emperor had much of a reputation for personal piety, both understood how Catholicism could support the social order at home and abroad. Moreover, protecting missions abroad could provide a convenient rationale for sending more forceful means of imperial expansion.

The colonial administration never encouraged the evangelization of Muslims in Algeria. Most of the time, the authorities explained this approach as a concession to local sensibilities. But conversion to Christianity would have strengthened the claims of indigenous Algerians to political equality. In stark contrast to elsewhere in the empire, organized Catholicism in Algeria remained, as historian Charles-Robert Ageron put it, "perhaps rather too ready to take 'no' for an answer."[7] The Catholic Church in Algeria became wealthy and powerful; but it existed almost wholly to serve the settlers.

In the South Pacific, missionaries followed the officers and merchants long at work in expanding European empires. Louis-Antoine de Bougainville had advocated French expansion in the South Pacific following his voyage from 1766 to 1769, partly to compensate for the loss of Canada. The exploits of naval officer Jules Dumont d'Urville as cartographer and botanist helped sustain French interest in the South Pacific beginning with his first voyage in 1822. Thereafter whaling, coprah (dried coconut kernels from which oil can be extracted), and the simple presence of the British helped keep the French interested. By the end of the 1840s, the French and the British had divided between them rule over hundreds of islands in the South Pacific. French missionaries first arrived in Tahiti in 1834. Local resistance led to their expulsion, and to the sending of a French gunboat to enforce their return in 1838.

The French declared Tahiti a protectorate in 1842, clearing the way for an expanded missionary presence. But the London Missionary Society had already been active in the South Pacific for half a century. Catholics had to compete, then as now, with a Protestant majority on many islands. Both Protestant and Catholic missionaries worked hard to blend South Pacific religious practices with Christian monotheism. Much would hang on the conversion of local chiefs. As in Nouvelle France, expressing an interest in Christianity facilitated chiefs' access to Europeans, which in turn facilitated access to European goods and weaponry. Chiefs who sought French patronage tended to embrace Catholicism,

---

[7] Charles-Robert Agéron, *Modern Algeria: A History from 1830 to the Present*, trans. Michael Brett (Trenton: Africa World Press, 1991 [translated from 9th French edition, 1990]), 71.

those who sought British patronage Protestantism. Competing religions and competing patronage networks led to open warfare in Tahiti from 1844 to 1847. Eventually, and grudgingly, the French permitted French Protestant missionaries to serve alongside English Protestants, in the hope of replacing them.

Paradoxically, the durability of the French settlements in West Africa and the existence of a *métis* Catholic elite impeded the expansion of the missionary empire. Islam took hold early in Senegal outside this elite, and never let go. In Senegal, Catholicism tended to support the existing social hierarchy. The more the conurbations of the Christian-dominated Quatre Communes grew, the more Muslim immigrants they attracted. Christianity remained a mark of Frenchness, and often of class. The excluded could resist Christianity on that basis.

Christians in Senegal, both European and *métis*, did not always adhere to Catholic beliefs, notably on monogamy. Nor did they always prove spiritually subservient to white priests from the Hexagon, few of whom bothered to learn any of the local languages. Many *métis* celebrated both Christian and Islamic holidays and prayed both to Jesus and Mohammed. "An appearance of Christianity, Mahomedan manners, and fetishist superstition," wrote a frustrated Abbé Lambert in 1841, "that's all there is to religion in Senegal." Official Catholic disapproval of his living openly with a Senegalese woman did not prevent Louis Faidherbe, the governor of Senegal, from having their son baptized or giving him the Faidherbe family name. The ordination of the first three Senegalese priests in 1840 did not do much to enforce Catholic orthodoxy. Only at mid-century, with a new generation of clerics inspired by Libermann and with more overt support from the French army, would Christianity advance in West Africa, and then only to a limited degree.

In Southeast Asia, missionaries and geopolitics blended from the beginning. France had sent missionaries to the region beginning in the seventeenth century, following the Portuguese. Indeed, in 1787, Nguyen Anh, the future emperor of Dai Nam (approximately present-day Vietnam) and founder of the Ngyuen dynasty, sent French priest Pierre Pigneau de Behaine to France to plead for help him defeat a rival faction in the south. According to the Treaty of Versailles (1787), the French agreed to send an expeditionary force in exchange for a concession at Tourane (today Da Nang). The sinking financial fortunes of the French monarchy as revolution loomed prevented King Louis XVI from actually sending support. But French missionaries continued to make converts. Neither the Nguyen nor the French collected data, but converts certainly numbered in the hundreds of thousands, particularly in Tonkin, Cambodia, and the Mekong Delta.

Indeed, by the 1830s, French missionaries proved so successful that they provoked a backlash. Emperor Minh Mang came to construe Christianity as a threat to the Confucian foundations of the dynasty and began a ferocious campaign of repression. As would often prove the case in such campaigns, many more indigenous Christians died than foreign missionaries. Some missionaries were accused, probably accurately, of joining plots against the Nguyen. But the Catholic Church gained some spectacular new martyrs, and a good bit of political capital. Père François Gagelin managed to get a letter smuggled out before his execution in 1833 to exhort the devout to make his martyrdom known. Most notoriously, Père Joseph Marchand in 1835 suffered the death of a thousand cuts, a hideous torture of inflicting knife wounds over a protracted period of time. The campaign of repression continued into the 1850s. French naval incursions in 1843 and 1847 failed to convince the Nguyen crown to change its ways.

After 1851, Catholics in the Hexagon pressured the new emperor of the French to protect their coreligionists in the region. As we will see, with the British consolidating their hold over India and the Opium Wars extending European imperialism in China, Napoleon III also had earthly reasons for intervening. In 1858, a French force sailed to Southeast Asia to enforce an ultimatum calling for, among other things, the protection of Christian missionaries. Repulsed at Tourane, the French in alliance with the Spanish operating out of the Philippines turned south to seize Saigon (today Ho Chi Minh City). French soldiers and sailors, as we will see, henceforth became the primary agents advancing French imperial interests in Southeast Asia.

2.3.2   The Officers' Empire: Senegal and Southeast Asia

Before 1871, the French military remained something of a constant in a fast-changing French society. The French army in the Hexagon stayed neutral in the various changes of regime. A rudimentary system of conscription by lot that allowed for the purchase of substitutes supplied adequate numbers of men in the ranks from the lower socioeconomic classes. The aristocracy no longer had legal standing after the Revolution of 1830, though many young noblemen continued to pursue military careers. The meritocratic Napoleonic tradition lived on. The army and navy continued to provide real avenues for advancement, professional and social. While service in the empire continued to be less prestigious than in the Hexagon, it also spared poorer officers social expenses well in excess of their salaries. The highly romanticized Légion Etrangère (Foreign Legion), first formed in 1831 and still in existence today, served alongside the regular colonial army. By definition comprising men who declared themselves foreigners, the Legion provided its members with an avenue of settlement in the colonies.

Throughout its existence, the colonial army bred military entrepreneurs, who sometimes followed imperial policy and sometimes made it. No one did more to forge the role of the officer-entrepreneur in the colonies than Louis Faidherbe, whose military and political career spanned the July Monarchy to the Third Republic. The son of a hosier who died when he was a child, Faidherbe landed a place at the prestigious École Polytechnique. He served in Algeria and Guadeloupe before his posting to Senegal in 1852. Keenly interested in geography and what would become anthropology, Faidherbe contributed regularly to scholarly journals in Paris. His strategy of expansion in Senegal enjoyed considerable support from the business community, particularly in Bordeaux, still seeking to revive its fortunes after the fall of the mercantile empire. Like many of his fellow officers in West Africa, Faidherbe set aside the social norms of the Hexagon. His fifteen-year-old common law wife, Dioucounda Sidibe, helped him learn three Senegalese languages. Later, at the age of forty, he married his eighteen-year-old niece, Angèle Faidherbe. She raised Louis (his son by Dioucounda) alongside the three children they had together as a blended family.

Faidherbe was the architect of a colonial Senegal that expanded inland from the Quatre Communes. Beginning in 1852, he implemented a plan to build forts and trading posts along the Senegal River – on the semiarid Sahel, where the forest transitioned to the desert. With the acacia gum trade in decline because of competition from Egypt and from synthetics, the new colonial economy would rely more on the increasing demand for peanut oil, and later palm oil. Control over the river and its peoples would ensure transport. Commerce and security, the argument went, would create a virtuous circle of expanding French influence. Peanuts and palm oil could not provide in the nineteenth century the economic bonanza that enslavement and sugar had provided in the eighteenth. But Senegal would provide a springboard for further expansion in West Africa.

Assuredly, Faidherbe did not spare the patriarchal rod of colonial expansion – including burned fields and summary executions. Indeed, he founded the first *école des otages* (school of the hostages) in Saint-Louis in 1855. The French authorities would compel chiefs and other notables to send male children to be taught French alongside practices of French colonial rule. But with barely 1,000 Europeans under his command, he had to rely mostly on diplomacy, notably threats to individual chiefs coupled with offers of protection. In conscious contrast to Algeria, he never sought to draw settlers beyond the bare minimum. Senegal thus constituted the first large-scale experiment in indirect rule. In this ethnically and linguistically diverse domain, adjacent to the Arabs and Berbers of the Sahel, Faidherbe had plenty of local animosities to exploit. His own unusual proficiencies in languages helped him considerably. Like earlier French imperialists dealing with Africans, Faidherbe never lacked partners. Generally, he sought to co-opt rather than disrupt local political and social structures.

According to its own brutal calculus, French imperialism had few more cost-effective imperialists than Faidherbe – expansion with commercial potential at little expense to the Hexagon. In 1857, he founded what would become the famed light infantry, the Tirailleurs Sénégalais. Its soldiers served at a tiny fraction of the cost of white soldiers, and comprised volunteers, prisoners, human tribute from deals negotiated with chiefs, and enslaved persons purchased by the French, then legally freed for military service. The reputation of the Tirailleurs for ferocity became the stuff of legend, which also established some convenient distance between conquerors and conquered. Africans could fight other Africans in the name of France. Eventually recruited throughout sub-Saharan Africa, the Tirailleurs served the French empire until the late 1950s.

In Southeast Asia, the navy came to play a role in governance analogous to that of the army in Algeria or Senegal. Only the navy, after all, could guarantee communications over the vast distances of the Pacific. The French navy had its own reputation to restore and preserve. While France did not seriously attempt to match British naval supremacy in the nineteenth century, a strong navy remained essential to its Great Power identity. The navy could point to successes in the Crimean War of 1853–6, and to the assistance it provided to nationalists in the wars of Italian unification. In 1857, Napoleon III approved an enormous naval expansion costing some 250 million francs (worth more than \$3 billion today).[8] As sail gave way to steam after mid-century, the navy needed coaling stations around the globe. Supporting colonial expansion meant more colonial expansion.

The enhanced role of the navy fostered changes on the ground, as enclaves in Tourane and Saigon proved inadequate to match French strategic interests. British control over India became more serious following the repression of the Sepoy Rebellion of 1857–9. France sought

---

[8] Exact conversion of expenditures to present-day foreign currencies is always difficult, in part because whole societies in Europe were much poorer in the nineteenth century than those societies today.

an answer to British India, as well as a competing path to influence in China. In the Treaty of Saigon (1862), the Nguyen emperor agreed to French direct rule over Cochinchina. Cambodia, a weakening vassal state of the Kingdom of Siam, became a French protectorate at the request of King Norodom in 1863. Eventually, *Indochine* (Indochina), hitherto an amorphous geographic term covering the lands between India and China, came to mean the French empire in Southeast Asia. The question henceforth became how to make that expanding part of the empire politically and economically viable.

2.3.3 The Emperor's Empire: The Royaume Arabe and the Bagne

If empire simply means hierarchical contracting that preserves difference, it is fitting that Emperor Napoleon III would have no one consistent colonial policy. Perhaps Louis-Napoleon's most ambitious imperial scheme occurred relatively late in his reign, a reboot of the entire French presence in Algeria through a particular variety of modernized monarchy. Advising the emperor on what became known as Arabophile policies was Ismaël Urbain, a model salesman for a multicultural empire. Born in Guyane to a white merchant and a *métis* woman, Urbain had learned Arabic as a young man and had worked for the army as an interpreter. Later, he converted to Islam and married an Algerian Arab.

The Arabophile imaginary exemplified by Urbain sought to replace the settler colony with a *Royaume Arabe*, an Arab kingdom united to France through the person of the emperor. "Algerians," comprising majority Arabs, as well as Berbers, Jews, and settlers, all would be French nationals in some broad, imperial sense. They would build the Arab kingdom together. They would not do so as equals, nor, given that France was not a republic, was it necessary that they be so. "All peoples are perfectible, so long as they seek to progress along the line of their normal development," wrote Urbain with confidence. This new Algeria would remain forever distinct from but connected to the Hexagon through law and trade, and, most importantly, through the dynasty.

Early on, Napoleon III signaled a new approach to the Islamic world. In October 1852, with his regime still in transition from the Second Republic to the Second Empire, he ordered the release of Abdelkader from his French prison. Supposedly overwhelmed by this generosity, the national hero of Algeria proclaimed: "Others could defeat me, others could put me in chains, but Louis-Napoleon was the only one who could win me over." According to the fine print always necessary to read in imperial contracting, Abdelkader could not return to Algeria. He was encouraged to migrate to Ottoman Syria, where he supported French and British intervention in 1860 to protect communities of Christians. In 1861, the Ottomans created the Christian-led Mount Lebanon Mutasarrifate, an opening for future French imperial interests in Ottoman Syria and throughout the eastern Mediterranean. The Second Empire had done well by doing good in liberating its former foe.

To be sure, in 1860 Napoleon III had named Pélissier governor of Algeria. Now a general and *maréchal de France* (the highest military honor), Pélissier had achieved notoriety in the *enfumade de Dahra* back in 1845. But the reputedly senile marshal was considered likely to do what he was told. Napoleon III was the first French head of state actually to visit the empire. He traveled to Algeria in 1860 and 1865, in imperial processions elaborately staged by the Armée d'Afrique. He wrote public letters to Pélissier in 1861 and to his successor, Crimean war hero and *maréchal de France* Patrice MacMahon, in 1865, outlining his vision. His letter to Pélissier advocated a hybridized Algeria: "In a word, instead of following the example of the North Americans who chase to extinction the bastard race of Indians, we should follow the example of the Spanish of Mexico, who assimilated themselves with the indigenous people." In the letter to MacMahon, he could not have put the matter more plainly: "Algeria is not a colony strictly speaking, but an Arab kingdom. The indigenous people as well as the colonists have an equal right to my protection, and I am as much Emperor of the Arabs as the Emperor of the French." Eventually, according to the scheme, civilian rule would replace military rule.

The Royaume Arabe had a spotty record in practice. MacMahon retained traditional military views on how Algeria should be governed. *Pénétration pacifique*, the sexualized term used at the time, came to mean renewed expropriation through the Tell. Heinous episodes of colonial violence continued, such as the massacres of men, women and children following the French siege of Laghouat in 1852. A serious Kabyle rebellion in 1864 required the French to increase the Armée d'Afrique from 60,000 to 85,000 men. An incident of Algerians attacking settlers in Djelfa (some 300 km south of Algiers) in 1861 resulted in the deaths of three Europeans and the serious injury of eight others. To Pélissier, the incident proved the existence of Muslim fanaticism, which merited the swift execution of seven men deemed responsible. In fact, the incident revealed the precarity of European settlement beyond the coastal cities. Djelfa also made it difficult to take very seriously the assurances of the allegedly multicultural emperor.

Natural disaster did not make regularizing French rule easier, particularly for Arabs and Berbers. A horrific drought in 1867, followed by plagues of locusts, famine, cholera, and typhus after the rains returned, killed hundreds of thousands. Starving, desperate survivors fled from the countryside to overcrowded cities. The government in Algiers never made a serious effort to determine just how many people died, though no one doubted that the vast majority were rural Arabs and Berbers. Realistic estimates provide a range of 500,000 to 1 million people dead, or between one-quarter and one-third of the entire population by 1871.

The most important legislation on Algeria during the Second Empire came in its late, "liberalizing" phase, and had effects directly opposite of those claimed. The Sénatus-Consulte provided a way to legislate by circumventing the lower house. The emperor appointed members of the Senate for life, and its decrees had the force of law. The Sénatus-Consulte of April 22, 1863 proposed to clarify land ownership by legitimizing titles grounded in Islamic law. As implemented, largely through the Bureaux Arabes, the law actually facilitated appropriation. By definition, the Sénatus-Consulte was French law, which few Muslims had the means of contesting successfully in French courts. Over time, interpretations of the law increasingly favored appropriations as a matter of state necessity. *Refoulement*, or pushing back the Arab population to lands the colonial authorities thought appropriate to their numbers, became policy protected by the law.

The Sénatus-Consulte of 1865 sought to clarify the legal status of the residents of Algeria, all of whom acquired French nationality. However, Muslims and Algerian Jews could become citizens only if they accepted French civil law on matters such as marriage and inheritance. Many devout Muslims considered doing so tantamount to apostasy. Settlers, on the other hand, could become full French citizens after three years of residence. Their children born in Algeria became French citizens automatically because of the long tradition of *ius soli*, the law of the soil. Consequently, the Sénatus-Consulte of 1865 evolved into a French version of Jim Crow. At best, the Royaume Arabe returned to the later views of Tocqueville and his heavy-handed advocacy of an Algeria safe for European settlers, only "liberal" in its grudging willingness to accept a few Muslims willing to assimilate, body and soul. Settlers continued to arrive, adding to a population that reached perhaps 200,000 by the end of the Second Empire, roughly half of them from the Hexagon.

His position as head of state implicated Napoleon III in another area of French imperial expansion – the prison colony or *bagne*. As president of the Second Republic, he told the National Assembly: "It seems possible to make the punishment of hard labor more effective, more morally improving, less expensive, and at the same time, more humane, by using it in the development of French colonization." In fact, like Saint-Domingue, the *bagnes* became laboratories of imperial domination. Political convicts as well as common criminals could be sent there.

Previously marginalized Guyane acquired new relevance as a penal colony. Thousands of kilometers from the Hexagon and adjacent to the jungle, Guyane offered few avenues of escape, and fewer still that would enable escapees to return to France. Tropical diseases, coupled with poor nutrition and mistreatment, meant that transportation to Guyane could amount to a death sentence. Of the 6,288 prisoners transported there between 1852 and 1856, 3,574 contracted yellow fever and 1,721 died of it. Even thereafter, between 7.6 and 9.9 percent of the prison population per year between 1858 and 1862 died of the disease.

According to an 1854 law, those not carried off by disease would carry out what architects of the *bagne* called "the most painful work of colonization." Prisoners labored under conditions rivaling slavery under the Ancien Régime, making roads and buildings, and draining swamps. The carceral regime enforced discipline through methods including beatings and public executions. Positions as guards in the *bagne* tended to draw sadists. Many prisoners who survived their sentences were subject to *doublage*, meaning they would remain in Guyane as colonists for the rest of their lives. Most notoriously, the Bagne de Cayenne, more commonly known as the L'île du Diable or Devil's Island, created a carceral hell within a carceral hell for political prisoners. It had a death rate in its early years estimated at 75 percent. The French would close it only in 1953.

In 1867 the Bonapartist regime announced that it would create a second major *bagne* destination, in New Caledonia, formally acquired by France in 1853. The official newspaper, *Moniteur Universel*, put the matter plainly on February 14, 1854: "The takeover had as its goals assuring for France the position in the Pacific that the interests of the military and commercial fleet require as well as realizing the views of the government on the penal system." Small numbers of French missionaries already served in New Caledonia. These had arrived nourished with tales of Kanak cannibalism that of course got better with the telling. Convicts deemed incorrigible only added to this unique colonial mix.

New Caledonia became part of the French and British partition of the South Pacific. It also constituted a kind of response to the British penal colony turned settler colony in Australia, even though transportation there, long in decline, ceased altogether by 1868. The discovery of important nickel deposits in New Caledonia provided an additional incentive to continue transportation, which created a lightly regulated, extremely inexpensive labor pool for dangerous work. Humanitarians, on the other hand, could comfort themselves with the idea that the milder, South Pacific climate would prove less lethal than that of pestiferous Guyane. Missionaries could find converts, capitalists could find minerals, captains could find another coaling station, prisoners could find redemption. The most optimistic saw New Caledonia as the *bagne* with a human face. Many of the 22,000 people transported there between 1864 and the end of transportation to New Caledonia in 1897 might have begged to differ. Nevertheless, as we will see, New Caledonia would evolve into its own variety of settler colony, with more settlers as a percentage of the total population than Algeria.

2.3.4 *The Capitalists' Empire*

Many historians paint Napoleon III as some sort of Saint-Simonian, though the term in this case obscures as much as it clarifies. Henri de Saint-Simon (1760–1825) advocated an eclectic mix of social theories – Ancien Régime ideas of social cohesion among unequals, attention to the material needs of the burgeoning working class, and the creation of an efficient economy through professionalized, technocratic management. The emperor wore economic doctrine as lightly as he wore doctrines either of authoritarianism early in his career or of liberalism later. He advocated infrastructure to facilitate trade, notably the building of roads and railroads. Few regimes in France ever had a more sincere belief in free trade or in the limits of state intervention in the economy. As a nation of savers, the French had plenty of capital to invest abroad. Arguably, "informal" empire, capitalist expansion without formal rule, proved at least as important as formal empire in extending French influence in the world. But informal and formal empire collided at intervals that arguably made formal empire look even more incoherent than it was.

Perhaps only chattel slavery and the *bagne* rivaled the opium trade for infamy in the history of European imperialism. Opium grown in British India was exported throughout Asia, particularly to China. Simply put, Europeans blackmailed Chinese elites into granting them monopolies over the opium trade, whereupon the Europeans did all they could to foster mass addiction. Europeans then used the profits to offset trade deficits in Asian goods, such as tea and silk. "Free trade" fostered no uglier commerce. Europeans dealt with Chinese recalcitrance through gunboat diplomacy, notably the Opium Wars of 1839–42 and 1856–60. France joined its "frenemy" Britain in the Second Opium War, with the additional familiar objective of protecting French missionaries. Atrocities were committed on both sides, notably in the treatment of prisoners. In 1869, the French and British destroyed the splendid Summer Palace near Beijing, as a cheaper alternative to occupying the vast city. The ensuing Convention of Peking (1860) restored "free trade," and compelled the Chinese to pay a large indemnity. Missionaries would have a free hand. For the French, the path lay open for the expansion of trade in opium and much else operating from Indochina.

The Bonapartist imaginary even envisaged new opportunities in the Western hemisphere, including an arguably absurd scheme for a canal joining the Atlantic and Pacific oceans through Nicaragua. The most ambitious scheme, however, involved setting a Habsburg on a Mexican throne that he would owe to French military and financial support. Through its Habsburg protégé, ascendant France would replace decadent Spain as the "civilizing" influence in Latin America. If the idea succeeded, said Napoleon III in 1862, "we shall have restored the strength and prestige of the Latin race on the other side of the ocean." Moreover, supporting Maximilian, brother of Austrian Emperor Franz Josef, could give France an ally against the rising power of Prussia.

But mostly, the ill-fated Mexican venture had roots in French finance. The French currency, the *franc germinal* established by Napoleon in 1803, proved remarkably stable over a politically unstable century. That stability depended on a bimetallic gold-silver standard, which fixed the value of the franc to the two metals, in turn fixed in exchange to each other. Changes in the world supply of bullion, such as those resulting from the California Gold Rush beginning in 1849 and the Australian gold rushes beginning a few years later, threatened this stability. The French sought new sources of bullion to rebalance, based on some very dated estimates of the riches of Mexico. Informal empire through a French-sponsored emperor, the theory went, could stabilize the whole situation. For the moment, the situation offered massive opportunities for speculation, notably in the state debt of Mexico. French speculators told themselves that they could buy Mexican debt cheap and sell dear as the bullion flowed. Best of all for French imperialists, the United States, hitherto the rising power in the hemisphere, descended into the preoccupation of civil war in 1861. Opportunity seemed to present itself on all fronts.

The biggest problem with the scheme, of course, involved failing to gain the support of the Mexican people before or after the coronation of Maximilian I as Emperor of Mexico on April 10, 1864. France would eventually send 40,000 troops to Mexico to support him. Maximilian was far from the most reactionary member of his family ever to sit on a throne, but the Mexican people had not thrown off Spanish rule to be governed by another Habsburg. Maximilian, after all, descended from the Austrian branch of the dynasty that had first conquered Mexico back in the sixteenth century. Only the most reactionary elements in Mexican society rallied to him, and even these became disillusioned following his endorsement of modest land reform. Moreover, the elected president of

Mexico, Benito Juárez, never relinquished power and turned the French intervention into a bloody guerrilla war. The United States never recognized the Habsburg regime, and began aiding Juárez as its own Civil War drew to a close.

The French, seeing the point of evaporating returns, began to disengage. They withdrew their forces in 1866, abandoning Maximilian to his fate. His own brother, the Austrian emperor Franz Josef, likewise refused help, not that he could have delivered much anyway. The Mexican government court-martialed the former emperor and executed him by firing squad on June 19, 1867. Édouard Manet's various paintings of the execution probably remain better remembered than the incident itself, for reasons that have more to do with tastes in French art history than the politics of the French empire. French holders of Mexican debt suffered unrealized dreams and losses if they did not sell in time; but they had paid little for the debt in the first place, and often had been paid some return before its value disappeared. They also knew full well that republican Mexico would need to return to the capital markets eventually, and that doing so would require some recognition of existing debts. French imperial capitalism would survive.

Probably the most ambitious exercise in French imperial capitalism was later so completely appropriated by the British that it is scarcely remembered as French. Dreams had floated since antiquity of a waterway joining the Mediterranean and the Red Sea, shortening by thousands of kilometers the sea routes between Europe and Asia. In the nineteenth century, the French revived this dream. A Suez Canal would support the long-standing French dream of dominance in the eastern Mediterranean. Napoleon Bonaparte had led a disastrous invasion of Egypt from 1798 to 1801 toward that end, in which he basically abandoned his army to seek his political fortunes in the Hexagon. That invasion left an inexplicably positive memory among his compatriots (including his nephew), a memory carefully nurtured by French Orientalists. A canal would provide the French with the additional bonus of a cultural highway to the exotic East.

Until late in the nineteenth century, Egypt largely ruled itself as a tributary province of the Ottoman Empire. The French achieved a surprising degree of informal influence in Egypt, through an expanding community of expatriates of 68,000 people by the end of the Bonapartist regime – more French than lived anywhere in its empire proper except Algeria. These expatriates managed trade through Christian communities throughout the eastern Mediterranean. Alongside the British, the French profited from the "cotton boom" in Egypt brought about in part by the North's blockade of the South in the American Civil War. French financiers continued to export capital to Egypt at lucrative rates. French lawyers were particularly involved in "modernizing" Egyptian business law, most often to the advantage of Europeans through concessions, enclaves of extraterritorial French sovereignty. The khedive of Egypt, Muhammad Ali and his heirs, made use of French military advisers to help in his struggles against internal rivals. Indeed, relations between the French and khedive remained cordial enough for him to send a battalion of Sudanese soldiers to support the Mexico misadventure.

As an exercise in mid-century imperial capitalism, the Suez Canal was the brainchild of one man, Ferdinand de Lesseps (1805–94). Born of a distinguished family of diplomats, the young Lesseps had served as such in Egypt, where he became interested in reviving the idea of a canal. He had few backers at the outset. Napoleon III was not eager to disrupt his relationship to the British, particularly if doing so involved a massive and risky investment in one of the largest infrastructure projects in the history of the world. Even the British were reticent at first, because they tended to prefer railroads as the instrument of colonial expansion in Africa.

Lesseps therefore set about raising capital on his own. In 1854, and with the authorization of the khedive, he established the Compagnie Universelle du Canal Maritime de Suez, a limited liability company. This company ran the canal until the Egyptians nationalized it in 1956. Having formed the company, however, Lesseps did not bring a very sophisticated understanding of capitalism to the task. He approached the House of Rothschild, perhaps Europe's premier bankers, for 200 million francs in capital (more than $3 billion today). When told of the standard interest rate of 5 percent, he left in a huff, reportedly telling Baron Rothschild: "Keep your counting rooms. I'll raise the money without you." A far better salesman than financier, Lesseps in fact did so through the public offering of shares. The French became by far the largest investors, followed by the khedive himself.

Actual construction of the canal began in April 1859. Through it all, Lesseps employed his diplomatic skills in a complex balancing act among the Ottoman and Egyptian authorities, the investors, and the French and British governments. Of course, nearly all of the actual labor and a good bit of the engineering came from Egyptians. Khedive Mohamed Said Pasha and his nephew and heir Isma'il Pasha used mass conscripted labor. This form of servitude had the lonely advantage of being seen as less onerous than conscription into the Ottoman army. No one knows how many workers died in the construction of the canal, though General Abdel Nasser's later claim of 120,000 dead remains widely believed in Egypt and beyond. Its ferocious cost in blood and treasure notwithstanding, the canal opened in 1869. Isma'il Pasha commissioned Giuseppe

Verdi to write his opera *Aida* in honor of the opening, and it premiered in Cairo in December 1871. French imperial capitalism appeared to have scored its greatest triumph since the colony in Saint-Domingue.

But imperial victory proved fleeting. European bankers, French and increasingly British, tempted the khedive with ever more debt, which he had ever more trouble servicing. Debt thus led to more debt, which had to be paid in gold or European currencies. Everyday Egyptians increasingly resented the burden debt service placed on them as taxpayers. As the debt cycle continued, the khedive's situation became desperate. In 1875, the British prime minister Benjamin Disraeli arranged the purchase of the khedive's shares, thanks to a loan from the same House of Rothschild spurned by Lesseps at the origin of the project. But the financial troubles of Egypt continued, as the British and French persisted in tempting the regime with foreign capital and the strings of supervision that came with it. In the wake of a nationalist revolt in 1882, British and French forces moved in as a form of foreclosure. Egypt became a de facto British protectorate. The French presence in Suez would continue through the company until 1956, but with the French as junior partners. British imperial capitalism had prevailed.

Napoleon III fell from power in 1870, for reasons that had nothing directly to do with the French empire. He blundered into the Franco-Prussian War of 1870–1, which helped create a united Germany, the very thing that France had provoked the war to avoid. The empire had evolved considerably between the defeat of the first Bonaparte emperor and the defeat of the second. France had established a settler colony in Algeria and had begun to do so in New Caledonia. It had sought to reinvent its presence in West Africa. French Indochina could at least aspire to the status of a French answer to British India. French missionaries spanned the globe, followed by French merchants and financiers. But beyond a vague presumption of needing imperial domains to sustain a Great Power identity, the question of just why France held and desired them remained unanswered. Or, put differently, there remained too many answers that never really sufficed, even in combination. Or, put differently still, Babar had far too many identities.

3   The *Mission Civilisatrice* to 1914

On July 28, 1885, Jules Ferry rose to speak on colonial policy at a boisterous session of the National Assembly of the Third French Republic. He was at that time a back bencher, his government having fallen at the end of March thanks to an unexpectedly difficult phase of imperial expansion in Indochina. But Ferry remained the foremost advocate for colonialism. This issue that day concerned funding extraordinary expenditure for an expedition to Madagascar. Not all of Ferry's colleagues understood just why, with Imperial Germany at its doorstep, France should send an army to conquer an island larger than the Hexagon itself off the southeast coast of Africa, particularly as it already occupied several surrounding islands. Even the vanilla boom in Madagascar lay decades in the future, long after the French established colonial rule. Ferry had a good bit to explain.

Ferry's speech laid out a vision for empire far beyond Madagascar. He argued that France turning its back on colonialism meant France turning its back on the world. To do so would be "to abdicate, and in a shorter time than we might think, believe me, to fall from the first to the third or fourth rank of nations." The silence that spoke in his speech was the loss to Imperial Germany of two wealthy provinces, Alsace and Lorraine, which had been French since the time of Louis XIV. Prospects for imperial expansion seemed far brighter than those for *la revanche* (revenge) on the Kaiserreich. Ferry also had economic concerns. French capitalism needed new, global markets. Trade in far-off lands would require security. France could not remain a Great Power without a great navy. No warship, he reminded his colleagues, could carry more than a fourteen-day supply of coal, meaning that the navy required secure bases around the world.

Ferry's speech is best remembered, however, for what he added to this mix, in his attempt to forge the most coherent theory of colonialism since mercantilism. He brought to colonial debates an argument controversial even at the time – that racial superiority constituted not simply a justification but an obligation for colonial expansion: "I repeat that there is for the superior races a prerogative, because there is a duty toward them. They have the duty to civilize the inferior races." Few of those present doubted the accepted truths of *races supérieurs* and *races inférieurs*. Nor was the idea of improving people of different colors new to the imperial enterprise. What, after all, had missionaries been trying to do for centuries?

Ferry sought to synthesize a new colonial doctrine, in which the French empire would do well by doing good. That synthesis became known as the *mission civilisatrice*, or civilizing mission. Historians now use the term mostly in an ironic sense. France, the theory went, would carry republican values wherever it brought the tricolor flag. French imperialists would intervene in the evolution of human progress, raising whole peoples to become worthy of those values. France would also teach the virtues of commerce, enriching both Hexagon and empire along the way. Military strength on land and sea would protect the civilizing mission. France would become a greater power than ever – now with a republican conscience.

The *mission civilisatrice* would face the daunting task of reconciling republican universalism and the difference on which empire rests. As we saw, since the First Republic abolished slavery in February 1794, republicanism had implied assimilation. French citizens became French citizens, whatever their color. A vastly expanded empire and nineteenth-century race doctrine argued differently. Ferry would win the immediate argument on Madagascar, which stage by stage would evolve into a French protectorate before becoming a formal colony in 1896. The national debate on what the empire should become continued.

Essentially, the same agents of imperial expansion as earlier in the century would carry out the *mission civilisatrice* – the state (now republican), officers, missionaries, and capitalists. Different agents served different functions in different places. Soldiers mattered more than capitalists or missionaries most of the time in Africa. The French built colonial Indochina with a very different mix of agents. There, with the collaboration of colonial officials, missionaries, soldiers, capitalists, and indigenous elites, the French constructed perhaps their most developed colonial state.

But the more lands the Third Republic conquered, the more difference it would have to manage as empire. The more difference it had to manage, the greater the challenge to republican universalism. It came to matter increasingly just who Babar was, a question increasingly connected to his color. Republicanism in France had always had a predominant color – white. But the fine points of republican whiteness would achieve new significance as French republican rule extended over more and more people who clearly were something else.

3.1   The Third Republic as Regime and Empire

Adolphe Thiers (1797–1877), the great phrasemaker of the founding of the Third Republic, had remarked back in 1850: "The republic is the form of government that divides us the least." Plenty still divided the French two decades later. The Second Empire disintegrated in defeat in the Franco-Prussian War of 1870–81, with the emperor captured by the Prussians and packed off to inglorious exile in London. The Paris crowd saw the chance to reenact its own revolutionary past and declared France a republic. Doing so was not going to change the fortunes of France in a war already lost. Nor was the last-minute departure by hot air balloon of left-leaning republican hero Léon Gambetta to lead continued resistance from the city of Tours. When the dust began to settle in 1871, a majority of Frenchmen probably preferred some kind of monarchy. One Bonaparte may have departed, but Bonapartists had not. There were also Bourbon and Orléanists claimants to a new throne. There was not enough room on a French throne, Thiers allegedly quipped, for three backsides.

Moreover, the Paris crowd refused to accept defeat in the war, seizing the city and declaring what became known as the Paris Commune. They forced a provisional government led by Thiers to operate out of Versailles. In Karl Marx's famous essay "The Civil War in France" (1871), he praised the Communards as "the glorious harbinger of a new society," as proletarians crushed because their time had not yet come. Most historians today, however, see the Paris Commune as something that looked more backward than forward, to the days when a Paris crowd that drew its strength from the socialism of artisans could hold the imagination of the world. The Versailles government would eventually defeat the Commune through a siege led by General Patrice MacMahon, who like General Cavaignac in 1848 had learned his craft in Algeria. Atrocity stories on both sides, as usual, got better with the telling. But suppressing the Commune was certainly a bloody business. The traditionally accepted figure of 20,000 Parisians dead is probably more in the range of 5,700–7,400.[1] The *bagne* also received a new wave of involuntary immigrants (some 3,800 people) in the aftermath of the Commune.

But the French remained divided. The republican regime would not really establish itself until 1879, and then as a collection of compromises. France indeed would become a republic, its leaders elected by universal male suffrage. But long gone was the 1848 dream of *la République*

---

[1] See the painstaking analysis in Robert Tombs, "How Bloody was the *Semaine Sanglant* of 1871: A Revision," *The Historical Journal* 55 (2012): 679–704.

démocratique et sociale. The French forged a socially conservative republic, with low taxes, low levels of state services, and quite low levels of economic justice. The Third Republic would care deeply about three policy areas – education (for the proper formation of citizens), railroads (to serve both commerce and national security), and the military. Empire notably did not count among these three initially, and never in terms of the allocation of public resources. Through its long life, the regime could never agree on a consistent policy on so dire an issue as famine relief in the empire. Before World War I, the republic would spend only about 7 percent of its state budget on its imperial domains. Of this, about half went to Algeria, the most populated *départements* of which legally were not the empire at all. From its first days to its last, the conservative republic would seek to maintain and expand its empire on the cheap.

In the Anglophone world, it has long been tempting to conflate the entire history of the Third Republic with its demise in 1940. Certainly, it was an effervescent parliamentary regime. Governments had an average life span of 250 days between 1879 and 1940. A strong National Assembly produced fragile governments. According to a common quip at the time, the President of the Republic, the nominal head of state, was someone who got to wear evening clothes during the day because he spent most of his time in public ceremony. Yet beneath the apparent turbulence of high politics, the Third Republic for most of its life proved a resilient agreement among middle class white men to get along on political matters. To date, only the monarchy has exceeded the Third Republic in longevity. Persons tended to change a great deal more than basic policy, in both the Hexagon and the empire.

The colonies had representation in the National Assembly, though in small numbers. The colonies sent from seven to twenty representatives from Paris between 1875 and 1931, with the number slowly increasing over that time. But even in 1931, some 606 deputies and 307 senators represented some 41.8 million French in the Hexagon, whereas some nineteen deputies and seven senators represented an estimated 64.7 million people in the empire.[2] Indigenous peoples were held to be represented indirectly by deputies for whom they could not vote, as were all women and minors.

Yet even this modest representation of the empire remained controversial through the whole life of the Third Republic. Adolphe Messimy, later minister for colonies and war minister, reminded his colleagues in 1907 that if they followed a principle of equal representation, the colonies

---

[2] Jacques Binoche-Guedra, "La Représentation parlementaire colonial (1871–1940)," *Revue Historique* 280 (1988): 529.

would send some 700 deputies to Paris. He argued that such a hypothesis, "by its very absurdity," showed how colonial representation could upend French political life. The idea that one day the empire could colonize the Hexagon had deep roots.

In fact, empire never wholly united the French. Thiers and Gambetta tended to support colonial expansion. But a rising socialist movement in the latter part of the century, while more ideologically inclusive than after the Great War, generally opposed enlarging the empire. Most socialists saw imperial expansion, not inaccurately, as the instrument of enhanced capitalist oppression at home and abroad. Prewar socialist hero Jean Jaurès visited Algeria in 1895. While he did not reject the *mission civilisatrice* as such, he lamented: "We have been unfaithful [*infidel*] tutors of the Arab people." Appropriating the words of Maximilien Robespierre during the French Revolution, he reminded his compatriots: "The peoples do not love armed missionaries." Feminists such as Hubertine Auclert, who had lived in Algeria as the wife of a magistrate, criticized patriarchal rule in the colonies, even as she bitterly protested granting "black savages" in the *vieilles colonies* the suffrage denied to "cultivated white women." In the *vieille colonie* of caste-ridden Pondicherry, universal male suffrage would eventually aid the cause of Indian nationalism.

Imperial conquest had opponents in the Center and on the Right as well as the Left. Georges Clemenceau, whose position on the political spectrum would shift considerably over a long career, made many a scathing speech about the arrogance of imperial expansion. Directly opposing Ferry, he maintained that "these adventures, costly and sterile expeditions, launched haphazardly in every sense," could hardly send the proper message of French universalism to the world. "You want to found an empire in Indochina," he thundered, "we want to found the Republic." A serious scandal in 1893 over financing the proposed Panama Canal, in which Clemenceau was mostly innocent, temporarily damaged his political career and did not endear him to imperialism. A withering, racist critique of empire before 1914 came from right-wing nationalist Paul Deroulède, who saw colonial expansion as a giant distraction from reconquering Alsace and Lorraine. "I had two sisters," he maintained in one version of the story, "and you are offering me twenty *nègres*."[3] However, the electorate allowed the Parti colonial, a faction in the National Assembly, influence well beyond its numbers.

---

[3] The French reads: "*J'avais deux sœurs et vous m'offrez vingt nègres.*" In a more classist but potentially less racist version of the story, he posited "twenty domestic servants" (*vingt domestiques*).

Most of this chapter will focus on parts of the world in which colonial expansion and the struggle for coherence under the Third Republic had the most dramatic results – Africa and Indochina. In North Africa, the French would seek to reestablish, yet again, the settler colony in Algeria, and would acquire new protectorates in Tunisia and Morocco. In West and Central Africa, it would expand inland from the coastal settlements. To unite their North African and West African domains and to compete with their "frenemies" the British, the French would annex most of the Sahara Desert. In Southeast Asia, the French would create Indochina in its full colonial sense through combining its colony in Cochinchina and its protectorate in Cambodia with protectorates in Annam, Tonkin, and Laos.

The rise of modern science also had implications for empire, in the form of race doctrine. Race based on color, of course, was not new to the imperial enterprise. Sieur François Delbée back in 1671 certainly understood the color of the persons he loaded on to his ships, as did those persons themselves. But the Ancien Régime and even the Enlightenment maintained flexible views on race relative to what came after. "Scientific" knowledge refined race theory with new forms of claims to truth. Paradigms of nineteenth-century race theory would in turn shape governance in the imperial domains.

While "scientific" race theory is sometimes blamed on the great English theorist of evolution, Charles Darwin, his successors drove his relatively fluid views in more dogmatic directions. French theorists, construed as some of the brightest lights in European academia in their day, participated fully in the construction of what would become known as Social Darwinism. Émile Durkheim, one of the parents of modern sociology and himself only obliquely interested in empire, stressed *faits sociaux*, social facts largely beyond the control of individuals. Social facts are not immutable but exist in the context of elemental constructions of the role of the individual in society. Applied to the empire, a given colonial policy could expect to change the colonized society only incrementally, and over a very long time frame. Alfred Fouillé taught at the ultra-elite École Normale Supérieure, which has trained many of the most powerful guardians of the French Republic to our own day. Fouillé argued in the early 1890s that all races could progress, but that some did so much faster and farther than others. "They might be compared," he wrote, "to runners on the field of civilization; those who are ahead can run all the more quickly because their head start is already greater." Fouillé particularly opposed racial hybridity, which he saw as individualizing and concentrating racial competition, creating "a personality divided against itself, incoherent."

Other theorists articulated ways in which race should directly shape colonial policy. Gustave Le Bon, still known for his work on the psychology of crowds, argued that mental evolution proceeded at a glacial pace, largely impervious to colonial decrees. Consequently, the French "must consider as dangerous chimeras all our ideas of assimilating or Frenchifying an inferior people. Leave to the natives their customs, their institutions, and their laws." Léopold de Saussure, the brother of semiotician René de Saussure, served as an officer in the French navy in the Pacific and wrote *La Psychologie de la colonization française* (1899). He developed a full-blown attack on the very idea of assimilation, contending that the "Latin" races, speakers of Romance languages, had a tendency for assimilation inherited from the Romans. The interest of Enlightenment *philosophes* in rendering the world rational had exacerbated this tendency. The Spanish affinity for assimilation, he continued, had resulted in imperial decline, leading to the then-recent disaster of war with the United States in 1898. France, therefore, should leave assimilation to "natural" processes, in which conquered people would become as French as they could or wanted to be. Most, Saussure concluded, would rightly be left behind.

From such theories came an alternative colonial doctrine to assimilation – association, the theory underpinning the story of Babar. French imperialism would accept racial difference, and hierarchies produced by that difference, as permanent within any foreseeable time frame. France would not try to make French the peoples over whom it ruled, beyond the bare minimum required for governance. French rule would accept local law, customs, and institutions – including looking the other way at indigenous versions of slavery.

The Third Republic, like the Fourth and the Fifth, would cherish the formation of colonial elites as its own version of Darwinian social selection. A tiny number of indigenous people, fluent in French and the best and brightest of them educated in the Hexagon, could rise to positions of responsibility. Hybridity did not necessarily mean exclusion, in the empire or the Hexagon itself. Indeed, a *métis* from Senegal, General Alfred Amédée Dodd, would lead the conquest of the ancient Kingdom of Dahomey (today Benin) from 1890 to 1894. Ideally, colonial elites would help the French rule and develop the colonies whence they came. Colonial theory imagined Babar long before de Brunhoff wrote his first children's story, which was published in 1931.

The tension between assimilation and association structured both the colonial and the postcolonial history of the French empire. Both doctrines had formidable logical challenges. Under assimilation, if "France" was "France" – whether in Paris, Dakar, Hanoi, or Tahiti, what would happen to immense differences in language, economy, religion, and culture? Competing cultures would either fight each other to the death or merge somehow into hybridity. But in the end game of assimilation, everyone would be "French." Theoretically, the white daughter of a Hexagon blue blood could marry without prejudice the black son of a peanut farmer from Senegal. Very few partisans of assimilation in the Hexagon believed in taking the doctrine quite this far. Association, on the other hand, seemed to beg an intractable question. If imperial rule was about respecting local culture, why did it exist at all except to extract resources? Republican empire participated in plenty of extraction but could never feel comfortable admitting extraction as its principal goal. On the other hand, improving whole peoples of myriad colors over an indefinite timeframe would not appear to justify the costs of empire in blood and treasure.

The *bagne*, that brutal institution of extraction, flourished under the Third Republic. At a stretch, social engineers could argue that the *bagne* served a domestic *mission civilisatrice* by ridding the Hexagon of those unworthy of citizenship and putting their labor at the service of the empire. Guyane came to be seen as too lethal for all but the most incorrigible criminals, though it could continue to receive special prisoners such as Captain Alfred Dreyfus.[4] Other prisoners were more likely to be sent to New Caledonia – some 22,000 between 1863 and 1931. The vast majority of those transported were men, though some 1,000 were women. Many were recidivists, though some 4,000 people were transported after the repression of the Paris Commune. With nickel production rising and the Kanak population falling rapidly because of the spread of European diseases, the island needed labor.

Strewn throughout the empire, from New Caledonia to Madagascar to Senegal to the Hexagon itself, were an array of militarized disciplinary units first organized under the July Monarchy and known collectively as the *biribi*. The best known were the *bataillons d'infanterie légère d'Afrique* (light infantry battalions of Africa) better known as the "Bat d'Af" or ironically as *les joyeux* (the joyous ones). More labor than combat units, the Bat d'Af structured a perilous life of torture. Endless hard labor under a blazing sun was its own punishment, as were wretched sanitary conditions, intentionally poor nutrition, and beatings from guards and fellow prisoners.

[4] Dreyfus was falsely convicted in 1895 and then again in 1899 of spying for the Germans. The Dreyfus Affair served up a toxic combination of anti-Semitism, anti-republicanism, clerical reaction, and anti-clericalism. Dreyfus himself served some five years on Devil's Island before his pardon in 1899.

While some youth found themselves in the Bat d'Af through miscar-
riages of justice, more common were hardened criminals in their thirties.
The Bat d'Af considered old men those who made it to their forties. The
prisoners themselves helped build a violent dystopia. Ubiquitous tat-
toos demarcated a complex social order – from the strongest, presumed
to play the "active" role in organized rape, to the *djèges*, derived from
an Arabic word for "chicken," passed from prisoner to prisoner to play
the "passive" role. Debilitating sexually transmitted diseases thrived in
such an environment. The French Republic would not disband the last
of its disciplinary units until the 1970s. Few regimes anywhere and no
republics ever excluded anyone more ferociously than the Third Republic through the *bagne* and the *biribi*.

3.2   The *Mission Civilisatrice* in Africa

Throughout its long history, the French empire acquired the most
territory in the shortest period of time in Africa between 1870 and 1914.
At the fall of Napoleon III, France in Africa ruled coastal Algeria, the
Quatre Communes of Senegal and parts of the hinterlands to varying
degrees, and a collection of trading posts along the West and Central
African coast, in today's Guinea, Côte d'Ivoire, Benin, and Gabon. By
the time France entered World War I in 1914, it ruled most of West
Africa and the Sahara, and a large expanse of Central Africa.

The Third Republic sought to make sense of its vast domains in Africa
through forming two colonial federations – Afrique-Occidentale française
(AOF, or French West Africa, 1895) and Afrique-Équatoriale francaise
(AEF, or French Equatorial Africa, 1910). At 4,689,000 km^2, the AOF
was more than eight times the size of the Hexagon (some 544,000 km^2).
The AEF at some 2.500.000 km^2 was over four times the size of the
Hexagon. The French populations in both federations remained microscopic.[5] France also ruled a small but strategic domain in the Horn of
Africa (French Somaliland, today Djibouti, a protectorate after 1884),
and the massive island of Madagascar (some 587,000 km^2, somewhat
larger than the Hexagon, 1897). In North Africa, the French ruled protectorates in Tunisia (1881) and Morocco (1912) as well as Algeria. The
Third Republic mobilized the *mission civilisatrice* to try to make sense of
these vast domains.

---

[5] For example, as late as 1953, the AOF had an estimated total population of some 16 mil-
lion people. Some 30,000 Europeans also lived there, about half in Dakar. Anonymous,
"Démographie de l'A.O.F.," *Présence Africaine* No. 15 (Hommage à Jacques Richard-
Molard) (1953): 68.

At a certain level, French expansion in Africa has a simple explanation – geopolitics. The "Scramble for Africa" had its origins in two European conferences (1878 and 1884–5) held in Berlin and called by the German chancellor, Otto von Bismarck. The first further authorized the partition of North Africa; the second helped establish two foundational doctrines of imperialism under late nineteenth-century international law. Under the doctrine of effective occupation, for a new imperial domain to be recognized internationally, the colonizing power actually had to govern, not just claim it. The conference thus legitimized the *mission civilisatrice* as a foundation of governance. As a corollary to the doctrine of effective occupation, the Berlin conferences articulated the doctrine of the hinterland. Effective occupation, typically along a coast, carried with it the right to annex enough of the hinterland to protect the territory originally occupied. This doctrine of course begged the question of how much annexation would suffice to guarantee security. In effect, the doctrine of the hinterlands constituted an invitation contrived by the European powers to partition the entire African continent.

Like other aspects of Great Power competition before 1914, colonial acquisition was not always rational. France had acquired a host of far-flung and potentially costly new domains of debatable strategic or economic utility. France did not need to conquer all of Madagascar to secure more coaling stations for its navy. Promises of vast reserves of gold there proved optimistic. Who even at the time could have believed in vague schemes for settlement? Who could argue that France needed a new settler colony? Few of the French could pronounce lengthy Malagasy names, even the relatively simple name of Queen Ranavalona III, whom the French deposed in 1896 to establish direct rule, let alone that of Rainanandriamampandry, a former commander of the royal garrison whom the French had executed. The economic value added by conquering the Sahara Desert seemed less than self-evident.

In short, France acquired new African domains because its European rivals did. In 1890, for example, the British recognized French predominance over Madagascar in exchange for the recognition of a British protectorate in Zanzibar. Yet reducing colonial acquisition to the projection of European politics on to the world stage homogenizes colonial expansion, since it accords imperial domains a single function. The massive expansion of the French empire in Africa might have been irrational to a political scientist, but it had profound historical effects on colonizer and colonized that were felt long after independence. The *mission civilisatrice* had real meaning in French imperial rule. Colonial officials, officers, missionaries, and capitalists all sought in one way or another to remake Africa in their own images.

3.2.1   The Civilizing Colonial State

Like other kinds of state power, colonial authority in practice would be checked in many ways. For example, in protectorate Tunisia in the 1890s, something so apparently simple as consolidating consular courts for handling matters involving Europeans had to be negotiated through a complicated web of relationships with the dey (still *in situ*) and with Italy. Italians, more numerous than the French in Tunisia until the 1930s, would not submit to French consular courts unconditionally. As a "civilizing" agent, the colonial state would mean different things to different persons in different places at different times. The line between civilian and military rule was seldom clear, and sometimes non-existent. But many colonial officials and officers took republicanism seriously, as they understood it, throughout the empire.

Regime change in the Hexagon in 1870 had immediate repercussions in Algeria, and indeed gave rise to the settler notion that they represented the "true" French Republic. Settlers had never forgiven Napoleon III for the very idea of the Royaume Arabe, however modest and contradictory the actual results. Further, settlers came to consider military rule altogether too friendly to the indigenous population because of the Bureaux Arabes and the reliance of the military on local magistrates or *caids*. Settlers thus eagerly embraced civilian rule under a republic. Indeed, Algiers staged its own settler Commune in late 1870, led by a lawyer exiled to Algeria for his activities back in 1848, Benoît Vuillermoz. The Commune rejected two military governors proposed by the provisional government in Tours. "*Algérie farà da sé*" (Algeria will go it alone), telegraphed Vuillermoz to Paris in November 1870. The fact that *farà da sé* is Italian and not French seemed to say it all. The settlers were African republicans fixated on a white-led regime, not Hexagon republicans transported to the other side of the Mediterranean. The Crémieux Decree of October 24, 1870 added to their numbers, by making full French citizens of an estimated 35,000 indigenous Jews. Nearly all Algerian Jews descended from families settled there for centuries and led much of their lives in the Arabic and Berber languages of their neighbors. Nevertheless, the Crémieux Decree gave them a separate and superior legal status.

But no sooner had Paris regained control over the Commune of Algiers when it had to confront the largest Arab and Berber uprising until after World War II. The Muslim population, already enraged by the confused and unhelpful response of the colonial government to the famine of 1867, feared a civilian regime for precisely the same reasons the settlers embraced it. Further, defeat by Prussia and the disintegration of the Bonapartist regime had shown the vulnerability of the French state. Mahieddine Ibn el Kader, the son of Abdelkader, called for a general uprising. Its leader in the field beginning in March 1871 was a Kabyle (Berber), Sheik Mokrani. Though the call to *jihad* or holy war divided the Arabs, it drew both Arab and Kabyle support.

While some 100,000 indigenous Algerians ultimately fought the French, the uprising proved perhaps a foredoomed enterprise after the suppression of the Paris Commune in May 1871. The new regime in Paris could send thousands of battle-hardened troops across the Mediterranean, many experienced in colonial warfare. They defeated the rebellion over the next six months. Mokrani died of exposure in the desert, and some 212 indigenous Algerians were deported to the *bagne* in New Caledonia. Some of their descendants still live there, known as the *Kabyles du Pacifique*, because Kabyles were required to remain after Europeans and Arabs were amnestied. Repression swiftly followed suppression in Algeria – a new round of land appropriations amounting to some 500,000 ha, and a collective fine of some 35 million francs (some $70 million today), to be collected from an impoverished population. "Civilizing" republican Algeria meant annihilating indigenous institutions as completely as possible.

European immigration began to trail off into the early twentieth century, never to recover. For example, Bône (today Annaba), drew 10,529 new Europeans settlers in 1866, but only 1,765 in 1911. The European population would increase, but much more slowly and mostly through reproduction. An increasing share of the European population was thus born in Algeria, without direct connections to Europe. Settlers continued to prefer cities, an impediment to the colonial regime's ambition to colonize the rural Tell. Proportionally fewer rural settlers appropriated more and more land. The gradual mechanization of agriculture would further deepen the urban/rural divide. In 1896, approximately 578,000 persons of European descent lived in Algeria, or a little under 11.6 percent of a total population of 5 million people.

The colonial state sought to guarantee white rule by reformed spatial governance, through an institution originally developed under the July Monarchy. The term *commune de plein exercise* has no real counterpart in English. Originally, they were enclaves of civilian municipal rule in the uplands of the Tell previously governed by the military. Under the Third Republic, the *commune de plein exercise* became primarily an administrative instrument of solidifying settler authority. Settler-led municipal councils taxed Arabs and Berbers and distributed the proceeds for the benefit of the settlers. Jules Ferry himself described them as the equivalent of robbery in broad daylight of the Muslim majority. In the region of

Bône, for example, the *communes de plein exercise* comprised a population only about 20 percent European in 1907. *Communes mixtes* had primarily indigenous populations, less autonomy, and existed in rural areas. They served the basic function of making more land available for white settlement. The *communes mixtes* around Bône comprised a population that was only about 4 percent European in 1907. *Communes indigènes* were even more remote and remained mostly under military rule. The French would extend this form of territorial organization throughout West and Equatorial Africa into the twentieth century.

In the AOF, France had acquired so much territory so fast that a federal framework had a certain logic. The federation comprised millions of hectares of savannah, desert, and rain forest, and peoples of seemingly numberless ethnicities, languages, and forms of political organization. A single governor-general based in Dakar could preside over highly differentiated colonial rule within the federation. As in Indochina, the Hexagon sought a self-sustaining colonial regime paid for through trade and the taxation of the indigenous peoples. In French Sudan (today's Mali), for example, the colonial state pursued financial self-sufficiency through *une politique cottonière* (a cotton policy). Colonial officials, who favored peasant production in the interest of civil peace, found themselves at odds with investors, who favored plantation-style cultivation, with African labor managed by Europeans.

As in the Hexagon, the Third Republic in Africa cared deeply about specified areas of public policy, but parsimoniously. Throughout, Paris advised colonial officials to establish schools *"sans surcroît de dépenses,"* without spending too much money. This kept colonial education rudimentary and occupational. The *écoles des otages* (schools of the hostages) proliferated in the AOF, typically under more sanitized names. But local notables continued to send their sons there to be educated under the watchful eye of the colonial state.

Colonial education had the long-term function of making French the literal *lingua franca*, the indispensable unifier of the empire. Proficiency in French would do much to shape whether colonial subjects could look forward to other opportunities, such as better-supported schools. In the republican tradition, the best and brightest would have access to elite education in the Hexagon. That said, colonial education had its critics among colonists even at the time. Why, wrote one of a high school in Algiers in 1882, "should we take to our breast the children of these vipers," and in a quick shift of metaphor, "these young Arabs who will return to their lairs, like young jackals that we want to tame, the moment they become free?" Colonial schools, in fact, trained most of the anticolonial elite and postcolonial leadership, in Africa as elsewhere.

Nothing about French rule in Africa since the Ancien Régime had done much to alter the traditional systems of servitude on which many African societies depended. Even in the Quatre Communes of Senegal, French national territory where indentured servitude had been abolished back in 1848, escaped persons were commonly returned to their masters. The return of a republic after 1871 carried with it renewed calls for the complete and enforced abolition of all forms of servitude, led in the Senate by the still-active Victor Schœlcher. AOE Governor-General Ernest Roume agreed, writing in 1890 that France "does not recognize the individual's right to contract a personal engagement that forever deprives him of his own freedom." In practice, however, the matter proved not so simple. The frugal republic was never going to go out of its way to subsidize the transition to relatively expensive wage labor, above all in colonies short on specie. Indeed, demand for unpaid labor would increase as economies developed. In addition, the more French rule extended through West Africa, the more it had to depend on contracting with local chiefs who had no intention of surrendering forms of servitude on which their own rule rested. "Slavery" in its myriad meanings had decades to run in the AOF.

The Third Republic characterized itself as a regime not of men but of law. Of course, men, so gendered, made law. But what should law even mean in the empire? Nearly all guardians of the Republic believed that simply assimilating millions of colonial subjects immediately into the law of the Hexagon was neither practical nor desirable. "We should try to uplift the native," wrote the AOE governor-general Martial Merlin, "but in a way appropriate to his mentality and his needs." In West Africa, the juridical *mission civilisatrice* involved imposing French colonial criminal law while preserving most Islamic and other forms of African civil law. Maintaining indigenous civil law helped preclude claims to full French citizenship. Doing so also gave indigenous bodies considerable authority in everyday life. In 1903, the French established the Chambre d'homologation, a branch of the appeals court, to supervise delegated justice.

The most notorious juridical instrument of *la mission civilisatrice* was a fully separate discourse of criminality for non-whites, the *indigénat*. Another term not easily translated into English, the *indigénat* was neither native law nor French law. Indeed, it was not really law at all in the sense of an explicit code guaranteed by an independent judiciary or predictable procedures. Mostly, it meant the will of the colonial administrator, often as interpreted by him. Infractions under the *indigénat* could include anything that obstructed the collection of taxes, the refusal to participate in conscript labor, and most gestures that appeared to question the authority of France, such as refusing to accept colonial money as legal tender. The colonial administrator could judge attitudes as well as deeds. For example, those who paid their taxes with a poor spirit could attract punishment even if the taxes were paid. The full purpose of the *indigénat* was to define the *indigène*, or the native inherently ineligible for citizenship. The very flexibility of the *indigénat* helps explain why the French applied versions of it so broadly – in Algeria and Cochinchina in 1881, in Senegal and New Caledonia in 1887, in AOF in 1904, and AEF in 1910. Few aspects of colonial rule drew more resentment among the colonized.

3.2.2   Civilizing Officers

Throughout the nineteenth century, and under every French regime, the empire promised young white men virility, adventure, and conquest, discreetly but clearly including sex. Mars and Venus combined in numberless ways in the French empire, in consensual and non-consensual situations. *Pénétration coloniale* was not just a metaphor, nor was it understood solely as such at the time. At the very least, the empire reinforced the tendency of the French state to look the other way in all manner of same-sex relations – whether the violent relations of the *biribi* or the presumed activities of the governor-general of Morocco, General Hubert Lyautey.

Statistically more common, probably, continued to be heterosexual unions of various sorts between French men and colonized women. Maurice Delafosse, an ethnographer and colonial official, took a wife in a *marriage à la mode du pays* (marriage according to local custom) in the Côte d'Ivoire. Like Faideherbe, he legally recognized their children, one of whom (Jean Delafosse) would reach ministerial rank in the Côte d'Ivoire after independence. The colonial army did not consider itself above using African women as a form of war booty. In December 1887, the Tiraillleurs sénégalais captured jihadist Mamadou Lamine Drame, and distributed his various wives among his captors. The military encouraged more consensual unions among its elite colonial corps, particularly the Tirailleurs Sénégalais. The very existence of the *mesdames tirailleurs*, the theory went, could help disrupt local practices of slavery.

In more public matters, virility had always helped make colonial policy as well as implement it. Back in the 1840s, the masculine, adventurous spirit of Jules Dumont d'Urville responded to his frustration with service in the Napoleonic navy, the untimely death of some of his children, and his own health issues (including gout and kidney infections). With royal sponsorship, he explored the South Pacific up to the coast of Antarctica. He named the section of the coast the Terre Adélie after his beloved wife, a name it retains today. D'Urville's "discovery" provided the foundation for largely theoretical French claims to a slice of the continent.

Later, masculine yearnings for adventure likewise surely motivated Pierre Savorgnan de Brazza, who led the French colonial penetration into Central Africa in the 1880s. Born in Rome in 1852 as "Pietro" to wealthy Italian parents, Brazza's early *wanderlust* led him first to the École navale, the academy in Brest, then to a career in the French empire. Up to a point, Brazza simply followed in the footsteps of Louis Faidherbe in Senegal. With the support of powerful patrons in Paris, Brazza carried out two expeditions along the Congo River that morphed into expeditions of conquest. In September 1880, he signed a treaty of protection with the *makoko* (monarch) of the Anziku kingdom, some 200 km inland from the coast. Brazza promised protection both from other Europeans and from rival kingdoms. The *makoko*, in return, transferred "his territory to France, to whom he cedes his hereditary and supreme rights." The French government, it bears noting, had not authorized Brazza to make any agreement with a foreign sovereign.

But Paris could not easily relinquish even unauthorized new domains. The government not only ratified a treaty it played no role in writing but also sent Brazza back to the Congo in 1883 as *Commissaire de la République* with a subsidy of 1,275,000 francs to extend French claims through the Upper Congo. Though always more an explorer and entrepreneur than a day-to-day colonial administrator, Brazza had laid the groundwork for the AEF, founded in 1910. Brazza and his successors made regular if only sporadically successful attempts to interest French private capital. Economic exploitation took place through concessions, monopolies over agriculture and forests granted for a price by the French state. Unlike Ancien Régime concessions, however, the state did not formally subcontract its own authority over internal security.

Through it all, Brazza and his deeds enjoyed a level of media coverage in the Hexagon all but unimaginable even to Faidherbe in his early years. As shown in Illustration 3.1, he had a good understanding of the polyvalent messaging on masculinity made possible by photography. Mass-circulation publications such as *Tour du Monde* and *Le Petit Journal* found hundreds of thousands of readers among a Hexagon population with one of the highest literacy rates in the world, thanks to the investment of the Third Republic in primary education. Numerous stories illustrated with elaborate engravings made Brazza an international figure and a national hero.

Even more than Faidherbe, Brazza crafted his image through his own writings. In his prose, exoticized Africans became ideal subjects for the *mission civilisatrice* – children, lovely and insightful in their way, who

Illustration 3.1 Colonial masculinity: Pierre Savorgnan de Brazza, 1889.
Source: Bibliothèque nationale de France (public domain).

wanted only a benevolent but firm guiding hand to advance themselves. In their childlike fascination with blue beads he brought with him as presents, Africans made Brazza aware of the arbitrariness of value itself: "Our European precious stones had value only because they were rare, and blue beads were very rare in the Ondoumbo country." Brazza prided himself on his ability to extend French interests without bloodshed, preferring what he called "prestidigitation [magic tricks] and pyrotechnics" to violence. A well-phrased threat of violence could preclude the need for violence. When such a skilled imperialist offered so much colonial expansion at so little expense, Brazza made the Hexagon an offer it did not want to refuse.

Other officers followed in Brazza's media-blazed path. Probably the most famous episode illustrated the most difficult moment of imperial competition between France and Britain. In the "scramble for Africa" following the Berlin conferences, Britain annexed along the north–south axis of the Nile River, between the Cape Colony in South Africa and its de facto protectorate in Egypt. France, in turn, annexed along an east–west axis between its West and Central African domains, across the Sahara toward the protectorate it established in 1884 in French Somaliland (today Djibouti). Colonial troops rather than white troops, notably the Tirailleurs, provided the French military muscle. In July 1898, the British and French met at Fashoda (today Kodok, in South Sudan). Charismatic officers became media figures in their respective empires – Herbert Kitchener commanding the British and Egyptian-Sudanese forces, and Jean Baptiste Marchand, conqueror of the Sahara, commanding the French forces.

As word of this testosterone-fueled standoff in Fashoda trickled back to Europe, warmongers in both empires began to polish swords. Practically speaking, however, Marchand's force of some 132 men stood little chance against Kitchener's force of some 1,500. Nor, truth be told, did France have an interest in fighting a Great Power it would surely need at its side in the event of a conflict with Germany. At the time, Clemenceau was complaining about the folly of disputing marshes along the Nile while the Germans held Strasbourg. He was not alone. France backed down in the confrontation with Britain, much to the consternation of the Parti colonial and the popular press. "We have behaved like madmen in Africa," President Félix Faure later admitted, "led astray by irresponsible people called the colonialists." Indeed, later events would prove the wisdom of Clemenceau's fixation on European security interests. Reconciliation after the French retreat at Fashoda laid the foundations for the Entente Cordiale, the alliance that would hold the Western Front in World War I.

Charles Mangin, an enterprising officer present at Fashoda, proposed a radical scheme that could transform the empire itself. In his book *La Force noire* (The Black Force, 1910), Mangin advocated making the Tirailleurs Sénégalais and other colonial forces the backstop of French national security. In the end, he argued, 40 million French with uncertain allies faced 65 million Germans. A standing army of at least 500,000 West Africans could help France redress this imbalance. While Mangin hardly considered West Africans his political equals, no one held them in higher regard as soldiers: "Not only do they love danger, the life of adventure, but they are remarkably susceptible to discipline. The attachment of the Senegalais to France is absolute." The scheme proved controversial at the time, if only for racial reasons. Settlers everywhere and their supporters in the Hexagon ferociously opposed greater reliance on soldiers of color. Besides, given the close links between military service and citizenship since the French Revolution, what political claims might colonial veterans make on the Republic? The Third Republic would adopt Mangin's idea only during World War I, and then only partially and nearly *in extremis*.

Probably the most famous and influential imperial officer under the Third Republic was Hubert Lyautey. As we will see, many of the actual methods of indirect rule were developed in Tonkin by his mentor Joseph Gallieni. But Lyautey cut a more public figure. Well educated and articulate, no colonial officer ever felt more at home in the salons of Paris or in the pages of the most prestigious literary journals – much to the resentment of less urbane colleagues. Only through the fables of Cyrano de Bergerac or the tales of Napoleonic glory, Lyautey wrote of his service in Madagascar, could Europeans understand "this combination of constant danger and celebration" in which colonial soldiers served France. Known as a right-wing Catholic monarchist, Lyautey in fact cooperated with the Third Republic in imperial adventures over a military career spanning five decades. His book *Du Rôle colonial de l'armée* (1900), Lyautey laid out his imaginary. In an age of conscript armies, he argued, patriotic officers properly trained in the empire could play an indispensable pedagogical role in maintaining cohesion in the Hexagon. In the empire, colonial officers commanded, but played equally important roles as educators, builders, jurists, even agronomists. Their selfless devotion to a thankless task could inspire decadent compatriots in European France.

As someone who practiced empire as much as he preached it, Lyautey served as the equivalent of a viceroy in protectorate Morocco for most of the period between 1907 and 1925. Morocco was the last African addition to the empire before World War I. A by-then familiar narrative of debt, external "supervision" of repayment, followed by a precipitating crisis (here the murder by a mob of the French physician Émile Mauchamp in Marrakech in March 1907), led to the establishment of a formal protectorate in Morocco in 1912. As with Tunisia in 1881, the French could not annex Morocco because of Great Power politics: Spain and Germany competed for influence there. Nor, to be sure, did the Third Republic want the additional expense of direct rule in Morocco. Lyautey himself saw Morocco as the much-improved answer to Algeria, which he saw as virtually a cesspit of the flotsam and jetsam of Europe tyrannizing the alienated Arabs and Berbers who detested them.

In Morocco, the *mission civilisatrice* involved acclimatizing Moroccans to the idea of a permanent French presence as the power behind the throne of the sultan. French rule would appropriate Moroccan Arabic terms to emphasize the urban over the rural – the land of government (*makhzan*) versus the land still ruled by tribes (*sība*). Lyautey had a particular gift for presenting himself as an instrument of the will of the sultan, particularly Mawley Yusuf, who with implausible deference Lyautey referred to as *saidna* (our master). "Soft power" exercised through sub-contracted private organizations such as Catholic-run schools and the Alliance israélite universelle (serving the substantial Moroccan Jewish community) sought to create a Francophone indigenous elite closely bound to France.

Throughout the protectorate, the French would rely on markets and micro-intervention, down to village and tribal levels. Intelligence officers would establish elaborate networks of informants, pitting not just Arabs, Berbers, and Jews against one another, but tribe against tribe. Neverthe-less, armed resistance across terrain ideally suited to guerrilla warfare was always just around the corner, as the French would discover at inter-vals in Morocco as elsewhere. Indeed, at the end of the day, Bugeaud would have recognized the regime Lyautey created in Morocco. The *razzia* would always prove the ultimate enforcer of colonial authority. "Pacification" became what later generations would call an Orwellian term, here meaning constant, grinding guerrilla war. Lyautey would live long enough to see as much in the interwar period.

3.3   The *Mission Civilisatrice* in Indochina

While the showdown at Fashoda might have been a temporary blow to the pride of French imperialists, of far greater import was the very exis-tence of the British Raj in India, the second locus of British world power after the British Isles themselves. The relatively small French enclaves that persisted in Pondicherry, Chandernagor, Yanaon, Karikal, and Mah, for example, served simply as the exception that proved the rule of British mastery over the Indian subcontinent. Coupled with other stra-tegic domains such as Singapore and Hong Kong, to say nothing of the expertise of British imperial capitalism, Britain's power in Asia in the second half of the nineteenth century began to look hegemonic.

While the parallel is far from exact, the French saw Indochina as a kind of response to British India. As such, Indochina required a coher-ence that the vast French empire in Africa did not. Coherence, in turn, required a colonial state and a functioning capitalist economy integrated into Asian markets. Such an economy would require expensive infra-structure, notably canals, ports, roads, and railroads. The parsimonious Third Republic wanted all of this paid for at minimal expense to the French taxpayer. Imperial entrepreneurs who did as they pleased might suffice to conquer Indochina, but not to develop it. The *mission civilisa-trice* would need, in some sense, to "civilize," or at least develop, French imperialism itself.

3.3.1   Conquest, the Tache d'huile, and Governance

The road to French expansion in China and Asia lay broadly through Tonkin, the northernmost province of Vietnam. Theoretically under the rule of the emperor in Hue, Tonkin was part of the Sinosphere, with centuries of tribute to and trade with the colossus to its north. France had to weaken the hold of China on Tonkin in order to extend its influence in China. To do so, the French sought to make the emperor of Vietnam more dependent on themselves. A quixotic and probably ill-advised expedition up the Red River in 1873 by Francis Garnier resulted in his death and set in motion a complicated competition for Tonkin among France, the Black Flag (paramilitary Chinese not under direct imperial command), and the Vietnamese crown in Hue. The French showed they could handle the emperor through the Treaty of Saigon, signed in March 1874. They agreed to evacuate Tonkin, for the time being, in exchange for the relegalization of Christianity, new concessions, and the "temporary" French direction of imperial customs houses. An accompanying commercial treaty signed in August 1874 guaranteed "free trade" the length of the Red River and French military aid in "protecting" Tonkin.

Of course, these treaties presumed that Vietnam needed protection from China, the real impediment to French expansion in Southeast Asia. To overcome this impediment, the French would turn to gunboat diplomacy in the undeclared Sino-French War of 1884–5. At intervals, the French fought the Vietnamese, Black Flag forces, and imperial Chinese troops. The Vietnamese crown discreetly supported the resisters, despite having signed the Treaty of Hue with France in June 1884, which formalized the protectorates of Annam and Tonkin. The French suffered several reverses on the ground, and ultimately had to commit some 35,000 troops to the enterprise.

Paradoxically, these reverses eventually made it possible for Ferry to secure funding for French expansion in Southeast Asia from an increasingly skeptical National Assembly. France, after all, could not permit itself to suffer defeat at the hands of a decadent Chinese empire, Black Flag "bandits," and a Vietnamese imperial crown supposedly under French protection. The French navy and marines helped carry the day, thanks to retaliatory landings in Taiwan and a "rice blockade" of the Yangtze River, which threatened to disrupt the domestic rice supply of China. Finally, in signing the Treaty of Tientsin in June 1885, the Chinese agreed to French supremacy in Tonkin. This rendered manageable the threat from Black Flag forces. In a spectacular piece of imperial theater, on June 6, 1885, in the presence of the court in Hue, the French melted down the seal given to the Nguyen dynasty by the emperor of

China. They replaced it with one of their own, sent from France and carved from a meteorite. In case anyone missed the point, the seal proved that French rule too could descend from heaven, literally.

By then, Ferry's government had fallen, and his career never fully recovered from the difficulties of extending French rule – what became known as *l'affaire Tonkin*. But not even Clemenceau publicly advocated relinquishing the new protectorates. France renegotiated its protectorate with Cambodia as well, according to a convention signed in June 1884. Khmer governors would report to the French resident general, who would be responsible for the management of taxation and public order. King Norodom is supposed to have said to his protectors: "Your protection is the cremation of the monarchy." A brief war followed in 1893 with the Kingdom of Siam (today Thailand), which used imperial ambitions in its own survival strategy. The French also faced renewed conflict with the Black Flag. In response, the French "rescued" the Laotian dynasty by establishing a protectorate there in 1893. In doing so, the French established a buffer zone against further expansion from Siam. France now ruled vast domains in Southeast Asia, at some 737,000 km^2 a good 40 percent larger than the Hexagon.

As we have often seen, giving an imperial domain a color on a map did not mean exercising effective control over it. The number of French present remained tiny. In 1875, Saigon, the commercial capital of Indochina, counted 7,583 French residents, 1,114 long-term and 6,469 temporary. Cambodia counted at most 150 French at about the same time. Even the French military presence seemed modest to occupy all of French Indochina, with a combined population by 1888 of probably 15 million people. The French maintained a mere 12,500 French troops in Tonkin, 2,300 in Annam, 2,000 in Cochinchina, and 600 in Cambodia (and presumably only a handful in Laos).

But this modest presence proved sufficient in the event of direct confrontation. Following a foolish dispute in 1885 with the imperial regents over the door through which the French military governor should enter the palace in Hue, the regents fled with the fourteen-year-old Emperor Ham Nghi in tow. From their refuge in Tan So, they issued a call for general resistance in support of the adolescent emperor, with the extermination of Christians thrown in for good measure. What came to be known as the Can Vuong (aid the sovereign) movement for a time drew support not just from royalist mandarins,[6] but from many thousands of peasants. The base of the movement in the countryside proved both its

---

[6] Mandarins, invented by the Chinese, were highly educated, elite civil servants who handled much of everyday governance in Tonkin and Annam.

strength and its weakness. Can Vuong showed that the French could melt down as many imperial seals as they liked, but their authority outside the cities would remain circumscribed. "If we are unlucky enough to lose and die," one Can Vuong response to French overtures warned, "we will become supernatural devils [*qui thieng*] for killing bandits." But the dispersed nature of the rebellion encountered numberless local rivalries that made coordination difficult. By 1889, the French had mostly prevailed in the field, for the time being.

Imperialism could never sustain itself by brute force alone, if for no other reason that the parsimonious Third Republic found force expensive. Even by 1894, the French had only about 5,000 European soldiers in all of Tonkin, and some 12,000 colonial soldiers in all of Indochina. Enterprising officers led by Joseph Gallieni from 1892 to 1896 tried to reinvent colonial expansion in Indochina by making it less bellicose and thus cheaper. Founding principles became *occupation progressive* and *pénétration pacifique*. The austere, devoutly republican Gallieni likely would never have owned up to the sexual connotations of the latter term; but his method made expansion a kind of seduction, always underpinned by the threat of violence, to be employed as sparingly as possible. *Action lente* (slow action) involved establishing fortified points in communication with each other across the territory to be pacified. Following the envied British example, most of the occupation would be carried out by inexpensive colonial troops.

Fortified posts would protect markets, at which the occupier would pay above-market prices to draw in peasants. The market, the theory went, would seduce the rural population into literally buying into the colonial system. Militarily, *action vive* (fast action), attacks with columns supported by artillery, would be reserved for achieving and performing mastery over the recalcitrant – the metaphor not so much rape as summary execution. "The pirates," Gallieni wrote, "rarely hold out when faced with concentric attacks and do not resist the artillery which terrorizes them."

Otherwise stated in a less sexualized metaphor, colonial expansion would occur in the manner of a *tache d'huile*, an oil spot dropped on water. The oil would spread slowly but certainly, strategically covering the water. But the oil would remain oil and the water would remain water. Underneath the water, constant micro-intervention informed by extensive local intelligence would pit one group against another in what remained a divided Tonkin society. "If there are morals and customs to be respected," Gallieni wrote, "there are also hatreds and rivalries that we need to know how to disentangle and use to our advantage." Long-standing practices rose to the level of policy, known as the *politique des races.* The problem with the *tache d'huile* metaphor was its tendency to stasis, or worse, the endless dissipation of the oil to insignificance. Nevertheless, Gallieni was considered successful enough in Tonkin to be made governor of Madagascar in 1896, where he could apply his method in a much larger and likewise diverse colonial domain.

For the Gallieni method to work, French rule in Indochina had to transition from occupation to governance. The "pacification" of Annam and Tonkin had cost France a great deal of money. The Third Republic was determined to build a regime in Indochina that could first pay for itself, then add to the riches of imperial France. This would prove a tall order given the fragmented nature of French power. France directly ruled Cochinchina through the Ministry of Colonies. A community of some 5,000 Europeans in Saigon elected a *conseil colonial* that controlled much of the budget. The French ruled Annam, Tonkin, and Cambodia as protectorates (through the Ministry of Foreign Affairs), though the navy remained the power behind the throne everywhere.

With pacification barely underway, the French government in 1887 fundamentally reorganized colonial authority through creating a federation, the Union Indochinoise, with its capital in Hanoi. Jules Harmand, the first civilian commissioner for Tonkin, would write of the Union in 1891: "The great possessions should be organized as true states, provided with all the structures necessary for the survival and the functioning of states and made to possess all the characteristics that define states, except one – independence." Such a prescription, of course, begged the question of just what, save pure repression, would prevent quasi-independent states from actually becoming independent. Yet the same basic principle guided French rule in Indochina until 1954 – the quest for economic independence somehow reconciled with political dependence.

In April 1891, Paris made the governor-general "the trustee of the powers of the Republic in French Indochina." Each province of the Union would have a resident superior accountable to the governor-general. Subject to broad supervision from Paris, the governor-general could make law and draw up a budget for the entire Union, command the military authorities, and communicate directly with French diplomats throughout Asia, without going through the Foreign Ministry, the Colonial Ministry, or the Ministry of War. Fully realizing these powers in his five-year term, Paul Doumer (1897–1902) created a cabinet for the Union, with ministries of finance, public works, agriculture, and several others. He created a civil service, modeled after that of the British in India, and opened it to what the state deemed worthy Indochinese. As in India, more than a few Vietnamese civil servants would turn on the colonial regime in the next century. But for the time being, the Indochinese

Union had a governance structure more coherent than anywhere else in the French empire save the non-colony of Algeria.

Doumer and his successors partly eviscerated traditional power structures in the Indochinese protectorates and partly co-opted them. In Tonkin, a July 1897 decree from Emperor Than Thai made the Tonkinese mandarinate subordinate to the resident superior rather than the crown. An imperial decree of September 1897 "reformed" the monarchy in Annam, among other things by inserting French officials into all policy discussions. Taxation already lay mostly in French hands. In Cambodia, a July 1897 royal decree stipulated that the resident superior had to countersign all important documents pertaining to French rule. After 1899, the French established a similar relationship with the Laotian monarchy.

The French struck a series of bargains with the mandarinate, which continued to play an important role in governance in Annam and Tonkin. They mostly preserved the professionalized nature of the mandarins, notably the Confucian examination system based on classical literature. The mandarins retained most of their high status and power, so long as they facilitated rather than thwarted French rule. Most mandarins accepted the bargain. Indeed, as Doumer wrote, "It is they who were the first to be conquered morally." The mandarins proved pivotal in the gradual shift in the nineteenth century from writing in Vietnamese with Chinese characters to Chur Quoc Ngur, the Romanized system originally invented by a Portuguese missionary in the seventeenth century and still in general use today.

Public finance illustrated the ruthlessness of the Indochinese Union. Europeans paid little to nothing in direct taxation, and in any event remained too few to have much impact on the Union budget. The Union government made extensive efforts to regularize the taxation of land and of persons. It also sought to monetize the *corvée*, a common practice of taxation through unpaid labor. But the complexities of land ownership and the limited reach of the state in the countryside (where most Indochinese lived) meant that direct taxation would never suffice to create a self-financing colony.

The Union therefore relied on three monopolies (*régies*) of commodities considered essential – salt, alcohol, and opium. Salt was essential for preserving food in subtropical and tropical Indochina. For centuries, peasants had brewed alcohol mostly from rice, for festivals and general consumption. As we have seen, opium had a sordid imperial history decades before the French established the opium *régie* in 1893. The drug continued to enjoy considerable popularity, particularly among significant Chinese populations in cities. A small concession on the coast of southern China, Kouang-Tchéou-Wan (today Guagzhouwan) with its capital of Fort Bayard (today Zhanjiantg) obtained by the French in 1899 facilitated the still-lucrative opium trade throughout East Asia. In Cochinchina, the authorities estimated in 1907 that some 20,000 of 90,000 Chinese living there used opium in one form or another, and that these 20,000 consumed five times the amount of the non-Chinese population. The French would definitively dismantle the opium *régie* only in 1950, and only then because France had signed a convention on drugs sponsored by the United Nations. All monopolies created endless opportunities for bribery, smuggling, and simple circumvention. Mere colonial repression, for example, was never going to stamp out centuries of rural home brewing.

Whatever its caprices, inefficiencies, and outright immoralities, the colonial revenue machine more than achieved its goal of making the Indochinese Union self-supporting. In Marxian terms, the state extracted enough surplus value from Indochinese workers to support a budget three times that of the AOF. Moreover, it established a reserve that could cover budget deficits in hard times and, perhaps more important, provide the foundation for borrowing for infrastructure. Indeed, before World War I, the Union turned a profit for the Hexagon – not just for capitalists but for the French state itself. The Union contributed some 13 percent of its general budget to Paris, about what the Union spent on public works. Not since Saint-Domingue had French imperialism seemed so ruthlessly profitable. Colonial revenue and anticolonial resentments tracked each other accordingly.

3.3.2   Subcontracting the Mission Civilisatrice: *Missionaries*

As we have seen, Christian missionaries in Indochina, almost entirely Catholic, long predated other bearers of a European colonial presence. But they were never purely the instruments of the states whence they came. The empire of the missionaries was Augustine's City of God, not the City of the World. Generally speaking, syncretic Buddhist and Confucian traditions proved more friendly to missionaries than monotheistic Islam. By 1887, there were an estimated 377,000 Christians in Indochina (some 270,000 in Tonkin and Annam, 90,000 in Cochinchina, and 17,000 in Cambodia). With additional conversions and natural increase, there were some 500,000 Christians in the Indochinese Union by 1900. As had also been the case for centuries, interests of church and state remained intertwined in the Hexagon, even after the formal separation of church and state in 1905. French power projected around the world protected missionaries before and after that tumultuous episode.

Even at its most anticlerical, the parsimonious Third Republic relied on the free labor of priests and nuns in Indochina.

Missionaries would go where other imperialists feared to tread, sometimes bending their own religious traditions along the way. For example, in the spring of 1887, Père Jean-Baptiste Guerlach went on his own mission among the Bahnar and Sedang peoples (non-Vietnamese ethnic groups who speak languages related to Khmer), in the Central Highlands of Annam. After a ceremonial meal with two Sedang chiefs, Guerlach "adopted" two of their sons to affirm the alliance between the chiefs and the mission. The next day, Guerlach had an altar built replete with a crucifix, candles, and a statue of the Virgin Mary. He asked Jesus to bless his new sons. Thereafter, he and the two chiefs cut their thumbs, dripped blood into a cup of wine, stirred it with a chicken bone, and drank it. The ritual imitated, and doubtless to some profaned, the Catholic sacrament of communion. But to Guerlach, the ends of conversion justified these means.

This appropriation of the sacrament proved only the beginning of Guerlach's adventurism in the Central Highlands. He played a key supporting role in an episode worthy of later fictional renderings such as Joseph Conrad's *Lord Jim* (1900) or Francis Ford Coppola's *Apocalypse Now* (1979). In 1888, the businessman-turned-colonial-adventurer Charles-David Meyréna declared himself King Marie I of the Sedang, complete with a constitution, flags, and postage stamps. His fantasy kingdom reached the media in expatriate circles in Indochina and in Europe. While Meyréna's enterprise self-destructed in the end and he died in exile in 1900, it attracted enough attention to concern the French authorities. The aftermath of the episode coincided with seriously damaged relations between church and state in the Dreyfus Affair beginning in 1894, in which most senior Catholic officialdom unwisely supported the anti-Dreyfusards.

From the time Meyréna arrived in the Central Highlands, Guerlach served as his guide and translator. He and other Catholic missionaries had been conspicuously present at quasi-royal occasions, as translators and as witnesses affixing their signatures to what the secular authorities saw as documents of sedition. Guerlach defended himself publicly in the French language newspaper *Courrier d'Haiphong*. His signatures, he maintained less than plausibly, simply documented his presence and did not indicate any kind of endorsement. As a missionary, he considered that he had carried the flag of France with him into these remote lands. Indeed, Guerlach contended, the Third Republic itself was at fault for permitting Meyréna to carry on so in the first place. The clergy in Vietnam largely sided with Guerlach. In itself, Meyréna's ephemeral

Kingdom of the Sedang was not going to much shape French rule in Indochina one way or another. But it illustrated a more enduring quarrel between the Third Republic and the Catholic Church, abroad as well as at home.

As republicans gained the upper hand in the Hexagon in the aftermath of the Dreyfus Affair, skepticism toward Catholic missions in Indochina grew. Freemasonry, a widespread, generally pro-republican, and conspicuously male fraternal movement, drew many French imperialists. The Catholic Church had forbidden believers to join back in 1783, though Catholic Freemasons were not unknown. Léon Gambetta, Jules Ferry, and Paul Doumer were all Freemasons, as were most of the leading journalists in the French language press of Indochina. Journalists helped keep Mayréna in the news, perhaps longer than the facts merited.

Stories of Catholic misdeeds, particularly in parts of the Union where the colonial state did not exercise much effective control, got better with the telling. Mayréna, critics contended, represented only the tip of the iceberg. They held that Catholic power ran rampant across Indochina, remaining answerable to no one, at any rate no one in Paris or Hanoi. Priests and nuns kidnapped children and sold them. They decapitated Vietnamese who would not kneel to them. They would not even bury the corpses of the unbaptized. Perhaps worst of all, they hesitated to teach French to the indigenous, preferring Vietnamese written in the Catholic-invented Chur Quoc Ngur. To be fair, more than a few Catholic clergy long identified the godless Third Republic with the work of Satan. In any event, critics knew as well as anyone that the clergy worked for a "Catholic" rather than a "French" Indochina.

In the end, however, practicality preserved the uneasy symbiosis between Catholic missions and the Third Republic. Before 1914, there were initiatives to enhance secular teaching, notably the Alliance française in language instruction and the Mission laïque in the instruction of teachers. But even by 1911, while the state schools taught some 5,500 male students, Catholic schools taught more than 15,000. Simply put, the state's stinginess in social programs required subcontracting. Where else could the colonial state look besides missionaries to staff schools and hospitals, let alone facilities for lepers? For their part, where could Catholic missions look for physical protection besides the colonial state? No Catholic forgot that the Can Vuong movement had called for the extermination of Christians, or the simmering resentments of Vietnamese nationalists. As in the Hexagon, the Third Republic and the Catholic Church in Indochina arrived at a modus vivendi by the time of World War I.

3.4   Capitalism and the *Mission Civilisatrice*

Parsing out the symbiosis between colonialism and capitalism in the French empire poses even more of a challenge than that between colonialism and missionaries. Ferry himself, as we saw, envisaged the spread of French universalism and French capitalism as two sides of the same coin. Disentangling public and private capital in the empire was never easy. Developing a capitalist economy anywhere in the empire required costly infrastructure and accompanying levels of risk unacceptable to many private investors. Yet the Indochinese Union had to develop a growing capitalist economy to hope to compete with British India. The colonial state, at the expense of colonial taxpayers, stepped in with formidable subsidies and sometimes repurchased commercially unviable but politically necessary concessions. Investors were seldom left to a purely free market.

As in the Hexagon, the Third Republic in the empire cared deeply about railroads, for military as well as economic reasons. No one forgot that Prussia had defeated France in 1870 because it assembled so many soldiers so fast through its railroad network. In addition, after formidable start-up costs, railroads could cheaply link buyers and sellers throughout the Union, and deliver goods to modern ports for export to Asia and beyond. But the reach of the colonial imaginary in railroads everywhere exceeded its grasp, with endless stories of boundless ambitions, crushing, dangerous, and generally forced labor, construction delays, immense cost overruns, and incomplete projects.

One of the first such projects illustrated these perils – a plan to build a railroad across the Sahara joining Dakar and Algiers. In February 1881, Colonel Paul Flatters, whose experience in the empire dated back the Bureaux Arabes in the 1850s, led a surveying expedition for the project. The expedition comprised some eleven white French, forty-seven North African soldiers, and some thirty Algerians as guides and helpers. Deep in the desert, the Tuareg (Berbers) set upon the French. Flatters and his officers were killed almost immediately. The Tuareg continued at intervals to torture fifty-six survivors as they endeavored to stagger some 1,500 km to the nearest French camp, selling them poisoned meat and human flesh represented as mutton. Weeks later, some twelve men from the expedition finally reached safety. Clearly, building colonial railroads would not be for the faint of heart. Yet the dream of connecting the West African domains by rail continued, and pieces of a network were actually built in the decades to come. Only the War of Algerian Independence in the 1950s put a definitive end to the scheme.

"Indochina," the newspaper *La Quinzaine colonial* remarked in 1901, "is made with steel and money: the steel of the rails and the money of the common budget [of the Union]." Doumer had certainly lived by this principle upon becoming governor-general in 1897. A proposed railroad line from Haiphong on the Gulf of Tonkin to Kunming, China (some 850 km) would serve several functions. It would provide an avenue of transport for the entire Tonkin province and from there north to Yunnan province, China. A robust Indochina, in turn, would preclude further British expansion east toward China from Burma. An even more ambitious French railroad project would connect the Yunnan line to a line from Hanoi to Saigon (the Transindochina line), over 1,700 km. Such a line would help unify all of Vietnam, the geographic backbone of the Indochinese Union. Any railroad network in Vietnam would straddle hundreds of kilometers of mountainous terrain and would require immense amounts of human and financial capital.

Doumer fully mobilized the colonial state to secure the necessary loans. In 1898, he persuaded Paris to permit the Union to borrow 200 million francs (over $750 million today), guaranteed by the Union's own revenues (from the colonial *régies*, as well as direct and indirect taxation). Doumer orchestrated the formation of a private consortium of financial and industrial interests. Metallurgical and railroad interests in the Hexagon stood to profit mightily from such an enterprise. According to an agreement made on November 11, 1898, the Government General of the Union would provide an annual subsidy of 3 million francs to service the loan, for which the colonial state assumed all the risk. Private investors could expect an unspectacular but steady and essentially risk-free profit at Vietnamese public expense.

Railroads underpinned an economy of extraction in Indochina. Foreseeable if unforeseen cost overruns required additional state subsidies. For most segments, actual costs were twice the estimates. For the Yunnan line alone (completed 1910), the Vietnamese people provided an estimated 39 million of the 64 million francs necessary to complete the project. The Transindochina line, completed only in 1936, cost more than double its original budget. These costs would have been much higher but for the work of tens of thousands of poorly paid or conscript laborers, known as *les coolies*, mostly from China and Annam. Falling rocks, landslides, derailments, and floods in the rainy season made for horrific risks. Constructing the Yunnan line took lives of some 12,000 of the 60,000 Indochinese and Chinese workers. Moreover, the monumental costs of the railroads had resulted in rates for passengers and goods well beyond the affordability of most Vietnamese and Chinese. Their labor had built a railway that few of them could expect to use, except in crammed, designated cars. More often, railroads proved simply another tool for the extraction of the surplus value of their labor (see Illustration 3.2).

Illustration 3.2 Railroad and mining in Tonkin (probably 1890s).
Source: https://humazur.univ-cotedazur.fr/omeka-s-dev/s/Humazur/item/
5042#?c=&m=&s=&cv=(public domain).

The development of a colonial economy in Indochina took place in
the regional context of East Asia. Export possibilities from Laos were
minimal. Vietnam had some coal, iron, and tin. With the rise of the
automobile, natural rubber would become increasingly important. But
rice for export to Asia became the most important driver of economic
development in Vietnam. Most of this was grown in Cochinchina, the
Red River delta in Tonkin, and Cambodia. An intra-Asian rice trade
long predated the French, of course. But the French sought constantly
to "modernize" rice cultivation, through costly infrastructure investments in canals, irrigation, roads, and railroads. "Modernization" also
meant consolidating as many smallholdings as possible into plantations,
often owned by wealthy Vietnamese. Doing so required turning peasants into wage laborers. In addition, colonialism throughout East Asia
confronted a highly complicated system of monetary exchange involving
specie – gold and silver, but also copper and even zinc. "Trade dollars,"
from Spain, Mexico, the United States, Great Britain, and India, also
circulated as coins typically issued in silver.

To modernize finance in Indochina, the French government in 1875 authorized a consortium of private banks to form one of the extraordinary institutions of the French empire, the Banque de l'Indochine. The early date is noteworthy, because the bank predated not just the formalization of the protectorates in Annam and Tonkin, but the consolidation of the republic in the Hexagon. Imperial finance had its own trajectory. Until the Great Depression, the Banque de l'Indochine answered to no one beyond its own board. Most of the time, this was not a problem in the Hexagon, because both the bank and its political backers shared the goal of making Indochina safe for imperial capitalism. But in significant ways, the bank became a law unto itself, quite independent of its own stated purpose of economic development in Indochina.

The Banque de l'Indochine combined public and private functions – treasury for the Indochinese Union, central bank, and international commercial bank. Given its size and vast assets, the bank essentially controlled credit throughout the Union. The bank and not the colonial state issued and regulated the official currency, the *piastre*. Imports all had to be paid in French francs, handled by the bank. The complicated means of determining exchange rates in the economic Sinosphere provided endless opportunities for arbitrage and huge profits for the bank. The Banque de l'Indochine was a pioneer in international banking, with branches in Hong Kong, Shanghai, Beijing, Bangkok, Singapore, Pondicherry, and elsewhere. The bank earned substantial fees for financial services generally, such as managing the indemnity paid to the foreign powers by China after the Boxer Rebellion of 1899–1901. When World War I began, the Banque de l'Indochine earned at least half of its profits from trade with China, and between China and other Asian entities. It made money for a small circle of investors in good years and bad.

Private capital follows profit, whatever the stated purpose of capitalist institutions. Investments outside Indochina often proved more lucrative than profits inside. By 1914, Indochina had become a net exporter of capital to the rest of Asia. In Marxian terms, capital created through extracting the surplus value of Indochinese labor went elsewhere rather than to developing Indochina. The Banque de l'Indochine wrote relatively few loans directly to fund agriculture, and most of those to plantations or to companies that refined agricultural products. Peasants constantly incurred debt, for seed, fertilizer, animals, equipment, and the means of subsistence between harvests. The lack of commitment on the part of high finance to "retail" agriculture threw peasants back on usurers, often Chinese, who could charge up to 2 percent compounding interest per month. Peasants often lost their land through varieties of debt trap and had to become agricultural laborers.

As subcontracted agents of empire, missionaries and the Banque de l'Indochine both served a second master, whether the Christian God or Mammon. The latter perhaps did more to shape the actual content of the *mission civilisatrice*. Before World War I, the Indochinese Union "worked," in the sense that it created a large sphere of French influence in Southeast Asia at little to no net expense to taxpayers of the Hexagon.

But where exactly was the "civilizing" in all this, in Indochina or elsewhere? Certainly, France by 1914 had effaced the defeats of 1815 and 1870–1, and had reestablished itself as a Great Power, in Europe and around the world. It extended its rule over millions of foreign people, and over territories many times larger than the Hexagon itself. It had contracted deals with numberless local elites and had begun building a Francophone bureaucratic and commercial class of indigenous peoples. But French rule deepened existing social cleavages in the empire along the way and created many new ones. If the point was to transplant republican values, the *mission civilisatrice* had at best a dubious record. It had done a fine job telling by word and deed the "inferior" races all about their inferiority. But could France actually claim by 1914 that it had raised whole peoples?

Otto von Bismarck, a more cautious German chancellor than some of his successors, remarked in 1888: "Your map of Africa is all very fine, but my map of Africa lies in Europe. Here is Russia and here is France, and we are in the middle; that is my map of Africa." In other words, he would take imperial acquisitions if they came but would not fight in Europe for them. Overseas empire did not cause World War I, at any rate not directly. To the extent that France vastly expanded its empire in the first four decades of the Third Republic as a matter of national security, it is difficult to see just what protection that empire afforded in the leadup to war. Austria-Hungary, which had no overseas empire, and Germany, which had a relatively limited one, ignited a European war in 1914 for European reasons. Bismarck had seen overseas empires first and foremost through the lens of European geopolitics, as would many statesmen who followed him. But as we will see, a general European war would transform the French empire, as it would empire everywhere.

4   Empire and the World Wars: 1914–45

As early as July 1946, the future French president Charles de Gaulle referred to a second *guerre de trente ans*. He alluded to the Thirty Years War of 1618–48, in which European civilization tore itself apart in wars of religion. According to this analogy, the two world wars of the twentieth century constituted a single conflict, with a single basic cause (Germany). There are arguments for and against this construct. In fact, the two world wars had distinct causes and differed considerably in their global character. World War I (1914–18), still commonly known in France as *la Grande Guerre* (the Great War), was effectively a European conflict that dragged in other parts of the world, notably the overseas empires. World War II, more genuinely a global conflict, began as two regional wars – an Asian war driven by Imperial Japan beginning in 1937, and a European war driven by Nazi Germany beginning in 1939. The two merged only in 1941, with the German invasion of the Soviet Union in June 1941 and the Japanese attack at Pearl Harbor in December 1941. Great Powers fought over "the world" in World War II in ways they really had not in World War I.

However, the case for a second Thirty Years War is more compelling in structuring the history of formal European empire. In combination, the two world wars broke European imperial power, at least in its nineteenth-century formulations. World War I showed the vulnerability of France as empire, a point not lost among a new generation of colonized peoples brought up under the contradictions of the *mission civilisatrice*. On a map, the French empire after World War I looked larger than ever in 1919, because of League of Nations mandates in the Levant and Africa. But in their way, the mandates highlighted the contradictions of republican empire itself.

After World War I, colonial policy focused increasingly on the *mise en valeur*, loosely translated as economic development toward the goal of supporting the Hexagon. Babar, the idealized subject of the *mise en valeur*, came from increasingly desperate imaginary presenting the empire as unbreakable. That imaginary shattered in 1940, when Nazi Germany conquered the imperial French conqueror, and Imperial Japan worked its will over the French empire in Asia. In the end, two non-European superpowers, the United States and the Soviet Union, would defeat Germany and Japan. While both superpowers were empires themselves, neither had fought the war to support European colonial adventures.

4.1   The Mobilization of Empire in World War I

Some of the first shots fired at France in World War I landed in Algeria on August 4, 1914, from the German cruiser *Goeben* and its escort ship the *Breslau* off the coast of Bône (today Annaba) and Philippeville (today Skikda). These state-of-the-art ships had been positioned in the Mediterranean to protect not very well-defined German interests. Partly to show friendship in hopes of persuading the Ottoman Empire to join the Central Powers, the German naval command ordered the *Goeben* and *Breslau* to sail to Constantinople (today Istanbul). The ships simply lobbed some shells at two Algerian cities along the way. They caused minimal damage and only a few casualties, not disrupting the General Mobilization, in Algeria or anywhere else.

Shortly thereafter, Governor-General Charles Lutuad issued a proclamation to all Algerians that perhaps said more than it intended to. To the "Algerians," meaning the white settlers, he stated with confidence: "You will defend Algeria up to the supreme sacrifice, because this land is your creation, because of the white farms [*les fermes blanches*], the crops, and the vines which in combination represent the fruit of your intrepid labor." He also explicitly addressed Muslims: "It is the land of Algeria, your native soil, which every day you help make so beautiful and fertile, that has received the first blows." Settlers naturally would give their all to defend the settler colony "they" had built. Muslims, to be sure, had been born there and labored there, particularly on European farms. But Algeria was not really "theirs" in the same way, if at all. Differentiated rule in the empire would mean differentiated mobilization for war.

World War I would illustrate time and again just how far empire reached. An unsuccessful naval raid in September 1914 by two German cruisers on a coaling station in Papeete in Tahiti destroyed part of the city. The French naval commander set the coal supply ablaze, and scuttled a gunboat, the *Zélée*, to prevent the Germans from entering the harbor. Most of the terrified residents of Papeete fled, limiting civilian casualties. Jane Dollet, a twenty-year old telephone operator, remained at her post, ensuring communications among the defenders. With the point of the attack now moot, the German cruisers soon departed. But the incident dislocated the copra trade in Papeete, much of which had actually involved German merchants. No corner of the empire, however remote, would remain wholly outside the vortex of World War I.

4.1.1 Colonial Soldiers

The colonial army (some 90,000 strong before August 1914) had long helped to guarantee the security of France and its empire. Like the British, the French used colonial forces primarily in the empire itself. As we have seen, recruiting colonial soldiers appealed to the parsimony of the Third Republic. Moreover, politicians feared defending the Hexagon directly with troops of color. But the first two months of the war forced a rethinking of this policy. Of nearly 1.3 million French soldiers who would die in the entire conflict, some 329,000 died in August–September 1914. Military planners throughout Europe had forecast a conflict that would be bloody, but short and above all decisive. The real war had resulted in stalemate, and in the German occupation of Belgium and most of north-eastern France. It would take years for the British to recruit and train a mass army. Imperial Russia had plenty of men but had suffered griev-ous losses in blood and territory. With its white menfolk of military age almost entirely in uniform in 1914, France had few places to turn except its empire to mobilize for a long war.

The war minister, Adolphe Messimy, put the matter bluntly: "Africa has cost us heaps of gold, thousands of soldiers, and streams of blood. We do not dream of demanding the gold from her. But the men and the blood, she must repay them with interest." The time had come, the argument went, for the empire to return the investment in *la mission civilisatrice*. The French applied the term *impôt du sang* (blood tax) to both the Hexagon and the empire. France indeed would extract consid-erable human capital from its empire. Some 475,000 colonial subjects would serve in the French army in World War I.[1] Some, such as Captain Khaled el-Hassani, a grandson of Abdelkader who joined a colonial cav-alry unit that arrived in France in September 1914, served as genuine volunteers. Likewise, Crown Prince Sisowath Monivong of Cambodia trained at Saint-Maixent, the French academy for non-commissioned officers, and rose to the rank of lieutenant in the Foreign Legion. Theo-retically a "white" corps, the Legion had flexible race policies when it wanted them.

---

[1] Approximate figures show the geographic distribution of the origins of colonial sol-diers: West Africa (166,000); Algeria (140,000); Indochina (50,000); Tunisia (47,000); Madagascar (46,000); Morocco (24,000), South Pacific (2,000). Richard Fogarty, "The French Empire," in Robert Gerwarth and Erez Manela, eds., *Empires at War, 1911–1923* (Oxford: Oxford University Press, 2014), 120.

But most colonial soldiers joined under the same conditions as before the war – some for the modest engagement bonus, others to escape problematic personal circumstances, many through some form of coercion from family or local notables. Apart from a marginal attempt at European-style conscription of Muslims in Algeria, the colonial authorities would convey the number of men they expected to be delivered by their local collaborators, along with financial inducements. Just how local collaborators acquired the expected bodies would remain their own affair. Recruitment methods were generally more brutal in sub-Saharan Africa than elsewhere. Like their white comrades, colonial soldiers joined for the duration of the war.

As assumption has long endured that France used colonial troops as cannon fodder, to spare the lives of white troops. While not entirely untrue, this assumption simplifies a more complicated reality. More than 70 percent of battlefield casualties occurred because of artillery fire, which could hardly discriminate by race and fell mostly on infantry. Colonial troops served almost entirely in the infantry, which had a mortality rate of 23 percent for the French army as a whole. According to one relatively uncontroversial estimate, some 19 percent of North African troops and 23 percent of "Sénégalais" (that is, other African) troops died in World War I, compared with about 16 percent in the French army in all branches of the service.

Certainly, the French army used colonial units differently from white units. Racism generally excluded troops of color from the technologically sophisticated branches of service, not just airplanes but artillery and most jobs in the navy. The army rarely used Indochinese and Malagasy troops in the front lines at all, employing them mostly in construction battalions, the *bataillions d'étapes*. This meant relatively low casualties and relatively low prestige. One exception involved colonial stretcher bearers, particularly from Indochina. The unarmed *brancardiers* often incurred more danger than regular infantry because they had to carry stretchers standing up. The Tirailleurs Sénégalais proved particularly susceptible to disease in the winter and were evacuated to southern France during the coldest time of the year. Malagasy troops, on the other hand, proved surprisingly resilient in the winter. It became increasingly common as the war continued to amalgamate colonial regiments and battalions into metropolitan divisions and army corps. Colonial units were particularly important beyond the Western Front, in Salonika in Greece and later in the Middle East. Colonial troops continued to occupy most of the empire, so as so "spare" white troops to defend the Hexagon.

Most of what we know of colonial soldiers' experience in the trenches of World War I comes from oral testimony recorded decades after the fact. Allowing for power differentials and cultural differences, colonial soldiers' recollections do not differ greatly from those of white soldiers. Impersonal forces put soldiers in the trenches – whether a local chief who needed to make his quota in French Sudan or conscription law in the Hexagon. Soldiers of all colors tended to remember most vividly facing the prospect of death or mutilation. Demba Mboup of the Tirailleurs Sénégalais recalled a dream the night before he was wounded: "I dreamed that I was attacked by two lions, but I saw Seriny Touba [a Sufi holy man] in my dreams. And when the two lions came, he put me in a basket and raised me up like this. But one of the lions scratched my left leg where I was wounded the next day. So Seriny Touba protected me." Tirailleur Aliou Diakhate remembered feeling distress that he could not stand up, bend down, and place his forehead on the ground for Muslim prayer. "So I took some earth in my hand," he recalled, "and I put it to my forehead. And I prayed to God in that way." A Muslim Tunisian infantryman saw the war itself in religious terms: "The Christian cheapens our existence. I beseech thee, my God, to save us, to cease our separation from our family and to recall us home from this unhappy army."

Some recalled a conviction that their service had changed something about the colonial bargain. Tirailleurs helped lead the recapture of the fort at Douaumont in the later stages of the Battle of Verdun in October 1916. As his unit was being moved to the south of France for the winter, Masserigne Soumare recalled: "In every town we crossed, the French were clapping their hands and shouting: *Vive les Tirailleurs Sénégalais!*" At least for the moment, white French understood what they owed to troops of color. Another soldier went so far as to articulate his own explanation of their service: "We were not fighting for the French; we were fighting for ourselves, to become French citizens." In the years to come, it would prove a short step discursively from equality within the empire to independence from the empire.

The most powerful African politician in the French empire at the time, Blaise Diagne, certainly thought a good deal about revising the colonial bargain. Diagne had a Third Republic resumé Babar himself might have envied. He was born of two black parents of modest socioeconomic origins, and his missionary teachers tagged him for academic success at an early age. Diagne got the chance to study in the Hexagon, in Aix-en-Provence. At the age of nineteen, he passed the exam to enter the colonial customs service. While in Madagascar in 1907, he entered into a completely public relationship with a white woman whom he would legally marry two years later. They had three sons together. He would say with pride as he turned to politics: "I am black, my wife is white, my children are *métis*, what better guarantee of my interest in representing the whole population?"

The voters of the Quatre Communes elected Diagne as their representative to the National Assembly in 1914 as the first "full African," that is, someone neither white nor *métis*. He owed his success to *originaire* African electors rather than the white and *métis* oligarchy. Despite some resistance among his colleagues in the Chamber to seating him, Diagne went right to work. What became known as the Loi Diagne, passed in October 1915, made men in the Quatre Communes subject to the same conscription law as other French citizens. Moreover, they could now serve in regular army units rather than in colonial units. A law of September 1916 made all residents of the Quatre Communes full citizens, wherever they had been born. The hated *indigénat* would no longer apply to any of them.

Diagne intervened most dramatically in renegotiating the imperial bargain in the last year of the war. Georges Clemenceau came to power in November 1917, a sign to the French and the world that France would win the war or die in the attempt. With the manpower situation ever worsening, the anticolonialist Clemenceau became more amenable to calling on the empire. Captain Abdel-Kader Mademba of the Tirailleurs Sénégalais, a protégé of Mangin and the first "full" black African to achieve such a high rank, lobbied for a recruitment drive in West Africa. Colonial officials opposed Mademba, fearing that the removal of thousands of men would increase the cost of labor. Clemenceau responded in character: "That's all well and good, but the Front interests me more." Clemenceau named Diagne *Commissaire de la République*, a title consciously harkening back to the French Revolution, when Paris gave its commissars full power to implement the will of the sovereign people. Exceptionally, Diagne could communicate directly with the government in Paris rather than through colonial officials. Supporters described his mission as *une croisade noire*, a black crusade to rescue France and its empire in their hour of need.

The *commissaire* certainly understood the theatrics of republican sovereignty in his six-month tour of the AOF, mostly Senegal and French Sudan along the Upper Niger River. He brought along an entourage of 350 people, colonial officials and military officers, some of them white. The spectacle of a black African in charge with a motorcade and speeches made in front of newsreel cameras left a powerful impression, as Diagne intended. He brought with him practical inducements for enlistment – bonuses for enlisting, modest family allowances, promises of jobs for returning veterans, and the establishment of new schools of agriculture and medicine.

Judged by the numbers, Diagne exceeded expectations. Originally assigned a target of 47,000 new recruits, he delivered 65,000 by the time the recruitment drive came to an end. Some, perhaps 14 percent according to one estimate, were genuine volunteers, who wanted to improve their status or genuinely believed in a republican empire. Many more, however, were raised through the traditional coercive means, the result of debt, crime, a form of taxation, or even extralegal enslavement to other Africans. The African troops raised in 1918 could not in themselves win the war. In the event, by the time they could be transported to Europe and trained, the war was nearly over.

But the principle turned out to matter. France needed the bodies of its imperial subjects and had proved willing, up to a point, to bargain with its African domains to get their help. The victory parade up the Champs d'Elysée in July 1919 featured colonial troops prominently, leaving little doubt as to their contribution. Diagne himself went on to a distinguished postwar career. In 1931–2 he served as under-secretary of state for colonies, and from 1920 to 1934 as mayor of Dakar. No person of African descent could have risen to such political heights at the time in the British Empire, let alone the United States.

4.1.2   Wartime Labor: The Empire and the Hexagon Meet Each Other

World War I brought the empire to the Hexagon in unprecedented ways. Before the war, millions of Hexagon French outside the major cities could expect rarely if ever to lay eyes on a person of color. With hundreds of thousands of colonial soldiers moving to and from the fronts of World War I, this changed. Moreover, a severe labor shortage resulted in a massive influx of workers from the empire. Some 300,000 people, almost entirely men, made the journey from Algeria, Indochina, Morocco, Tunisia, and Madagascar.[2] Some 140,000 Chinese worked either for the French or the British army in France, under a particular variety of imperial contracting for persons rather than lands. The war effort employed foreign workers in an array of occupations in industry and agriculture, often distributed by race. The authorities gave North Africans jobs sweeping streets, establishing an employment practice that persisted for decades thereafter. Many Indochinese found their way to munitions factories. Many Chinese worked in construction near the front lines. Not all jobs were unskilled. For example, some 5,000 Indochinese drivers served the French army, while others from the colonies served as trained nurses. Promises of wage equality to white French generally proved barren.

---

[2] As always, estimates differ as to numbers, here further complicated by the fact that some soldiers, particularly from Indochina, served as militarized laborers. Official estimates reported approximately: 78,000 Algerians; 49,000 Indochinese; 37,000 Chinese; 36,000 Moroccans; 18,000 Tunisians; and 4,600 Malagasy; with the remainder not classified. Tyler Stovall, "The Color Line behind the Lines: Racial Violence in France during the Great War," *American Historical Review* 103 (1998): 741–2.

Theoretically, a special section of the War Ministry assigned to the management of colonial labor guaranteed complete segregation. Originally, organized labor opposed the presence of colonial workers. The secretary general of the Confédération Générale du Travail, Léon Jouhaux, wrote in 1916: "This land must not become a cosmopolitan boulevard, where all races may meet with each other, with the sole exception of the French, because they will have disappeared." However, wartime exigency eventually won out. Segregation in the Hexagon would have to suffice, and then only to a degree. Colonial workers were to be housed separately in supervised compounds and escorted to and from the workplace, not unlike convict labor. But surveillance of such a large population proved impractical, mostly because of a lack of white French to supervise. Most of the violent racial incidents involved workers in port cities who declined to stay in their designated spaces.

Varieties of racial intermingling proved common in the end. The heavily censored media did not deprive the white French of endless images of fascination with colonial bodies, particularly black Africans. Many images depicted *marraines* (godmothers), white, middle-class volunteers assigned to look after soldiers in transit or on leave, providing multiform comfort to their infantilized charges. In addition, the war brought hundreds of thousands of white women into the industrial workplace. Colonizers and colonized often found themselves working side by side. One worker from Tunisia wrote: "The city where we are stationed is full of women, and here fornication is as abundant as grains of sand." Even the normally staid genre of published soldiers' testimonies authorized a male fascination with colonial physicality. Pierre la Mazière, who served as a nurse in the Dardanelles, effused of the black Africans he tended: "They are beautiful! If you exclude their flat feet and their calves which are too thin, they have splendid forms; the large legs of women, torsos bulging admirably with muscles. As for their skin, it is so soft and sweet that you understand in some way why the whites were wanting to touch it."

Nearly all colonial workers left France shortly after the war, voluntarily or involuntarily. Actual roundups resulting in deportation took place in Paris and Marseilles. Only about 25,000 colonial workers remained by 1921, most of them extralegal. But a pattern of importing labor from the colonies had been established and would greatly expand after World War II. In the meantime, concerns arose in the colonies as to just what irreverent ideas repatriated workers would bring back with them. One settler in Tonkin fretted that exposure to the Hexagon "will eventually create malcontents and revolutionaries, as well as the upsetting of our beautiful colony. They will no longer feel like planting rice in their fields after they have seen in France a number of things we should not have let them see or hear."

Illustration 4.1 Tirailleur Sénégalais during World War I (Caption: Glory to the French Empire) (exact date unknown).
Source: L'Armarium: Bibliothèque numérique, Hauts-de-France (public domain).

One artefact of World War I, the instant beverage Banania, is still available in every French grocery store. In 1912, Pierre-François Lardet began marketing the powder made from cocoa, ground banana and grains, and sugar. The government swiftly saw the benefits of providing frontline soldiers with a drinkable memory of home. In 1915, Banania began a new advertising campaign featuring a laughing Tirailleur Sénégalais and an invented "Africanized" slogan (*Y'a bon!*, or It's Good!). The campaign represented the Tirailleur as the alter ego of the bestialized monster who terrorized his German foes. To the French consumer, he was simple and cheerful, a well-behaved child who knew his place defending France. Postcards such as the one shown in Illustration 4.1 reinforced such messaging, with two captured German helmets thrown in for good measure.

Banania proved a stunning commercial success. It also became one of the most notorious symbols of French imperial condescension. Léopold Sedar Senghor, academic, poet, co-founder of the Négritude movement, and later the first president of independent Senegal, remarked famously: "I would tear that Banania laugh from every wall in France." Like comparable racist logos in the United States, the very success of the branding made its owners reluctant to change it. Today, Banania has reinvented the soldier as a sassy adolescent keeping multicultural France in line. He continues to wear a fez, to remind consumers of his otherness. Not everyone has found the reinvention satisfactory.

France, like its British ally, had placed an enormous bet on overseas empire before 1914. The French and British empires survived the war, while the German empire did not. The colonies had provided the blood, treasure, and commodities expected of them. But they had not in themselves won the war, which in any event seemed less and less "won" as the interwar years proceeded. Moreover, the mobilization of the empire had invoked or accelerated political and forces in the empire that the Hexagon would find it difficult to control. Numerous uprisings took place in the empire during the war, for example in the *département* of Constantine in Algeria, in the Sahara, the AOF, Madagascar, New Caledonia, and Indochina. Small, uncoordinated, and of multiple local origins, none of these revolts posed an existential threat to French rule. But they compelled the preoccupied and hard-pressed colonizer to take notice.

4.2   Empire between the Wars

As spaces colored on a map, the French empire emerged from World War I larger than it had ever been or would be again. The treaties of peace required Germany and post-Ottoman Turkey to surrender their imperial domains, which the victors divided among them in a fashion uncomfortably reminiscent of the previous century. France finally acquired the presence it had long sought in the eastern Mediterranean, through League of Nations mandates in Syria and Lebanon. In addition, France partitioned with Britain two former German territories in central Africa, Cameroon and Togo. But the new domains were not colonies under international law, much as the French might have tried to rule them as such. Governance in the mandates would be accountable to a new international body, the League of Nations.

Throughout the interwar period, imperial bargaining came under unprecedented pressure everywhere. To compensate for the grievous losses in blood and treasure of World War I, the French sought to reinvent their empire, to weld it to the Hexagon to form an economic and geopolitical whole. Theorists of the empire envisaged risks as well as opportunities in doing so. An economically integrated empire meant accelerated extraction. Jurists and sociologists pondered the future of the white race in such an empire, particularly children born of unions between colonizer and colonized. All of this occurred under prevailing discourses of empire that claimed to remain republican. The ubiquitous concept of *mise en valeur*, explained further later, combined a host of mostly existing policies. Alongside this attempted reinvention of the empire, anticolonial movements in the empire became more numerous, powerful, and articulate in the interwar period. Colonial authority repressed them everywhere, but not easily. In theory and mostly in practice, and as colored spaces on a map, the French empire remained unbroken through the interwar period. But its fragile character became increasingly clear in the Hexagon and beyond.

4.2.1 The League of Nations Mandates

The mandate system resulted from a stifled international revolution in colonial authority itself. Part of the allied ideological remobilization in the last years of the war led by the American president Woodrow Wilson called for "no annexations," meaning the habitual imperial partitions of the previous century. More cynically, wartime ideological mobilization cast German and Ottoman imperial authority as intrinsically illegitimate, in contrast with French or British imperial authority. Consequently, German and Ottoman imperial domains had to become something else – but what? Neither politicians nor diplomats nor jurists ever agreed as to just what the mandates were.

Legally, mandates were never colonies. The Covenant of the League of Nations called them "a sacred trust of civilization," though it left open just where sovereignty in them lay. The Great Powers delegated administrative power to one of themselves but left supervision of that power to the newborn League. Further, they invented what became a racial classification of mandates. Class-A mandates (all in the Middle East) had provisional recognition as independent states, Class-B mandates (in Africa) required more supervision, Class-C mandates (in Africa and the South Pacific) still more, approximating annexation.

Those who articulated and administered the mandate system never really agreed on whether its purpose was to modernize imperial rule or to replace it. As written, the Covenant appeared to place all mandates on a trajectory toward some form of self-rule. Race theory dictated that some peoples had far more capacity for self-rule than others, and that those different peoples would always have different trajectories.

The colonial administrators and soldiers who ran the French mandates thus considered themselves empowered to apply some very old techniques to the new system of rule. Indeed, many French officials had opposed the creation of the system at all since, as they argued, the *mission civilisatrice* already embraced the stated goals of mandatory rule.

The peace settlement in the Middle East brought a profound rupture in political geography, whose consequences the world still lives with today. Since Roman times, "Syria" had meant a land isthmus joining Anatolia and Egypt, with the Mediterranean on one side and the desert on the other. In January 1916, the British and the French agreed to divide all the Arabic-speaking Ottoman lands according to the Sykes–Picot Agreement, which informed the actual partition of the land isthmus after the war. An Arab-led revolt led by Emir Feisal of Mecca and supported by the British led to the defeat of the Ottomans in Syria, beginning in late-1917. A small French contingent of some 6,200 soldiers, many of them colonials, accompanied the campaign, which concluded with the Armistice of Mudros signed with the Ottomans of October 30, 1918.

Thereafter, a complex political game ensued among Arabs, British, and French. If only because of imperial overreach, the British needed an ally in the region, which suited long-standing French interests in the eastern Mediterranean. Even the anticolonial Clemenceau acquiesced, needing the support of the Parti colonial to remain in power. In the meantime, the indigenous elite had established the Syrian Arab Congress, whose goals included establishing a constitutional monarchy under Feisal that preserved the territorial integrity of Roman and Ottoman Syria. This put Feisal in the delicate position of trying to satisfy his British patrons, the French who disliked him and wanted half of his prospective domain, and his would-be Syrian constituents/subjects. One Damascus newspaper warned the future mandatory power: "Tell the Pope, the clericalists, and the politicians who aim at conquest that young Syria will never submit to old France."

Ultimately, allied military power decided the situation. The French deposed Feisal, whom the British later rehabilitated as King of Iraq. General Henri Gouraud defeated outnumbered and outgunned Arab forces at the Battle of Maysalun on July 24, 1920. Shortly thereafter, Gouraud made a triumphal and imperial-looking entry into Beirut formally to establish the future French mandate (see Illustration 4.2). He paid tribute to the Tirailleurs Sénégalais and the Maghreb troops who had guaranteed his victory. Gouraud advised mandate Syrians to follow the example of their colonial brothers: "Who could believe that these Moroccans and Senegalese, after having spilled their blood for four years on the battlefield, would sacrifice themselves again yesterday, if France were not a true mother to them?"

№ 84 Proclamation du Grand Liban
le 1er septembre 1920.

d, Librairie, Stamboul.

Illustration 4.2 General Henri Gouraud declares the state of Greater Lebanon as a mandate under the League of Nations, September 1, 1920.
Source: Wikipedia Commons (public domain).

Most devastating in terms of demography and sheer human suffering, was a wartime famine throughout Ottoman Syria that continued postwar. An allied naval blockade, Ottoman requisitions, and societal tensions between rich and poor aggravated an already dire situation of poor harvests. The famine killed an estimated 500,000 people of a total population of some 3.5 million. French mandatory rule thus began over a ruined, starving, and divided land and people. Destroying the Syrian Arab Congress maimed democracy in Syria for generations to come. The British and the French had so successfully altered the situation that to this day we take "Syria" as a geographic term to mean mandate Syria rather than Roman and Ottoman Syria.

French mandates ran into firmly established practices of colonial rule by soldiers and bureaucrats, who had little experience and not much interest in teaching peoples to govern themselves. Indeed, in the Class-A mandate for Syria and Lebanon, the French ruled in ways seemingly designed to make their continued rule indispensable. French authorities saw their new domain as tailor-made for the *politique des races*. The fact that the region had served as a highway for centuries joining Europe, the Ottoman Empire, the Russian empire, and the Arabic-speaking Middle East meant that it had a highly diverse population that practiced many religions (and sects within religions) and spoke many languages.

The *politique des races* in Mandate Syria required keeping these populations as separate and competitive as possible. The French established no fewer than six "states" in their mandate – Greater Lebanon, the State of Damascus, the State of Aleppo, the Jabal al-Druze State, the Alawite State, and the Sanjak of Alexandretta (ceded to Turkey in 1939). Each had its own "capital," essentially a French administrative center. Greater Lebanon in some respects lay at the heart of the entire enterprise. Maronites, indigenous Catholics not directly subservient to the pope in Rome, had constituted a majority in the Ottoman Mount Lebanon Mutasarrifate established in 1861. The French added territories along the Mediterranean coast to create Greater Lebanon in August 1920. Of course, the greater Lebanon became, the less Maronite it became. In 1926, the French promulgated a constitution that apportioned major offices among the major faiths and sects. This essentially religious/tribal distribution of power continues to provide what passes for governance in Lebanon today. Elsewhere, two sects of Islam, the Druze and the Alawites, got their own "states" ostensibly to protect them from Sunni or Shia majorities, but more plausibly to weaken states based in the major population centers of Damascus and Aleppo. The French took care to keep local government as weak as possible, to maximize dependence on mandatory authority. Much, to be sure, divided the peoples of post-Ottoman Syria. But they could sometimes unite in their shared resentment of French rule.

The French made only sporadic and half-hearted attempts to federate these quasi-states. Indeed, separate colonial bureaucracies competed for resources and influence allocated by the high commissioner operating from the mandate capital in Beirut. The League of Nations, in Syria as elsewhere, tended to look the other way in policies such as the *politique des races* that so brazenly contravened the spirit of the mandate. Various attempts to create constitutional government appeared through the 1930s, partly to satisfy the League of Nations. Satisfying some groups meant enraging others. The Parti colonial in Paris opposed anything that resembled actual self-determination. Certainly, returns on lackluster investment in Syria never came close to compensating for the costs of what had become an expensive as well as brutal occupation.

In July 1922, the League finalized Class-B mandates for the French in Togo and Cameroon. The French and the British had conquered both during the war and subsequently partitioned them along nineteenth-century lines, though here with most of the territory coming under French rule.[3] A Class-B mandate did not carry with it an explicit trajectory toward independence, but rather allocated to the mandatory authority specified tasks. It had to guarantee freedom of religion (and thus protection for Christian missionaries), see to the abolition of slavery, prohibit traffic in armaments and alcohol, prevent the militarization of the mandate territory, and guarantee free trade for all League members.

The French duly did not incorporate either of their African mandates into their existing colonial federations, and mostly adhered to League prohibitions on raising colonial soldiers. A *Commissaire de la République* in each mandate reported to the Ministry of Colonies. Otherwise, governance in Togo and Cameroon resembled French rule elsewhere in West and Equatorial Africa. The mandates produced much the same goods for export – cocoa, palm and peanut oil, coffee, and some cotton. The French built some roads and railroads, financed primarily through local taxation and built with conscripted labor. Missionaries and the colonial state continued at turns to cooperate and criticize each other. The French applied tailored versions of the *indigénat*, with the same resentments. Relatively little new land expropriation took place because the mandatory state simply inherited lands already taken by the German

---

[3] British-administered Togo joined Ghana following a referendum in 1956, while the French-administered Togo became the Togolese Republic in 1960. The mandatory period created English- and French-speaking elites in Cameroon, which remains a source of tension today.

colonial regime. Year in and year out, the French submitted rosy reports to the Permanent Mandates Commission of the League. Its first self-praising report in 1921, which preceded the formal establishment of the mandate, set the tone. France, the report concluded, "faithful to its traditions and to its colonial doctrine, devoted itself to the sacred task of civilizing the populations over which it has tutelage."

4.2.2   The Mise en valeur

As we have seen, the *Histoire de Babar* originally appeared in 1931, in the depths of the Great Depression. In this first story, we learn nothing of the future relationship between the city and the forest. Readers assume, perhaps, that association will guide that future, with the forest remaining the forest and the city the city. The best and brightest animals, now appropriately civilized, will get to wear green suits and rise to high status at home.

The 1931 Exposition coloniale internationale de Paris echoed the master narrative of colonialism inhabited by Babar. If the French were never going to move to the empire, a domesticated empire had to be brought to them. Colonial expositions already had a long tradition – Lyon (1894), Rouen (1896), Rochefort (1898), Hanoi (1902), and Marseilles (1906 and 1922). But at the end of the day, any truly "French" colonial exposition had to take place in Paris, as the political, economic, and cultural capital of the empire. The exposition was staged in the Bois de Vincennes just east of the city. Particularly given the continuing world economic crisis, the exposition constituted a massive investment, some 318 million francs, at least $700 million today. Yet it actually turned a considerable profit, attracting some 8 million visitors in its seven-month run.

The planners placed in charge none other than Hubert Lyautey, now *maréchal de France*. His own words summarized the point in the visitor's guide: "You must find in this exposition, along with the lessons of the past, the lessons of the present and above all the lessons for the future. You must leave the exhibition resolved always to perform better, grander, broader and more versatile feats for Greater France." The pavilions, designed by prominent white architects, presented a vivid colonial imagination. The Madagascar pavilion, for example, featured the Tour de Boucrânes (Tower of Skulls), some 50 m high, framed by enormous, sculpted heads of the zebu, a species of cattle. Visitors entered through a massive staircase. Missing were any connections to actual architectural practices in Madagascar. The most eye-catching pavilion involved a partial reconstruction of Angkor Wat in Cambodia, facilitated by imported molds of the original. The scale and Orientalized mystification of the pavilion made Angkor Wat probably the most recognizable site in the entire French empire. More unsettling were the *zoos humains,* a practice going back to the early modern period of presenting indigenous peoples like animals. While shorn of some of its most callous aspects, exhibits continued to display indigenous peoples in allegedly "native" settings. Anything hybrid, such as mixed-race persons or even non-citizen Francophone indigenous persons (the *évolués*), remained conspicuously absent. In all, the exposition provided an idealized, perfectly functioning empire, in which all fulfilled their hierarchically designated functions for the greater good, much like the forest of Babar the King.

At the level of policy, the exposition reflected what became known as the *mise en valeur,* a term not directly translatable into English. Literally, it means "put into value." In practice, it came to mean an array of political and economic policies intended to develop the empire in ways that would contribute to the security of a "global" France in an ever more dangerous world. Little in the interwar *mise en valeur* constituted new colonial policy. But the war had shown both the potential for mobilizing the empire and the need to continue doing so. The Great Depression and the collapse of world trade raised the stakes even further. The *mise en valeur,* the theory went, would move the empire from the margins to the center of French economic and geostrategic security.

The great popularizer of the *mise en valeur* was Albert Sarraut, a Third Republic perennial who over a long career served twice as governor-general of Indochina, once as minister of colonies, and twice as prime minister. His 671-page *La Mise en valeur des colonies françaises* (1923) remains the single most important statement on French imperialism between the wars. A fervent supporter of association, Sarraut envisaged the empire as "grandeur without servitude." He observed as governor-general in Hanoi back in 1918: "The colonies are states in the making."[4] He had in mind a somewhat more racially inclusive version of the British Dominions – home rule with foreign and defense policy directed from the metropole. The Hexagon would remain the center of a vast trading bloc, further consolidated by the French language, which would challenge English as a world language. Sarraut's empire must become ever more French, and in being so, "civilize in the full sense of the word, to affirm everywhere that inspiration where it finds once again the great characteristics of its national tradition."

Sarraut's idea of association had as a corollary a measure of top-down assimilation. As we have seen, social selection in the empire was also not new. The Third Republic in the colonies would select the best and the

---

[4] The French reads "grandeur sans la servitude" and "Les colonies sont des États en devenir."

brightest for assimilation to "Frenchness." Thereafter, they would return to their native lands, where their compatriots would recognize them as natural leaders. On the ground, the colonial state and colonial business could delegate more mundane functions to the partly assimilated *évolué*. So governed, each domain would find its unique place in the evolution of global France.

As minister for colonies in 1921, Sarraut put forward a plan for the economic development of the empire based on extravagant expectations of German reparations from World War I. Had his plan been enacted, France would have made massive investments in infrastructure, education, and public health. When actual reparations payments fell well short, the Hexagon left colonial finance largely unchanged. While the French state continued to favor credit in certain sectors, notably railroads, the colonies would have to raise capital much as before, through loans serviced by colonial taxation and the *régies*. The peoples of the empire continued to pay for infrastructure to which they had little direct access.

The *mise en valeur* further involved a renewed commitment to another familiar policy – what the British called imperial preference. Through tariffs and quotas, France would grant preferential access to commodities from its empire, and the empire would buy nearly all its finished goods from the Hexagon. In the AOF and AEF, this resulted in the expanded production of such commodities such as peanuts and peanut oil, cotton, cocoa, and coffee. There remained the problems of securing adequate labor and building the necessary infrastructure.

The colonial state made use of an instrument legal in West Africa since 1912, the *prestation*, labor extracted as a form of taxation. Colonial officials worked hard to reconcile this practice with the *mission civilisatrice*. "If our subjects have shown a sincere willingness to break out of their atavistic laziness and misery," wrote the AOF governor-general Jules Carde in 1928, "they are still far from attaining a modern rhythm of activity." French republicanism had never shied away from coercion toward the greater good. Practices reminiscent of Ancien Régime slavery remained, notably in the construction of the Congo-Océan Railway in the AEF from 1921 to 1934, connecting the interior of the French Congo to the sea. Official and unofficial estimates of the dead ranged between 15,000 and 60,000. A grim satirical cartoon from *Le Journal de peuple* of April 28, 1929 portrayed black bodies as railroad ties, while a corpulent white capitalist boasted that the railroad "only cost us 2,000 *nègres* per kilometer!"

Whatever its ethics, doubling down on old practices did manage to raise production throughout the empire. Before the Great Depression, rice exports from Indochina continued to increase, mostly to existing markets in Asia. As before, the benefits accrued primarily to French investors and their collaborators among Indochinese landowners. Imperial preference benefited their counterparts in West Africa. Production of other commodities also flourished, such as tin, tungsten, and coal, as well as certain kinds of wood. The continued rise of the automobile increased demand for latex from Indochina and Africa, and helped make Michelin the world corporation it remains today. Vanilla production increased dramatically in Madagascar, from 62 percent of world production in 1923 to 80 percent in 1933. Wine cultivation in Algeria increased enough to lead producers in the Hexagon to insist on caps in production. In 1913, the empire had been the third most important trading partner for the Hexagon, behind Great Britain and Belgium-Luxembourg. By 1928, the empire placed first.

However, imperial preference meant protectionism, a policy that usually starts well and ends poorly for everyone. Protection rarely encourages the efficient use of capital, human or financial. Guaranteed markets encouraged complacency, both in the Hexagon and in the empire. Imperial preference probably spared neither the Hexagon nor its empire very much in enduring the Great Depression, with its accompanying collapse of world trade. To be sure, the share of trade between France and its empire increased. The imperial piece of the pie grew relatively larger, but the pie itself shrank dramatically.

Modest investments in public health produced some of the most far-reaching effects of the *mise en valeur*. Colonized peoples had long had high birth rates. But even small reductions in rates of infant mortality facilitated rapid population growth. Increased agricultural production trickled down enough to improve nutrition somewhat in much of the empire. Even marginally improved nutrition bolstered resistance to disease. Rudimentary efforts at water purification and the dispatch of mobile medical units accomplished more than good publicity for the colonial authorities. Vaccinations against cholera and smallpox also reduced death rates. Medical gains eventually extended to tuberculosis, malaria, and sleeping sickness. The French established throughout the empire branches of the Institut Pasteur to research and treat tropical diseases. The colonial state also expanded medical training for indigenous doctors, notably in Vietnam and Morocco. Microbes came to constitute a particular kind of enemy impeding the progress of the French empire. In racially differentiated ways, colonizer and colonized could fight this enemy together.

It would be a mistake to overstate the change. Colonial health services always concerned themselves more with tiny white populations than with the indigenous masses. The French built a whole city as a "refuge" from tropical diseases in Dalat, at the southern end of the Central Highlands of Annam. Almost everywhere, colonial physicians fretted more about malaria, which particularly afflicted whites, than about sleeping sickness, which particularly afflicted Africans. In the AEF by the 1930s, at best a third of the population had even sporadic access to any French-provided health care. Famine and its attending diseases did not disappear in the French empire in the interwar period, notably a famine in Niger in 1931 that killed at least 15,000 people, and perhaps 30,000.

Nevertheless, throughout the interwar period, the population of the French empire beyond the Hexagon began a phase of rapid expansion, while the population of the Hexagon stagnated. The entire Indochinese Union numbered some 16.4 million people in 1914, by 1936 more than 23 million. In Algeria, the Muslim population expanded more than 26.5 percent between 1921 and 1936 (4.9 million to 6.2 million), whereas the non-Muslim population expanded by some 20.6 percent (792,000 to 946,000). By 1936, the Muslim population was increasing by some 2 percent per year, considerably faster than the rate of settler increase. Demography alone, in time, would force the questioning of colonial bargains.

4.2.3   Interwar Anticolonialism

Colonialism and anticolonialism grew up together everywhere empire planted its flag. Some of the most important forms of resistance remained the least immediately visible. Peasants could evade taxes, conscripted laborers could work with lassitude or intentional incompetence. *Évolué* working in offices could thwart colonial authority subtly in any number of ways. In the end, the *indigénat* probably angered native populations more than it altered actual behavior. To the last, the Third Republic remained a fervently bourgeois regime that wanted a vast empire on the cheap. It limited its own capacity to repress accordingly.

Nevertheless, something changed in the French empire after World War I. Colonized elites began to resist in ever more public ways, and to open new paths of communication with one another, typically in the French language. Paradoxically, the cosmopolitism of the French empire itself provided a wide audience to anticolonial intellectuals such as Aimé Césaire (1913–2008), a Martiniquais of African descent. Négritude, a cultural movement he helped found, reached across the African diaspora to place African-ness at the center of civilization itself. The imperial capital of Paris teemed with anticolonial intellectuals from all corners of the empire. Gradually, the colonizer lost control over the messaging of imperialism. The imperial powers, like it or not, had publicly committed themselves to some movement toward "self-determination" in the mandates. It became increasingly difficult to explain just why Muslim Arabic speakers in Syria and Lebanon had a trajectory toward independence, while Muslim Arabic speakers in Tunisia and Morocco, let alone Algeria, did not.

One could even argue that the Third Republic had done its work in the empire, with a host of unintended consequences. Crudely put, Babar had gone to school, but the lesson learned turned out not to be the lesson taught. The imperial republic had nurtured educated and articulate indigenous elites. Those elites would find their own voices and would emerge not just as the core of anticolonial resistance between the wars but as the core of the postcolonial leadership thereafter. Even in remote and rural Madagascar, a communist party published a newspaper, *Le Prolétaire malagache*, with a circulation of some 8,000. While hardly a mass movement, the party provided a means of articulating goals of anticolonialism and supplied postwar leaders of the movement for independence. When independence came, very few anticolonialists in Madagascar of any shade of opinion would seek a return of the monarchy deposed by the French in 1896.

Throughout Africa, the *mise en valeur* itself had accelerated the expansion of the *évolué*, which the colonial state continued to exclude from citizenship, ostensibly because they maintained Muslim or some other non-French civil status. But the Third Republic applied even this categorization differently. The *originaires* of the Quatre Communes of Senegal enjoyed full civil rights as Muslims. The three *départements* of Algeria were likewise French national territory, not colonies. Why did Muslims there not enjoy the same rights as the *originaires*? Anticolonialists could point to an ever-lengthening list of inconsistencies in imperial rule.

In colonial policy as in other areas, the Third Republic rested on a consensus of middle-class white men who wanted to govern in a certain way. In the Hexagon, this consensus seriously frayed over the interwar period. A broad center co-opting parts of the Right and Left still led. But a not-insignificant fascist Right and a supposedly still-revolutionary Communist Party made it ever more difficult for the center to hold. Politics in the Hexagon and the empire could mix in toxic ways. For example, anti-Jewish rioting in Constantine, Algeria, in August 1934 led to the deaths of twenty-five Jews and three Muslims, among them a twelve-year-old boy. Mohamed El Maado, an officer in the 3e Régiment des Zouaves (indigenous light infantry) with many connections to fascists in the Hexagon, fanned the violence. His goal was to give Muslims and settlers a common enemy in Algerian Jews, in the name of a trans-Mediterranean "French" fascism.

Powerful forces straddling the empire and the Hexagon blocked serious reform. The Socialist-led Popular Front government of 1936–8 proposed the modest Blum–Violette bill for Algeria, named for Prime Minister Léon Blum and Maurice Violette, a former governor-general. The bill would have granted full French citizenship to some 21,000 Muslims, a tiny elite of officers and professionals, who would have been able to maintain their Muslim civil status. The parties of the Left supported the bill, including the Communists. Most anticolonialists in Algeria supported it as well, as at least a small step in the right direction. But the settler electorate became politically hysterical and mobilized their supporters in Paris to prevent Blum even from bringing the bill to the National Assembly for formal consideration. This set the pattern for blocking reform in Algeria after World War II.

Anticolonial activists comprised an eclectic group with varied backgrounds and careers. Given the dangerous career they chose, many also lived remarkably long lives. Many had benefited from the educational opportunities offered by the imperial republic. Nguygn Sinh Cung, better known later as Ho Chi Minh (1890–1969), was born to a mandarin family, though the French deposed his father because of his anticolonial views. Ho himself attended a French high school (lycée) and spoke good, clear French. Only when refused admission to the École coloniale (the school of colonial administration) did he begin his long journey to anticolonial communism. Vo Nguyen Giap (1911–2013) masterminded the Vietnamese military victories over the French and later the Americans. He likewise attended a lycée and spoke good French, though he hotly denied allegations that he had ever studied at the prestigious Lycée Albert Sarraut in Hanoi.

Habib Bourguiba (1903–2000), later the first president of independent Tunisia, came from modest socioeconomic origins. His family worked hard to get him educated in French language schools. This led ultimately to a scholarship to study law at the Sorbonne in 1924. After 1927, he returned to Tunisia to practice, notably defending activists in criminal courts. An existing political group, Le Destour (constitution), drew elite followers among merchants, lawyers, doctors, and the entourage of the dey (still in place under the protectorate). Bourguiba helped found Neo-Destour in 1934, which advocated what Sarraut claimed should be the logical conclusion of the mise en valeur – independence with continued cooperation with France.

Félix Houphouët-Boigny (1905–93) of the Côte d'Ivoire was born to a family of hereditary chiefs. He converted to Catholicism and studied at the École de medicine de l'AOF, the medical school established for West Africans. But overt professional discrimination and years of service in colonial hospitals provided its own education in the disparities of colonial rule. As early as December 1932, he wrote an article under a pseudonym for a colonial newspaper entitled *"On nous a trop volés"* (They Have Stolen Too Much From Us). Yet in 1939, Houphouët-Boigny accepted an important position from the French, as *chef de canton* with jurisdiction over some thirty-six villages. For the time being, he took a reformist approach to blunting the edges of imperial rule.

Organized anticolonial resistance in Algeria proved particularly complicated. Certainly, a tone-deaf centennial "celebration" in 1930 of the French conquest helped unite Algerian nationalists. But their cause would prove divided before, during, and after the war for independence. Indeed, all the future fault lines of Algerian nationalism appeared during the interwar period – the religious versus the secular, leftist internationalist revolutionaries versus nationalists, Arabs versus Berbers. Activists held a host of mutually exclusive views on the role of the settlers in an "Algerian" Algeria and the future relationship with the Hexagon.

Settlers founded the Parti communiste algérien (PCA) in 1920, as a branch of the Parti communiste français. But the PCA did not open its doors to Muslims until 1936, by which time a decree from the Comintern in Moscow required all communists to set anticolonial goals aside and join a common front against fascism. Communism remained marginal in Algeria through independence, settler hysteria to the contrary. Messali Hadj (1898–1974) became involved in anticolonial activities while working the Hexagon, where he founded the Étoile Nord-Africain (North African Star). After his return to Algeria, he rebranded the organization as the Parti du Peuple Algérien. His advocacy of peaceful resistance did not keep him out of intermittent stays in French prisons. Abdelhamid Ben Badis (1889–1940) advocated a more Islamist version of Algerian nationalism. He wrote the first book on Algerian history in Arabic, perhaps best known for its phrase "Islam is our religion, Algeria is our country, Arabic is our language." Ferhat Abbas (1899–1995), the son of a *caïd* or local magistrate, served with the French army medical corps and trained as a pharmacist at the University of Algiers. Before World War II, he advocated a moderate strain of nationalism, what he referred to as "equality under French sovereignty." He saw the fate of Arabs, Berbers, settlers, and Jews as inextricably linked.

France fought two partly concurrent anticolonial wars in the interwar period. The protectorate in Morocco had never been "pacified," as the colonial euphemism had it, so much as governed under a kind of truce. After 1911, the Spanish and French effectively partitioned Morocco, with the Spanish occupying a strip in the north along the Strait of Gibraltar and the Rif mountains, inhabited mostly by Berbers. The Rif had substantial mineral deposits, notably iron ore. Spain sought is own *mise en valeur* in the Rif, not least because of the economic opportunities presented by its neutrality in World War I. Environmental damage and poor diplomacy with Berbers led to a revolt that, in turn, led to the proclamation in 1921 of a Republic of the Rif under the direction of Abd el-Krim (1882–1963). Hubert Lyautey, once again resident-general in French Morocco, initiated a delicate game of playing the Spanish and the Berbers off against each other, in part to prevent the rebellion from spreading across an ill-defined colonial border, a border that meant little to the Berbers.

As the war went badly for the Spanish, the French increasingly got drawn in, since a Berber victory against Spain could not go unnoticed across North Africa. Berber guerrillas probably never numbered more than 20,000 at any given time, though they knew the terrain and understood the opportunities of asymmetrical warfare. France would ultimately send some 160,000 soldiers to the Rif, some white troops from the Hexagon, but particularly colonial troops from Algeria and Tunisia, the Tirailleurs Sénégalais, and the Foreign Legion. In combination with some 90,000 troops from Spain, the rebels found themselves outnumbered by at least 12:1. Moreover, the colonial allies used the full array of modern weaponry – notably artillery and air power. The Spanish probably used poison gas, of French manufacture. Eventually, Hexagon politicians sidelined Lyautey and put General Philippe Pétain in charge. Critics at the time described his tactics as using a sledgehammer to kill a fly. Despite considerable collateral damage, Pétain never killed the fly, though a negotiated settlement did send Abd el-Krim to a comfortable exile in Réunion. Less publicized at the time was the reliance on colonial troops, and the deepening impression that France would defend its empire to the last drop of African blood.

Considerably more damaging to France on the world stage was the Great Syrian Revolt between 1925 and 1927. The League of Nations had given France administrative authority in Syria as a Class-A mandate, toward the stated goal of independence. All manner of Syrians who agreed on very little never forgot the difference between a mandate and a colony. The revolt began in the Druze state in August 1925 over the relatively minor matter of a Druze delegation presenting its grievances to the French High Commissioner, General Maurice Sarrail. The general owed his position more to his political ties to the Center-Left coalition then in power in the Hexagon than to his abilities as colonial administrator. Sarrail unwisely jailed the Druze delegation, sparking a revolt that spread through much of mandate Syria. France eventually won the military conflict, thanks to modern technology and more than tripling its troop deployment, from some 15,000 to 50,000 soldiers, again many from the colonies.

But the French had bombarded Damascus, Homs, and Aleppo, the major cities of the mandate, in full view of the international media. Moreover, as mandatory power, the French had to make an annual report to the Permanent Mandates Commission of the League. The commission took the exceptional step of rejecting the report for 1925 and demanding a full accounting. The French backed themselves into a defense of their actions as fulfilling rather than defiling the mandate, by claiming to protect Syria against terrorists. Few found such an explanation credible. Quincy Wright, a prominent American jurist who happened to be in Syria at the time and hardly an anti-imperialist, suggested in print that as a free people under the mandate, Syrians had a right to insurrection under natural law. In a sense, the mandate system "worked" as some of its founders intended, in that it provided an international forum for imagining colonized peoples as capable of self-rule.

In the French empire as elsewhere, the imperial powers could prevail as long as they were willing to spend enough blood, treasure, and political capital. The French military could not be defeated head on in the empire because of its technological superiority. Anticolonial movements could be kept in check through co-optation, well-paid informants, and indigenous police willing to collaborate with French power. The *indigénat*, backed by courts, prisons, and ultimately the guillotine, could keep the colonized masses in line. Most future nationalist leaders were in prison, in exile, or collaborating with the French when war returned to Europe in 1939. But the defeat of France in that war would change the contours of colonial bargaining, more swiftly and more profoundly than many colonialists or anticolonialists hitherto thought possible.

4.3   The Conqueror Conquered: World War II

The German military victory of 1940 shattered the Third Republic and ended a consensus as to just what "France" even was. The defeat resulted first in the occupation of the northern and western Hexagon, and after November 1942 and the Allied invasion of North Africa, European France in its entirety. The empire became its own battlefield in a genuinely global struggle. Throughout the French empire, the colonized had seen the colonizer humiliated and rendered subservient.

On its deathbed in May 1940, the Third Republic called out of retirement the World War I hero, Rif War veteran, and *maréchal de France* Philippe Pétain to form a government. All understood that he would not continue the war from the empire. Pétain in fact meant to use that defeat to transform France. He would govern from the spa town of Vichy in the Unoccupied Zone, embarking on what he called *la Révolution nationale*, a rejection of the liberal democracy that had lost the war. Vichy France sought active collaboration in the construction of Adolf Hitler's New Europe. Initial opposition was marginal in the Hexagon. In June 1940, Charles de Gaulle, recently promoted to brigadier general and a junior minister, on his own authority established *La France libre* (Free France), a government-in-exile in London. At first, he carried almost none of the empire with him. With the military front collapsing, the Third Republic, bourgeois to its last breath, had the gold of the Banque de France put on board ships that ended up in Martinique and Dakar. Eventually, the gold changed sides along with the colonies.

The mere existence of the French empire raised the stakes in the increasingly global conflict. The Eurocentric Nazi regime cared little about overseas empire, at any rate for itself. It did care about impeding British access to India and keeping the Allies out of strategic sites in Africa such as Casablanca and Dakar, where they posed a threat to the U-boat campaign. Germany's ally Imperial Japan cared a good deal about French Indochina, the linchpin of its expansion south. Officially, the Vichy regime remained diplomatically neutral. On July 3, 1940, the British weakened the ability of the French navy to intervene anywhere by a preemptive attack on the fleet at Mers el-Kébir, near Oran, Algeria.

Bit by bit, the combined efforts of the Free French and Allied military power convinced most governors and senior military officers in the empire to change sides. Remote domains adjacent to the British Empire, such as the New Hebrides (administered jointly with the British) and the French enclaves in India, declared their allegiance to de Gaulle right away. Most of French Equatorial Africa embraced Free France by the fall of 1940. The small French domains in the Western Hemisphere – Saint-Pierre and Miquelon, Guadeloupe and Martinique, and Guyane – were first isolated by the British navy, and eventually turned over to the Free French. The British navy, worried about the Japanese navy in the Indian Ocean, saw to the conquest of Madagascar and its surrounding islands by British imperial troops by September 1942. French West Africa proved much more conflicted, with most of the imperial domains siding initially with Pétain. Indochina sided unambiguously with Pétain. New Caledonia, beyond reach even of the Japanese onslaught that followed the Pearl Harbor attack of December 1941, was occupied by the British and turned over to the Free French in August 1941.

In some places, such as Syria and Lebanon in mid-1941, popular resentments remained constant and only colonial officials changed sides. These resentments initiated the crumbling of mandatory rule even before the end of the war. In Madagascar, the Free French imposed a ferocious regime of extraction based particularly on rubber. War with Japan had drastically reduced the availability of latex, pending the development of synthetic rubber, eventually produced in large quantities by the Americans. The Free French thus sought to reestablish France as a critical ally literally on the backs of their Malagasy colonial subjects. While not unsuccessful in the short run, wartime extractions laid the groundwork for a major insurrection in Madagascar in 1947.

In an attempt to convince the governors of West and Equatorial Africa not to go over to de Gaulle, Admiral René-Charles Platon pleaded: "The Marshal has only one card left, the empire. He wants to play it when the time comes. I beg of you, do not snatch it from his hands." Pétain's main assets, in the empire as in the Hexagon, were his personal prestige, the loyalty of colonial officials to what they considered the legitimate state, fear and/or hatred toward the British, and disdain for the Third Republic, which after all had lost the war. Indeed, Pétain had enough autonomy to name as his first minister of colonies Henry Lémery, a *personne de couleur* from Martinique. But the German occupier saw to Lémery's departure within a few months. The empire, surely, was a card. But whose card was it to play?

4.3.1 Collaboration with Which Empire?

Vichy's partial and circumscribed sovereignty made its writ in the empire inevitably problematic. How could a government that could not rule throughout the Hexagon rule an empire? The defeat of 1940 and the mere existence of Hitler's New Europe confused the imperial message in the colonies. In West Africa, for example, the Vichy authorities banned the Nazi propaganda film *Jude Süss* (the Jew Süss), lest the *indigènes* code Jews as white. Adding to the confusion, Allied naval superiority made communications between Vichy and its empire increasingly tenuous as the war continued. Moreover, Imperial Japan had proclaimed as war aims the destruction of European and American imperialism and the establishment of Dai Tōa Kyōekien, or the Greater East Asian Co-prosperity Sphere. For anticolonialists in the empire, would collaborating with Vichy help or hurt their cause?

Few settlers in Algeria had much use for the Third Republic by the time it expired. Like many of the French in the Hexagon, the settlers hailed the arrival of Pétain as divine providence, and at first eagerly sought collaboration. Early measures from Vichy proved popular, notably the abolition of the Crémieux Decree of 1870, which had given citizenship to indigenous Jews. This change also proved not unpopular with Muslim communities, as it returned some 120,000 Jews to the same legal status as themselves, including subjection to the *indigénat*. State employees lost their jobs. The regime ultimately deported some 1,500 Jews born in Algeria to camps in Europe. Vichy did not deport Jews directly from Algeria, rather Jews of Algerian descent who had the misfortune to migrate to the Hexagon. Mohamed El Maadi, who had stoked the anti-Jewish violence in Constantine in 1934, led a North African unit of the Waffen-SS, foreign units fighting for Germany.

The settlers likewise appreciated a Vichy crackdown on anticolonialists, such as the sentencing of Messali Hadj in March 1941 to sixteen years of forced labor. Pro-Vichy French would even fire on the Allies invading North Africa in Operation Torch beginning in November 1942. Yet as the tide of the war turned, particularly after the success of the North Africa campaign by the spring of 1943, settlers shifted their loyalty from Pétain to de Gaulle with remarkable speed. On June 3, 1943, the Free French established the Comité français de Libération nationale. They did so in Algiers, not in Dakar, Martinique, or Guadeloupe, which likewise remained French national territory. This moved French Algeria from the periphery to the center of the reborn republic as it regained its footing. The settlers embraced the return of white male democracy a good year before their compatriots in the Hexagon had the opportunity to do so following the D-Day landings of June 1944.

But de Gaulle understood that a global war for democracy had to have implications for the empire, above all in those bits of empire annexed to the metropole. The American army of liberation, in fact, had established some direct links with anticolonial activists in Algeria, much to the consternation of the Free French. In March 1944, de Gaulle imposed, more or less by personal decree, the most sweeping reform of colonial rule ever in Algeria. Some 65,000 Muslims could now become citizens without renouncing Muslim civil status. The *indigénat* would be abolished, and all adult Algerians, male and female, would acquire a (still unequal) franchise for local assemblies. Messali Hadj was released from the labor camp, and repressive measures against other activists diminished. Such measures displeased most anticolonialists as too little, too late. But settlers quickly grew suspicious of collaborating with the republican hero they had so recently cheered. In the end, World War II reinforced the propensity of settlers to consider themselves resolutely "Algerian" when dealing with the Hexagon, resolutely "French" when dealing with their Muslim compatriots.

Elsewhere, the Vichy years seemed to give free reign to colonial fantasy, at least at the official level. In remote Madagascar, larger than the Hexagon but with a European population of only about 23,000, collaboration occurred largely in a vacuum, with only occasional intervention from Vichy. For many years, both Zionist and anti-Semitic visionaries had floated the idea of Madagascar as a destination for Europe's Jews. For a host of logistical and ideological reasons, a Nazi version of this scheme proved stillborn. Vichy replaced the senior colonial administration with true believers in *la Révolution nationale*. The new regime also formed the Légion Française des Combattants et Volontaires de la Révolution Nationale, which brought together veterans, a few of them indigenous. In practice, it served as an arm of the colonial state, dedicated to articulating the new character of colonial rule. The Légion worked to create a cult of personality around Pétain, casting him as *my-amam'd'remy*, a paternal/maternal designation of Malagasy chiefs. Vichy propagandists also made much of alleged affinities between traditional, hierarchical Malagasy society and the new France envisaged by the National Revolution.

An exhaustive investigation by the colonial administration revealed some twenty-six Jews in Madagascar, whom the regime subjected to an array of Vichy anti-Semitic legislation but evidently did not deport. Freemasons, far more numerous because of the popularity of Freemasonry among republican colonial officials, constituted a convenient scapegoat for the sins of the republican empire. These lost their livelihood, and some their freedom. One Vichy radical adopted a term from the early 1890s to describe Freemasons: *mpkafous*, or heart-stealers. In the end, the speed and ease with which the British imperial forces seized and held Madagascar suggested that the collaborationist imaginary never reached very far beyond an inner circle of believers.

As we have seen, the Indochinese Union had the most developed colonial state of any imperial domain apart from those that doubled as national territory. But the collaboration of that state with Imperial Japan seemed to prove the Resistance adage that collaboration amounted to "give me your watch and I'll tell you the time." Vichy quickly made terms with the Nazi regime's Japanese ally. Two days before signing the formal armistice with Germany, on June 20, 1940, France agreed to close the border with China, including the Yunnan line, in order to cut off supplies to the Guomindang (Nationalists) in China. As early as March 1940, Japanese bombers had attacked the Yunnan line, in French airspace between Haiphong and Hanoi. In agreements signed on August 29 and September 22, 1940, France agreed to asymmetrical trade arrangements giving Japan generous access to Indochinese rubber, coal, and particularly rice, as well as permission to station troops in Tonkin and Annam. In July 1941, Vichy granted Japan military access to all of Indochina.[5] In exchange, Japan recognized French "sovereignty."

---

[5] The resulting occupation led to severe American economic sanctions, which in turn led to the attack at Pearl Harbor in December 1941.

Illustration 4.3 Vichy propaganda: work, family, and country in French and Vietnamese, 1942.
Source: Wikipedia.org (public domain).

In fact, the Japanese cared little about the day-to-day administration of their new de facto protectorate and gave Vichy colonial officials a wide berth. But "collaboration" with Vichy in Indochina meant collaboration with an Asian imperial power, one of whose stated war aims was the destruction of European imperialism. It did not escape notice throughout the French empire that the white colonizers now had Asian masters.

As in Madagascar, Vichy in Indochina directed much of its efforts toward the European population, which numbered some 34,000 people. The Légion Française had more influence in Indochina because it articulated the interests of a more powerful colonial state. Vichy Indochina tirelessly persecuted Jews, Freemasons, and Gaullist sympathizers. Some 187 members of the colonial civil service lost their jobs. A search for Jews uncovered about eighty, of whom forty-nine were serving in the military, twenty-seven of them in the Foreign Legion. As shown in Illustration 4.3, Vichy propagandists tried hard to graft Pétainist slogan of *travail, famille, patrie* (work, family, country) on to Confucian values of a harmonious, hierarchical society. Of course, this effort begged the question of just how an elderly *maréchal de France* would add much legitimacy to an Asian tradition dating back to the sixth century BCE.

By 1945, with Allied victory looking increasingly certain in Europe, with the American amphibious campaign closing in on the Japanese home islands, and with American bombing incinerating most of the major Japanese cities, the Japanese military made a quixotic effort to solidify its rule in Southeast Asia. On March 9, 1945, the Japanese removed the French colonial state and established "independent" kingdoms in Annam-Tonkin, Cambodia, and Laos. The fate of Cochinchina remained to be decided. In fact, the Japanese invoked the disintegration of colonial authority in Vietnam, and the beginning of a civil war that would last on and off for the next thirty years. Some French tried to change their loyalties from Vichy to Free France, notably about 4,000 French at Lang Son near the border with China. When the French commander, General Émile Lemonnier, refused to sign documents of surrender to the Japanese, they made him first dig his own grave, then beheaded him.

Yet remarkably, shards of Vichy rule in Indochina continued. In Dalat in the Central Highlands, Vichy, Free French, and Japanese forces actually fought together at the end of the war, to preserve "order" against a communist insurgency even then gathering strength. As would happen continually in the coming decades, the peoples of Vietnam would pay the price. A poor harvest, particularly in Tonkin, led to famine in 1945 and the death of some 1 million Vietnamese (2 million according to Ho Chi Minh). Meanwhile, at the Japanese surrender, over 300,000 tons of rice remained in storehouses in Cochinchina, Annam, and Cambodia. This stock had been intended for shipment to Japan, rendered impossible because of Allied naval supremacy. The gravity of the famine illustrated the degree to which no one held effective sovereignty in Indochina. At the very least, Free France would not find it easy to pick up where Vichy left off.

4.3.2   *Resistance against Which Empire?*

The subordination of French colonial power to Nazi Germany and Imperial Japan made resistance a complicated matter. Colonial officialdom at the outset almost uniformly embraced Pétain. But a great many people of all colors and of many political opinions in the colonies doubted that they would be better off in a world dominated by the Axis. Some helped Jews escape through the empire, notably Martinique. But particularly for colonized peoples, what would be the implications of "resisting" by joining the Free French, who promised little but continued colonial rule, however reformed? Should the peoples of the colonies seek to instrumentalize the resistance of Free France, and if so how?

Resistance through the Free French began in the AEF rather than the AOF. The AEF had the less developed colonial state of the two African federations, and had drawn relatively little public or private investment, even by the modest standards of the French empire. The more extensive colonial state in the AOF might have kept it more loyal to Pétain through the colonial bureaucracy. A British attack on the French battleship *Richelieu* docked in Dakar on July 8, 1940 helped to fan anti-British sentiment. In September 1940, French forces loyal to Vichy actually repelled a premature joint operation of the British and the Free French to seize West Africa. Only in July 1943 would the Free French, with African support, run Vichy out of Dakar.

In Free French lore, the core of the AEF rallied miraculously in the *trois glorieuses*, three days in August 1940 – Chad on the 26th, Cameroon on the 27th, and French Congo on the 28th. After the British attack at Mers-el-Kébir on July 3, 1940 and the clear adherence of Algeria and the AOF to Vichy, Free France assuredly needed a territorial base. The reconquest of the AEF even produced some of the last colonial heroes. Félix Éboué, the governor of Chad, had a Third Republic resumé Babar might have envied. Born the grandson of enslaved persons in Guyane, Éboué received his secondary education in Bordeaux and his professional education at the École Coloniale. The sole colonial governor of color in 1940, Éboué was likewise the first to transfer his allegiance from Vichy to Free France. Philippe Leclerc de Hauteclocque (a part pseudonym to protect his family in the Hexagon) was a career officer and veteran of the Rif War in Morocco. He led a band of colonial entrepreneurs on a mission to win over the African territories, notably Gabon. There, he helped Free French supporters among the white population win a small-scale civil war against supporters of Vichy. Later, some daring raids into the Italian colony of Libya led to the capture of Kufra on March 2, 1941. Of a theatrical disposition, Leclerc issued the Oath of Kufra: "Swear not to put down your arms until our colors, our beautiful colors, fly over the cathedral of Strasbourg."

Free French mythmaking overlaid a more complicated reality. Leclerc's band had no means of getting to Africa without British support, nor at that juncture any funding that did not come from London. The proximity of the British colony of Nigeria and the relatively small British part of the mandate in Cameroon gave Britain its own strategic interests in Central Africa. Éboué himself did not embrace Free France until he received a guarantee from the British that they would not encroach on French colonial domains that joined the Allied cause. Thereafter, however, Éboué did not hold back. "Rise up, sons of the Empire," he said in a broadcast of September 1940 from Brazzaville, "for the salvation of the homeland. Stand up with all your strength and all your love for France."

In announcing his adherence to Free France, Éboué had used a language that owed much to John Locke, and for that matter the American Declaration of Independence. Initially, the governor argued, "Chad submitted in sadness but in the strictest discipline" to the armistice and rule from Vichy. However, in the weeks that followed, the "metropolitan government" had required Chad to "multiply hostile measures toward Great Britain and to impose a policy of economic isolation on French Africa which would lead both native and European populations to ruin." Consequently, Vichy had abdicated its legitimate authority as colonial sovereign. This in turn freed the colonial officials from their existing obligations to the state in the Hexagon, making it possible for them to embrace de Gaulle.

But if one colonial authority could render itself illegitimate in Lockean terms, why not another? The situation seemed even more problematic in Cameroon, necessary to give Free France in Africa access to the sea. Cameroon had never been part of the AEF and legally was not even a French imperial domain, rather a mandate under the now-defunct League of Nations. So ambiguous had sovereignty in Cameroon become that Leclerc himself felt obligated to proclaim the "political and economic independence" of Cameroon, and to end his proclamation with "Long live free Cameroon!"

Ordinary Africans could be forgiven for not noticing a great deal of difference between their Vichy and Free French rulers. Promoted by de Gaulle to governor-general of the AEF, Éboué ruled with a familiar patriarchal hand, though he tried to mitigate its more brutal characteristics. Nevertheless, the *indigénat* remained in force until 1944. Extraction continued of colonial products through conscripted labor, the *prestation*. Indeed, as in Madagascar, compulsory labor in strategic rubber became more important than ever because much of the latex had to be drawn from trees in the forests rather than on plantations. In great need of specie, Free France saw to the mining of gold in the AEF with particular vigor. Expressions of the enthusiasm of Africa to join Free France could be viewed with some skepticism.

Fighting continued in sub-Saharan Africa, but it became increasingly marginal to the world conflict. Free France commanded colonial troops, some 27,000 in all, including troops previously serving under Vichy. New African recruits (some 17,000) were raised though the traditional means. All were paid a fraction of the wages paid to white troops. Nevertheless, troops of color fought for Free France in all the Allied campaigns until the end of the war. After the liberation of North Africa in 1943, the *blanchissement* (whitening) of Free French forces became a priority in anticipation of the invasion of the European continent. This occurred at the cost of the Free French not asking questions of former Vichy military personnel to which they did not want answers.

Throughout the empire, whether ruled by Vichy or Free France, men and women voted with their feet. They avoided conscription or forced labor through leaving for British Nigeria, Anglo-Egyptian Sudan, or Spanish Guinea. Organized labor unrest never seriously threatened Free French rule. A mutiny in December 1944 caused by pay and living conditions among Tirailleurs Sénégalais in Thiraroye, Senegal, resulted in the deaths of somewhere between 35 and 300 people. While Senghor wrote a bitter poem about the episode, it remains known precisely because it was exceptional. French sub-Saharan Africa would decolonize without a major war.

In contrast, the war for the independence of Vietnam began during World War II, through the rise of communist resistance to both Japanese and French rule. Ho Chi Minh spent the interwar years in exile, training in the Soviet Union and avoiding the French colonial authorities by operating from China. The Dang Cong san Dong Duong (Central Committee of the Communist Party of Indochina) met for the first time in Hong Kong in February 1930. On May 19, 1941, Vietnamese communists founded the more nationalist oriented Viet Nam doc lap dong minh (League for the Independence of Vietnam, more commonly known as the Vietminh) in Pac Bo, just 3 km from the Chinese border. Ho returned to China in July 1942, in hopes of obtaining the support of the Guomindang and Chiang Kai-Shek. But the Guomindang both feared the spread of communism and maintained a fantasy of reincorporating Tonkin at least into a postwar Sinosphere. They imprisoned Ho shortly after his arrival.

By 1943, however, the situation of the Guomindang had deteriorated sufficiently for them to release Ho, who returned to Tonkin to fight the Japanese. Together with Giap and fellow communist Pham Van Dong (1906–2000), the three began to organize an insurgency. De Gaulle inadvertently helped their cause by proclaiming from Algiers the necessity of reestablishing French colonial rule in Indochina as soon as possible. The Japanese coup of March 1945 created a political vacuum. Under Giap's direction, trained cadres fanned out through Tonkin, then into Annam and Cochinchina. As the Vietminh approached Hanoi, the

Japanese largely stepped aside in Tonkin, preferring in Jean Lacouture's words "Asian revolution to European revenge."[6]

The Vietminh had a surprising if temporary ally in the Americans, through the Office of Strategic Services (OSS), the precursor to the Central Intelligence Agency. Americans by 1945 made no secret of their impatience with European-style empire. Moreover, perceptive Americans understood that the Guomindang might well not emerge as the strongest power in postwar China, and that the United States might need new friends. In July 1945, the OSS through Operation Deer Team began to help train insurgents. Indeed, it was through a Deer Team radio that the Vietminh first learned of the Japanese surrender. At their meeting in September 1945, Major Allison Thomas of the OSS asked Ho whether he was a communist. Ho, who also spoke English because of his time in the United States and England, responded: "Yes. But we can still be friends, can't we?" However, anti-communist voices already on the ascent in Washington quickly brought this "might have been" scenario of cooperation to an end, much to the relief of the French.

In a public demonstration in Hanoi on September 2, 1945, the day of the Japanese formal surrender, Ho led a large public rally at which was read a Declaration of Independence of the Democratic Republic of Vietnam. A remarkable piece of anticolonial rhetoric, much of the declaration could have been written by Allied press officers, or for that matter rhetoricians of the American or French Revolutions. It called on the victors to live up their stated principles now that they had won their global crusade for democracy. It made direct reference to the "undeniable truths" of the Enlightenment, such as natural equality. Then, in the American style, it proceeded to lay out a charge sheet against French colonial authority. The French had "deprived our people of every democratic liberty," and enforced inhuman laws, meaning the *indigénat*. They had plundered natural resources and poisoned the Vietnamese people with opium and alcohol. Moreover, when faced with the threat of "Japanese Fascists," the French "went down on bended knees and handed over our country to them." In fighting Japan and preparing to fight postwar France if necessary, Vietnam had liberated itself.

In effect, the Vietnamese declaration continued Éboué's Lockean argument. French rule had rendered itself cruel and illegitimate. It then yielded to Japanese sovereignty that, at best, constituted submission to Asian rather than European imperial rapacity. The Vietnamese people,

---

[6] Jean Lacouture, *Ho Chi Minh: A Political Biography*, trans. Peter Wiles (New York: Random House, 1968 [originally published in French in 1967]), 102.

freed from both colonial yokes by the outcome of World War II, would henceforth determine their own destiny. The document expressed confidence that the Allies, having "acknowledged the principles of self-determination and equality of nations, will not refuse to acknowledge the independence of Vietnam."

But Free France had its own plans for the empire. De Gaulle had convened a meeting of twenty-one colonial governors of Africa, in Brazzaville, French Congo, from January 30 to February 8, 1944. Éboué was the only person of color present, and he would die of diabetes only six weeks later. De Gaulle's opening speech praised the *mission civilisatrice*, and colonial heroes such as Gallieni, Brazza, Lyautey, and Mangin. He declared a new day in "our Africa" (*notre Afrique*). But it would remain up to France "and to her alone, to proceed at the right time to make reforms in the imperial structure that she will decide upon in her sovereignty."[7]

Brazzaville would indeed produce ideas for reform that would have seemed radical before 1940 – the abolition of the *indigénat*, representative assemblies in all the imperial domains, representation for the entire empire in the National Assembly in Paris, and an amorphously expressed end to economic exploitation. Yet the great patriarch of Free French democracy left no doubt who would remain in charge. De Gaulle continued later in the conference: "any idea of autonomy, any possibility of evolution beyond the French bloc that constitutes the empire, even in the distant future, including self-government in the colonies, must be swept aside." He used the English term "self-government," suggesting the foreignness of the very concept. Yet Ho and millions in the French empire understood that 1945 was not 1919. It would prove difficult to explain just what the reforms supported by Free France offered that the *mise en valeur* had not, beyond sincerity. After World War II, the French empire would have to evolve into something else or expire. In the years to come, it would do some of both.

---

[7] The French reads: "il n'appartient qu'à elle, de procéder, le moment venu, aux réformes impériales de structure qu'elle décidera dans sa souveraineté."

5   Decolonization: 1945–62

Léopold Sédar Senghor (1906–2001) had perhaps the most brilliant resumé that could be put down to the imperial project of the Third Republic. Born to a merchant family south of Dakar, his family sent him at the age of eight to a Catholic boarding school. Aged twenty-two, he entered a seminary. Though he decided against a clerical path, Senghor remained a devout Catholic throughout his long life. In 1928, he moved to the Hexagon, where he would reside for the next sixteen years. He studied at ultra-elite Parisian institutions, first in the preparatory program at the Lycée Louis-le-Grand, then at the École Normale Supérieure. In 1935, he passed the *aggrégation*, which guaranteed him a job for life in the French education system. Senghor then embarked on an academic career that alone would have secured his fame – as a linguist, poet, essayist, and co-founder of the Afrocentric cultural movement Négritude. He served in a colonial unit of the French army in 1940, was taken prisoner by the Germans, then somewhat mysteriously repatriated to the Hexagon in February 1942 for "health reasons." In 1958, de Gaulle called on him as a linguist to serve on the commission writing the constitution for the Fifth Republic. In 1983, he became the first African elected to the Académie française, among other things the guarantor of the French language itself. Along the way, Senghor had become a true philosopher-king, serving as the first president of independent Senegal from 1960 to 1980.

His book *Hosties Noirs* (Black Hosts, 1948) included a poem written in January 1945 entitled "Prière de paix" (Prayer of Peace), dedicated to Georges Pompidou and his wife Claude. Georges Pompidou, later de Gaulle's successor as president of the Fifth Republic, had been Senghor's classmate at the École Normale Supérieure. Senghor's poem recounted an agonized survey of the French empire in the closing phase of World War II, and raised many questions about its future. The irresistible forces of liberation unleashed by the war could no longer be silenced by the immoveable object of imperial rule.

A profoundly pious poem, "Prayer for Peace," blended Catholic theology and Négritude. Africa, "crucified for four hundred years/And still breathing," had martyred itself for all of humanity. But in the Christian tradition, Senghor portrayed the martyr as triumphant, the exemplar of a better way forward. Like the communion Host, the *Hostie noire* as sanctified flesh reenacted the redemptive sacrifice of Jesus. "White Europe" assuredly surely needed redemption, above all those Europeans who "hunted down my children/Like wild Elephants," and then "exported ten million/Of my sons in the leprous holds of their ships" to a life of slavery. For generations after "freedom," their descendants under coercion grew sugar cane and cotton for the colonizer, "Since black sweat is fertilizer."

Yet the poet remained fully aware of his own deep connections to and devotion toward the land of the colonizer. "Oh Lord," he pleaded, "take from my memory France that is not France/This mask of meanness and hate that I can only hate." He pleaded with God to bless the nation that "opened my heavy-lidded eyes to the light of faith." Indeed, France had opened the world to him, introducing him to new "brothers" in places as far-flung as North Africa, Madagascar, and Indochina. "You from pacific seas and you from enchanted forests," Senghor continued, "I greet all of you with my catholic heart." The very word "catholic" comes from the Latin *catholicus*, meaning universal. He pleaded in conclusion for God to bless the sufferings of all the peoples of the world after the nightmare of World War II, and to "give their warm hands/A band of brotherly hands so they can embrace the land/Under the rainbow of your peace."

Of course, with the war not even over when Senghor wrote, we should not expect him to have laid out a program for the future of the French empire in a poem. But he certainly presented the problem. The sins of empire over the centuries could not be redeemed through simple reform. Plainly, the problem went beyond a "mask of meanness" that covered the face of a benevolent, inclusive, understanding, and somehow more authentic "France." Yet imperialism had happened, and colonized peoples could not return to some prelapsarian state before the invaders arrived – even if they wanted to and even if that state was as innocent as anticolonial rhetoric often claimed.

If colonialism was the problem, "decolonization" became the solution after 1945. Like "empire," "decolonization" meant different things in different times and places. The dissolution of the French empire into independent sovereign states was not everywhere a foregone conclusion. Few among the colonized, to be sure, would find sufficient de Gaulle's proclamations from Brazzaville in 1944. But many people of many colors who self-identified in some way as "French" would work to reinvent the empire in the postwar years. France would fight bloody wars of decolonization in Vietnam and Algeria. The second of these would destroy the regime in the Hexagon itself, the Fourth Republic. The new states of

West and Equatorial Africa, on the other hand, would arrive at complicated new sets of relationships to the Hexagon. As we will see, a surprising number of these relationships continue today. Decolonization would prove a process rather than an event or even a series of events. To date, it does not really have an end.

5.1 The Limits of Republican Empire

In the immediate aftermath of World War II, the French of the Hexagon by some indices discovered an affection for their empire that had rather eluded them for more than the two preceding centuries. In 1940, the École coloniale drew 355 applications. In 1944, with the Hexagon still being liberated, it drew 620 applicants in the first round of admissions, 700 in a special second round. The empire also acquired some surprising supporters. The Communist newspaper *L'Humanité* ran an article on August 30, 1944 (shortly after the liberation of Paris) proclaiming that France "could not accept any dispositions whatsoever that could diminish its sovereignty as a Great Power, nor its full right to administer the overseas territories over which it has charge, above all its right to defend these territories against all imperial designs." "Imperialism" here wore a British mask, held up by the Americans.

We can easily discern the logic behind this new affection for the French empire. It had provided the geographic locus for the narrative of continuous resistance to the German occupier. Moreover, thousands of colonial subjects had voluntarily donned a Free French uniform during the war – including later anticolonialists as prominent as Ahmed Ben Bella (1916–2012, the first head of government of independent Algeria) and perhaps the single fiercest critic of French colonialism, Franz Fanon. Gaston Monnerville (1897–1991) of Guyane was the grandson of enslaved people and would rise to the premiership and the presidency of the Senate after World War II. On May 25, 1944, twelve days before the D-Day landings at Normandy, he proclaimed: "Without the empire, France would be just a liberated country. Thanks to its empire, it is a country among the victors."

But the world had changed a great deal by 1945. The Soviet and American superpowers, each an empire in its own way, would have little patience for the European empires of the previous century. They would tolerate these empires only when they found it in their strategic interests to do so. Moreover, Allied propaganda portraying World War II as a global crusade for the liberation of peoples turned out to mean something after all. The mandates under the now-defunct League of Nations became trusteeships under the United Nations (UN), now with an explicit trajectory toward self-rule. Moreover, the Universal Declaration of Human Rights passed by the UN General Assembly in 1948 declared: "All human beings are born free and equal in dignity and rights." These rights clearly included self-determination. In response, French republican imperialism made a vast effort to reinvent itself, exposing the internal contradictions of republican empire in the process.

At a theoretical level, the very expression *la République une et indivisible* always sat poorly with empire, by definition a rule based on permanent and hierarchical difference. Every citizen in an ideologically consistent republic must have an identical stake in public power. That said, the internal contradictions of republicanism and empire did not unduly trouble the Third Republic. First to last, the regime construed itself as a national club for white men. As such, it had no trouble excluding all women and nearly all people in the empire. As most guardians of the Third Republic saw it, the empire was full of Muslims, savages, or both – people, but people profoundly ineligible for full membership in the republican community. The colonial doctrine of association recognized this accepted wisdom.

Yet reconciling republic and empire after 1945 meant facing formidable challenges. Some 120 million people lived in the French empire at the time – about 43 million in the Hexagon and 77 million elsewhere. At a meeting in Algiers in the summer of 1944 to discuss future constitutional arrangements, Socialist Jules Moch spoke the thoughts of many: "I cannot concede the placing of French delegates in a minority by *chefs nègres*." On the floor of the Constituent Assembly in August 1946, Édouard Herriot, a perennially influential figure under the Third and Fourth Republics, fretted famously: "If we give equality of rights to the colonial peoples, we will become the colony of our colonies" (*la colonie de nos colonies*). His colleague Senghor (an elected deputy from Senegal) sprang to his feet to accuse Herriot, accurately, of racism.

Yet one did not need overt racism to concede just what turning the French empire into a unitary republic would entail. The vast majority of the 77 million imperial subjects led very different lives from those of the 43 million citizens of the Hexagon. However reformers might spin the matter, most imperial subjects were impoverished and illiterate. If republicanism depends on commensurability, colonized millions were neither Herriot, nor Senghor, nor Babar. How to accommodate them as equals under a unitary republic? In the short term, the constituent adopted unanimously on May 7, 1946 the Loi Lamine Guèye, after the deputy from Senegal who proposed it. This law granted "all of the nationals of the overseas territories (including Algeria) the status of citizen, on the same basis as French nationals of the metropole or the overseas territories."[1] But the law left intentionally vague the question of the polity of which these 120 million French nationals would be citizens. Would they be citizens of a unitary republic or a reinvented empire?

Federalism provided a theoretical means of squaring the circle of republican empire. Sovereignty could have more than one locus. Citizens ostensibly could have an identical relationship to the central government. But significant powers would reside at other levels, as in states in the United States or the Federal Republic of Germany. The American experience certainly showed that federalism could accommodate racial inequality. Both the Fourth and the Fifth Republics would seek not so much actual federalism as reinvented empire with federal characteristics. At one level, federalism had remained anathema to the entire French republican tradition since its Revolutionary origins. *La République une et indivisible* could be governed only by a single *Volonté générale*, or General Will. When forced to choose between republic and empire, the guardians of the Republic tended to choose empire. In response, most former colonial subjects chose decolonization.

The constitution of the Fourth French Republic tried a confused mix of both a unitary republic and federalism, both underpinned by universal human rights. Legally, the French abolished their empire by proclaiming it a consensual union "composed of nations and peoples who place in common or coordinate their resources or their efforts to develop their respective civilizations." Intending at last to fulfill the *mission civilisatrice* of the previous century, "France undertakes to lead the peoples for whom it has taken responsibility toward the freedom to govern themselves, and democratically to manage their own affairs."

On April 11, 1946, Senghor himself presented to the Constituent Assembly Title VIII, the articles outlining the Union Française. Article 1 of the constitution declared: "France is an indivisible Republic, secular, democratic and social."[2] But Article 60 under Title VIII proclaimed: "The French Union comprises, in one part, the French Republic, which includes metropolitan France, the Departments and Overseas Territories, and in the other part, the associated territories and states."[3] The "French Union" and "France" were not the same thing. The departments included Algeria (now including the Algerian Sahara) and the

---

[1] The French reads: "tous les ressortissants des territoires d'outre-mer (Algérie comprise) ont la qualité de citoyen, au même titre que les nationaux français de la métropole ou des territoires d'outre-mer."

[2] "La France est une République indivisible, laïque, démocratique et sociale."

[3] "L'Union française est formée, d'une part, de la République française qui comprend la France métropolitaine, les départements et territoires d'outre-mer, d'autre part, des territoires et États associés."

vieilles colonies of Martinique. Guadeloupe, Réunion, Guyane, and the Quatre Communes of Senegal. Overseas territories included the West Africa and Equatorial Africa federations. "Associated states" comprised past and future protectorates – Morocco, Tunisia, Madagascar, and Indochina (with Vietnam, Laos, and Cambodia still cast as a single unit). Among the former mandates, Syria and Lebanon would become independent immediately. Togo and Cameroon became UN trusteeships, with the presumption of independence.

Title VIII described a decidedly unequal kind of federalism. While it hinted at some sort of international legal status for the new configurations, the French Republic in Paris would control foreign and defense policy. Like the Third Republic, the Fourth Republic was a parliamentary regime.[4] But the constitution created unequal parliaments. Only the Hexagon and the Overseas Departments and Territories would have representation in the new National Assembly. The French Union would have a separate assembly, half representing the 43 million metropolitan French, the other half representing the 77 million French nationals of the former empire. The Union Assembly remained purely consultative and had no budgetary authority. The president of the French Republic would preside over the Union, assisted by an advisory council comprising representatives of member countries. Further, the constitution created a differentiated citizenship. Adults in the Hexagon and the Overseas Departments remained full citizens of the French Republic. Others became citizens of the French Union. A constitution replete with references to universal human rights never specified the exact relationship between these two separate forms of citizenship.

The French Union proved a troubled enterprise from the outset. Nothing about the constitution circumscribed the deployment of French military forces, ostensibly to keep the peace but in fact to preserve French imperial authority. Algeria, in any event, remained national territory, subject to yet another version of the "special law" that had governed it since 1848. The "associated states" such as Morocco, Tunisia, and parts of Indochina found it difficult to tell just what their new status would give them that their prior status as protectorates did not. Morocco and Tunisia did not join the French Union, and legally remained protectorates until independence in 1956. After the French defeat in Vietnam in 1954, Cambodia, Laos, and even South Vietnam left the Union. As we will see, West Africa provided the most prominent supporters of reinventing the empire as some sort of hybrid between a unitary republic and a federation.

---

[4] Indeed, the reemergence of parliamentary sovereignty with a weak executive would lead de Gaulle to resign in disgust as president of the provisional government in January 1946.

5.2   The French War in Indochina

French authority in parts of the empire continued to ebb as World War II came to an end. Free French officials, having declared mandate Syria "independent" in September 1941, permitted long-promised elections in Syria in July 1943. These elections brought to power a bloc of nationalists seeking a complete end to any kind of foreign rule. Both the United States and the Soviet Union recognized an independent Syria in 1944. Despite some efforts to reestablish French administration by force in 1945, the mandates in the Middle East ended more with a whimper rather than a bang. Likewise, the French did not have a strong hand to play in Indochina. If Free France needed not just Vichy soldiers but Japanese soldiers to contain the Vietminh just in the Central Highlands, reestablishing French rule was going to prove a daunting task.

The wars of decolonization in Indochina and Algeria in some ways mirrored each other. The war in Indochina, far from the Hexagon, had a great deal to do with the emerging Cold War, but not a great deal to do with French identity. Losing Indochina after a century of rule did not make "France" any less "French." On the other hand, the war in Algeria, close to the Hexagon, had little to do with the Cold War and a great deal to do with French identity. After all, Algeria *was* France, or so the French had been telling themselves for more than a century. After Algerian independence in 1962, "France" meant something else.

Wars of decolonization proved almost always to be civil wars as well as wars against the colonizer. Different nationalists wanted different things, often profoundly different things. Further, imperial rule itself had never been possible without powerful people among the colonized maintaining a stake in that rule. The Declaration of Independence on September 2, 1945 did not immediately win over all the Vietnamese.

At least four powerful actors vied for influence in Vietnam as the postwar period began. The communist Vietminh had considerable political and military strength in Tonkin. But even as the fortunes of the Guomindang began to fade in China, its imperial ambitions in Indochina continued. The Viet Nam Quoc Dan Dang (VNQDD) had such close links to the Guomindang that few could tell where one left off and the other began. The VNQDD ferociously opposed the Vietminh. The British, operating out of Burma, had liberated much of Cochinchina and Annam. But they turned authority over to a French war machine that revived quickly under General Philippe Leclerc, the Free French war hero. The Americans, rightly worried about the prospects of Guomindang in China, did not want communism to extend its influence south. Already pondering about postwar competition with the Soviet Union, few American leaders found convincing Ho's flattering reference in the Declaration of Independence to the words of Thomas Jefferson.

Indeed, so strong had the forces against the Vietminh become that Ho and the French came to a temporary agreement to work together. Remarkable newsreel footage survives of a meeting in March 1946 aboard a French ship in the Gulf of Tonkin between Ho and the High Commissioner for Indochina, Admiral Thierry d'Argenlieu. Ho arrived alone and surrounded by an imposing-looking French flotilla. In a decidedly colonial-looking white uniform accessorized by a pith helmet, Ho looked every bit the cooperative subject. The Ho–Sainteny agreement of March 6 (so named for French diplomatic envoy Jean Sainteny), recognized Vietnam as "a free state having its own government, its parliament, its own army, its own finances." In exchange, Vietnam would join the French Union, which left elements of state sovereignty as important as foreign and defense policy under the control of Paris. More immediately to the point, the agreement permitted French troops provisionally to reoccupy Tonkin.

Not for the last time, an agreement to make peace in Vietnam proved a dead letter virtually from the moment the signatories rose from the table. The Ho–Sainteny agreement did result in the removal of Guomindang forces from Tonkin, doubtless part of Ho's motive in signing it in the first place. But d'Argenlieu bitterly opposed it, and in the tradition of French naval independence in Indochina, began to establish his own regime in Cochinchina. With power in Paris transitioning by that time from the patriarchal de Gaulle to a divided National Assembly, military entrepreneurs temporarily regained their historic autonomy in the south.

Few now believe that Ho, who after all had been practicing anticolonial politics for more than a quarter century by 1946, ever saw the Ho–Sainteny agreement as anything but an opportunity to reorganize and reload. The removal of the Guomindang from Tonkin accomplished, Ho purged noncommunists from the political scene, sometimes violently. The Vietminh began to provoke incidents with the French, and insurrectionary war resumed by the end of 1946. Ho called on his compatriots: "Whoever has a rifle must use his rifle! Whoever has a sword must use his sword! And if you don't have a sword, take up picks and sticks! Each person must fight with all his might against colonialism and save our homeland!" Even this call to arms echoed the French Revolution, the *levée en masse* mobilizing the nation in 1793. Taking the colonies out of the French empire would prove one thing, taking France out of the colonies another.

A subcontracted empire is an empire in decline. The French never used conscripts in Indochina, rather professional military from the Hexagon and colonial soldiers. Of some 479,000 soldiers who wore a French uniform in Vietnam between 1946 and 1954, some 223,000 came from the Hexagon, 123,000 from North Africa, 73,000 from the Foreign Legion, and 60,000 from the Tirailleurs Sénégalais. The French army in Indochina showed considerable skill in colonial warfare at the tactical level, notably in its focus on killing opponents rather than occupying territory. But French generals remained divided on basic strategy. Should the French consolidate their hold over Cochinchina, where they were strongest, or attack the center of Vietminh power in Tonkin?

The Vietnamese themselves remained divided, often violently. Even in Cochinchina, the French and Vietminh vied with Hoa Hao (a strain of Buddhist nationalism), Cao Dai (likewise a religiously based, syncretic form of nationalism drawing from Buddhism, Taoism, and Confucianism), and the Binh Xuyen (anticommunist, militarized gangsters who lived off organized crime). Swaths of the Mekong Delta proved all but ungovernable, as they would later after the Americans took over the war. Increasingly desperate by 1949 for some option that could unite anticommunists, the French called the ex-emperor Bao Dai out of exile in Hong Kong. They named him "head of state" (*quoc truong*) and tried to set up a new capital in Dalat. This move convinced almost no one.

Why did the French not simply abandon the empire in Indochina altogether, as they had Syria and Lebanon? The postwar fascination with empire in the Hexagon wilted quickly as its costs rose. In a January 1947 poll, 37 percent favored some form of Vietnamese independence, while about the same number favored the preservation of French sovereignty by force if necessary. The poll evidently did not ascertain the level of support if conscripts were to be called on to fight. Nor did reliable polls exist of indigenous sentiment, in Indochina or anywhere else in the decolonizing world. However, Indochina, like Algeria, became a matter of international concern, with global consequences.

Over about an eight-month period, the Cold War definitively spread to Asia, transforming the simmering war of decolonization in Indochina. On October 1, 1949, Mao Zedong proclaimed the People's Republic of China, which became a second locus for world communism alongside the Soviet Union. The Vietminh thus acquired untouchable lines of supply with their communist allies. In June 1950, the communist regime in North Korea led by Kim il-Sung, with Chinese and Soviet support, invaded the southern Korean peninsula. In short order, the United States discovered that it had not only "lost" China but also faced the prospect of Soviet and Chinese communism joining hands in Asia. The Americans thus acquired a stake in France not losing its war in Indochina. By the time the French phase of the war ended in 1954, the United States was providing at least 40 percent of the funding.

While most anticolonial movements embraced basically the same military doctrine, the transition from guerrilla war to a "people's war" in Vietnam was most associated with General Vo Nguyen Giap. As the Vietminh became stronger, its engagements could assume more conventional forms, in regular military formations. General Raoul Salan, for a time the French commander in Vietnam, described Giap's troops as "the best infantrymen in the world." After the victory of the communists in China, the French sought to restrict supplies to the Vietminh and regain control in Tonkin by building a series of forts along Route Coloniale 4 (RC4 on Map 4), parallel to the northeastern border with China. The project seemed uncomfortably reminiscent of the Maginot Line between France and Germany, which had failed to prevent the defeat of 1940. Raids along the colonial road became increasingly serious in 1950, leading to a daring communist assault on the exposed fort at Cao Bang and the abandonment of the fort at Lang Son in October. By the time the French gave up the project, engagements along Route Coloniale 4 had cost them 5,000 dead and 3,000 prisoners, two-thirds of whom would die in captivity.

French strategy descended into disarray as the Vietminh accumulated victories. The Free French hero General Jean de Lattre de Tassigny assumed command in December 1950, and partly reversed French fortunes in the strategic Red River delta. But in September 1951, he returned to the Hexagon, suffering from the cancer that would take his life in January 1952. The muddle resumed, and by May 1953, the republic charged General Henry Navarre with discreetly locating an exit strategy. Navarre, a veteran of the supposedly successful Rif War of the early 1930s, reasoned that one large victory would provide France with a strong position at the negotiating table.

The French military leadership used the term *stratégie du hérisson* (hedgehog strategy), not exactly a term that radiated imperial confidence. Though any commander with colonial experience should have known better by that time, Navarre believed he could draw the Vietminh into open country, where the technologically superior French could defeat them. He chose a large, remote basin of some 20 km by 6 km located about 300 km east of Hanoi near the border with Laos. The basin, surrounded by mountains and practically unreachable by roads, contained a town called Dien Bien Phu. The 17,000 French Union troops stationed there could only be supplied by air. This proved a job for the *parachutistes* or *paras*, later notorious in Algeria.

General Giap, for his part, now had some 50,000 battle-hardened Vietminh under his command, assured of resupply from China. Racist assumptions kept the French from appreciating that human labor could transport artillery and anti-aircraft weaponry up the surrounding mountains. The hedgehog, in short, became a sitting duck. After a horrific two-month siege, the French garrison finally surrendered on May 7, 1954. The Vietminh took nearly 11,000 French Union prisoners (see Illustration 5.1), of whom only about 3,300 survived for repatriation later that year. Dien Bien Phu proved one of the greatest defeats in French military history.

The Great Powers had already planned an international conference for 1954 in Geneva to manage the Cold War in Asia, notably in Korea and Indochina. The conference began on April 26, with the French position in Dien Bien Phu clearly deteriorating. After the surrender, the conference provided a ready-made venue for organizing the French departure. Like Korea, Vietnam would be divided, here along the 17th parallel, with a 5 km demilitarized zone separating the Democratic Republic of Vietnam in the north and the State of Vietnam in the south. The accords included vague plans for never-held "free elections" in 1956 to reunify the country. No actual treaties came from the Geneva Conference, because of the refusal of the regime in South Vietnam and their American backers formally to recognize the partition of the country.

In effect, the Geneva accords guaranteed that the war would not just continue but spread, if only for logistical reasons. Laos was effectively divided between a royal government and the communist Pathet Lao, ally of the new regime in the north. Further, the Vietminh enjoyed considerable support in the south, including a highly effective military contingent that would become known as the Viet Cong. Communists North and South, and for that matter their enemies, made no secret of their ultimate goal of national reunification. Because of the demilitarized zone, supply routes would have to pass through Laos and Cambodia.

Communism had at last achieved an internationally recognized locus in North Vietnam. Ho, Giap, and the new regime could rebuild Tonkin and northern Annam. Challenges included the migration of some 1 million Tonkinese Catholics to the south. Military aid continued to flow to the North Vietnam from China and the Soviet Union. Giap's formidable military machine once again reorganized and reloaded, well aware that time was on its side. The regime in the south held a universally castigated "referendum" in 1955, in which hundreds of thousands more people voted than were registered, or probably even existed. Nevertheless, the referendum paved the way for a Catholic from an old mandarin family, Ngo Dinh Diem, to establish the decidedly undemocratic Republic of Vietnam. This Vietnam left the French Union and became increasingly dependent on the United States. On April 7, 1954, during the siege of

Illustration 5.1 French prisoners, Dien Bien Phu, 1954.
Source: Wikipedia Commons (public domain).

Dien Bien Phu, President Dwight Eisenhower spoke ominously of what became known as the "domino theory." If Vietnam fell to communism, other countries in Southeast Asia could fall like dominoes. For Cold War reasons, the United States would pick up an anticolonial and civil war abandoned by the French.

For their part, relatively few of the French of the Hexagon seriously mourned the passing of a century of colonial rule in Indochina. France could let go of an expensive war (even with American subsidies) just as the postwar economic boom gathered steam. The human cost to the French of the Hexagon, while not negligible, had been limited by the reliance on professionals and colonial troops. However, the senior military command in France saw matters quite differently. The defeat in Indochina reenacted the well-remembered humiliation of 1940. France had lost one war of decolonization. The senior command, backed for the time being by an overwhelming majority of the French in the Hexagon, resolved that it would not lose another, come what may.

5.3   The War of Algerian Independence

The increasingly hysterical propaganda of the settlers to the contrary, the war of decolonization in Algeria never really became part of the Cold War. The United States had first established discreet links to anticolonialists during World War II, and few Algerian nationalists had close ties to the Soviet Union. Both superpowers removed any remaining doubts in the Suez affair of October–November 1956, when they took basically the same position in a major international crisis. Britain, France, and Israel joined forces to overturn the nationalization of the Suez Canal by the Egyptian president Gamal Abdel Nasser. An invasion quickly floundered, and both superpowers expressed displeasure with the whole enterprise. Following the Egyptian victory, both superpowers downgraded the Mediterranean as a site of Cold War competition.

But unlike the war of decolonization in Indochina, the war in Algeria profoundly reshaped where "France" was and what it meant to be French. Algeria had been French national territory since 1848. Even the southern desert regions (the Territoires du Sud) had become *départements* in 1947. Yet the ambivalence of the French about their non-colony settler colony continued. Not only had relatively few French of the Hexagon ever emigrated to Algeria, but also many French doubted whether the French of the Hexagon and the *Français de souche européene* (French of European roots) of Algeria really came from precisely the same national community. To be sure, the population of some 1 million *pieds noirs* (some 10 percent of the Algerian population in 1945) certainly considered themselves as "French" as anyone.[5] They owned most of the valuable land in Algeria and had powerful political friends in Paris and in the French military. Increasingly, they also considered themselves a people under siege, not least by a Muslim population increasing at about 2 percent per year, with their own numbers barely increasing at all. For the settlers, most of whom by that time were born in Algeria, preserving their position required support from a Hexagon that held them increasingly at arm's length as postwar events unfolded.

"L'Algérie de papa est morte,"[6] said de Gaulle in April 1959, to the editor of the Algerian newspaper *L'Écho d'Oran*. That he felt the need to say so showed just how invulnerable the *pieds noirs* had considered themselves in the postwar world. The French had repressed the last widespread violent revolt in Algeria back in 1871, although active anticolonialism remained thereafter. Many *pieds noirs* believed that the strong French state and minor reforms at the local level would suffice to keep their separate and unequal compatriots in check. Yet beginning in 1945, Algeria would bit by bit descend into violence that would ebb and flow, and continue until Algeria became ungovernable.

Sétif, a mid-sized city in the high plateau between Algiers and the city of Constantine, in certain ways exemplified *Algérie de papa*. A key stop on the trade route joining Tunisia, Algeria, and Morocco, Sétif profited from agriculture, mining, and small industry. The appropriation after 1871 of more than 446,000 ha of land facilitated the establishment of some 30,000 settlers. But they were always a minority, increasingly so as economic growth drew in Arabs and Berbers from the countryside. Yet the settlers considered themselves comfortably and permanently in control. Discontent grew under the surface, notably among young and disadvantaged new arrivals. Ferhat Abbas (1899–1985), who had worked as a pharmacist in Sétif, issued a manifesto in 1943 calling for Algerian sovereignty in an entity linked to France, and the following year formed an organization advocating this goal. Other anticolonial activists, many less moderate than Abbas, had links to Sétif. One such activist, Benyoucef Benkhedda, even described Sétif during the World War II as "the political capital of Muslim Algeria."

On May 8, 1845, city leaders in Sétif planned a celebration of the German surrender intended to perform a national union of ex-Pétainists,

---

[5] *Pied noir* (black feet) became a colloquial term mostly after World War II for the settler population. It has various stories of origin, most involving the appropriation of a pejorative name.
[6] Literally "Dad's Algeria is dead," though the expression is actually more complex. Alternative translations such as "Grandpa's Algeria" or "the Algeria of yesteryear" are probably more accurate.

Gaullists, settlers, and Muslims as French Algeria entered the postwar world. They assigned only about twenty gendarmes to control a demonstration of some 8,000 people representing a volatile mix of political leanings. While some wanted to celebrate role of Algerian soldiers in the defeat of Nazi Germany, others wanted to protest French rule, and yet others both. The chief of police forbade political banners of any sort. Banners appeared anyway, some advocating Algerian independence. The gendarmes received orders to seize the offending objects. A fight ensued, with shots fired by parties unknown. Five days of mayhem ensued: 103 Europeans were killed, some discovered as mutilated corpses. Several European women had been raped. If such violence could erupt in Sétif, it could erupt anywhere – a point lost neither on nationalists nor the French. Unrest spread through the *département* of Constantine, notably the smaller city of Guelma some 225 km to the east.

The French army, assisted by settler militias, responded with a chosen policy of terror – a disproportionate response calculated to intimidate the Muslim population. Tirailleurs Sénégalais, if we are to believe the atrocity stories, earned anew their reputation for ferocity. In addition, the French waged war from the air, including dive bombers. There was also an unknown number of simple vigilante murders, for example settlers breaking into prisons and simply killing all Muslim prisoners on the spot. French army estimates claimed some 500 Muslims dead, though a later French investigation put the figure at 1,000–1,300. Cairo radio, already broadcasting Algerian nationalism throughout the Middle East, reported 45,000 Muslims dead. Whatever the actual number, the French sent the message they wanted to send – that terror could still provide a way for a small population to rule a large one. The French would stop at nothing to preserve French rule. Yet the policy of terror itself showed fragile Algérie française actually was.

A series of postwar political reforms enraged settlers as too much and nationalists as too little. The Statut de 1947 passed by the National Assembly in Paris sought, yet again, to regularize the situation of Algeria in the French Republic. The statute declared all Algerians "French," equal in rights and responsibilities. Yet they would not be represented equally even in a new Algerian Assembly. Two electoral colleges would send sixty delegates each, one representing 464,000 European voters and 58,000 Muslim voters with European voter status, and the other representing 1.3 million Muslim voters. Each college would in turn send fifteen delegates to the National Assembly in Paris. While the Algerian Assembly would have notable powers over finance, its decisions were subject to review from Paris. Other proposals, such as the abolition of the *communes mixtes*, the expanded teaching of Arabic, and the enfranchisement of Muslim women, would require a two-thirds majority vote in the Algerian Assembly, all but unattainable given the conservative, patriarchal bent of its composition. The old alliance between settlers and powerful friends in the Hexagon continued to stifle further reform. Allegations of vote rigging, probably well founded, followed every election. By 1953, even the moderate Ferhat Abbas concluded famously: "There is no other solution than the machine gun."

Anticolonial political activism continued in Algeria, under many of the same interwar leaders. Organizations remained fissile throughout the struggle for independence. Venomous and sometimes lethal disputes impossibly mixed the personal and the political. The nationalism of Messali Hadj (1898–1974) developed into a critique of capitalism and imperialism more broadly. Ben Badis had died in 1940, but nationalism inspired by Islam had not. Some devout nationalists considered secular socialism as apostasy. Even after Abbas conceded the necessity of the machine gun, he continued to hope for close relations between France and an independent Algeria. The Algerian Communist Party, still under settler influence, sought to portray itself as above racial division. This proved an increasingly problematic position as the struggle intensified, as shown by the tangled political positions of its most famous sometime adherent, the author Albert Camus. The party embraced the national cause haltingly, and late. No single leader emerged among Algerian nationalists at any point on the political spectrum who was comparable in stature to Ho Chi Minh.

However, Algerian nationalism as a broad cause found new avenues of international expression. These would prove crucial as the war for independence continued. The Arab League, founded in 1945 and based in Cairo, provided a refuge for exiles and a crucial platform for communicating with the outside world, notably by radio throughout the Arabic-speaking world. The UN, particularly the General Assembly, helped oversee and encourage decolonization everywhere. Eventually, it would provide its own diplomatic front as an international forum.

On October 24, 1954, less than five months after the French surrender at Dien Bien Phu, a new militant organization announced itself, the Front de libération nationale (FLN). On November 1, it issued the declaration commonly associated with the beginning of the "armed struggle" phase of the Algerian War of Independence. Notwithstanding certain rhetorical similarities to Ho's September 1945 Declaration of Independence, its Algerian counterpart showed both how much the world had changed, and that Algeria was not just another French imperial domain, to be relinquished gracefully through a simple recognition of independence. Much more than Ho's declaration, the Algerian declaration stressed the existence of a timeless and united national polity, language used by the successor states to the multinational empires of Central and Eastern Europe after World War I. "Independence" would mean "the restoration of the sovereign Algerian state, social and democratic, bounded by Islamic principles."[7] This suggested, quite inaccurately, that the Regency of Algiers under the Ottomans bore a meaningful resemblance to a modern nation-state. European successor states had made similar claims.

Originally distributed in both French and Arabic, the declaration owed much to French revolutionary language. It called for immediate negotiations leading to the "recognition of Algerian sovereignty, one and indivisible." Even the stated reluctant embrace of violent struggle echoed the Jacobin cries from 1793 of *la patrie en danger* (the country in danger). Nationally self-conscious Algeria, finally breaking its chains of subjugation, faced "a single and blind enemy, colonialism, which refused always to accord the least freedom to the means of peaceful struggle." The nascent Algerian Republic, like its French forebear, had to fight or die. Likewise in the Jacobin tradition, the struggle begun by the vanguard minority would purify the republic, here "by the annihilation of all the vestiges of corruption and reformism, the cause of our present regression."

As written, the declaration showed a deep respect for the universal principles of the Declaration of the Rights and Man and Citizen of 1789. Independence would mean "respect for all fundamental liberties without distinctions of race and religion." More specifically, independent Algeria would respect French cultural and economic interests (*culturel et économiques*), though the document added the potentially ominous requirement that these be "honestly acquired" (*honnêtement acquis*). The new republic would not require settlers or their descendants to leave. Rather, it would permit them either to choose Algerian citizenship or continue to live in Algeria as foreigners under Algerian law.

The Vietnamesse declaration of 1945 had expressed a vague confidence in the alliance of liberalism and communism that had won World War II as the guarantor of independence. In contrast, the FLN declaration stated as an explicit priority the internationalization of the Algerian struggle across the Cold War camps. It also appeared to embrace pan-Arabism, at least across North Africa to Morocco and Tunisia. Under the auspices of the UN Charter, the FLN would seek "the affirmation of the sympathy of all nations who support our struggle for freedom." In time, the FLN victory on this discursive battlefield, based in diplomacy and world public opinion, would prove decisive.

---

[7] The French reads: "la restauration de l'État algérien souverain, démocratique et social dans le cadre des principes islamiques."

In the meantime, the FLN declaration also inaugurated what became known as the Toussaint Rouge (the red All Saints' Day). Some thirty attacks, mostly in the countryside in the Aurès mountains and the southern portions of the Constantine, claimed what by later standards proved a modest number of victims, five *pieds noirs* and two Muslims. But the FLN message had been sent and received. All Algeria had become a battlefield – cities, villages, countryside. No settler, and no Muslim who considered siding with the French, should henceforth feel safe. French authorities, for their part, led by a young minister of the interior, François Mitterrand, promised the repression of armed rebellion within a "France" comprising all of French Algeria. The future president of France would approve the execution by guillotine of fifty-six prisoners toward that end.

Opinions within the FLN differed as to the precise meaning of armed struggle. To some, duty lay in provoking incidents they knew would elicit a brutal French response. Such episodes would then force Muslims to take sides and identify themselves as part of the solution or part of the problem. According to two witnesses present, Youcef Zighout stated at a meeting in Constantine on June 25, 1955: "The fraternization between the Algerian and French populations is not only a temptation [*un luerre*] but a force for demobilization. This ambiguity must cease." As good as his word, Zighout masterminded a series of attacks in Constantine the following August.

The best known began on August 20 in Philippeville (today, Skikda), a medium-sized city of 74,400 people, some 28,000 of European origin. An Arab-led crowd armed with farm implements, hunting rifles, and bottles of gasoline first attacked the police station, then went on a rampage. The Government General ultimately arrived at a figure on 123 European dead, 71 of them civilians, along with 21 Muslims deemed pro-French. The Philippeville attacks provoked precisely the ferocious French military response sought by Zighout – combining tanks, artillery, machine guns, helicopters, and aircraft. The French made no effort to locate those responsible, though they managed to kill Zighout himself. Overall, however, the French made war indiscriminately on Muslim parts of the city. As always in the history of colonialism, atrocity stories on both sides got better with the telling. But even today, the most cautious historians can only provide wide ranging estimates of Muslim casualties, somewhere between the French figure of 1,200 dead and the FLN figure of 12,000.

Bit by bit, *Algérie de papa* became ungovernable. The FLN tactic of provoking disproportionate responses began to yield strategic effects. Moreover, like other anticolonial movements, the FLN developed the means of self-financing – extortion labeled "taxation" on Algerian workers in the Hexagon and enforced by FLN operatives there. Hexagon wages, in other words, subsidized the cause of national liberation in Algeria. By 1956, violence spread to the cities of Algeria, where most of the European population lived. Some settlers began to take matters into their own hands, notoriously by a bombing in the Casbah of Algiers on August 10, 1956 that killed some seventy men, women, and children. Settler bombings begat FLN reprisals. The French poured colonial troops, such as the Tirailleurs Sénégalais and the Foreign Legion, into Algeria. Parachute units that had served in Indochina and known simply as *les paras* became folk heroes and villains. Crucially, the Hexagon also began to send conscripts and reservists, implicating the general population in colonial warfare in unprecedented ways. The white menfolk of the Hexagon and their loved ones now directly had to face the ambivalence about occupying Algeria that had existed since 1830. At the same time, the French actively recruited Arab and Berber militias, deepening an evolving civil war.

Settler political strength in Paris remained apparently unmovable. In February 1956, the Socialist prime minister Guy Mollet visited Algiers in search of a reformist solution. Some 20,000 hostile settlers greeted him at what was supposed to be a solemn ceremony of commemoration at the World War I monument in the center of the city. Opinions differ as to whether the demonstrators actually threw rotten tomatoes at the head of government, but the settlers had made their point. By 1955–6, Algeria had become the graveyard of political ambition, and claimed such victims as the renowned anthropologist turned governor-general Jacques Soustelle. His immediate successor, the Free French war hero General Georges Catroux, was not able to assume office at all because of the visceral reaction from the settler population to his nomination.

The discovery of massive gas and oil deposits in the Algerian Sahara just as the war intensified raised the stakes. By 1956, it had become clear that whatever political entity held those deposits would become a major producer of hydrocarbons. The fact that the French had needed to ration gasoline during the Suez Crisis further focused minds in the Hexagon. If Algeria remained French, hydrocarbons offered the prospect of energy independence at a time when one-third of the French trade deficit came from imports of crude oil. If, on the other hand, an independent Algeria claimed these resources, the new state would have vast wealth through a globally tradable commodity.

In contrast to the war in Indochina, the War of Algerian Independence never developed into a "people's war," in the sense of conventional formations meeting on the battlefield. To the last, it remained a war of insurgency and a civil war. The French assembled a formidable military machine. Helicopters and motorized vehicles could move troops quickly almost anywhere in Algeria, accompanied by unchallenged airpower. The French would station some 400,000 colonial and metropolitan troops in Algeria, to fight alongside at least 150,000 soldiers in Muslim militias. Until the end of the war, Muslims fighting on the French side almost certainly outnumbered the number of active fighters in the Armée de Libération Nationale, the military wing of the FLN. Generals with extensive colonial experience, notably Raoul Salan and Jacques Massu, developed a strategy of counterinsurgency long studied thereafter. The stress on mobility, terror, the gathering of intelligence, and killing insurgents rather than occupying territory owed much to Bugeaud's strategy more than a century earlier.

In strictly military terms, the French enjoyed considerable success. What became known as the "Battle of Algiers" of 1956–7, best remembered through Gillo Pontecorvo's classic 1966 film, proved a resounding short-term French victory. Led by Massu's *paras*, specifically the 10e Division parachutiste, the French so devastated the FLN leadership in the Algerian capital that it never fully recovered until after independence. In October 1956, the French air force successfully forced to land a plane from Morocco bound for Tunis carrying five senior FLN leaders, including the future head of government, Ahmed Ben Bella. Not everyone believed King Mohammed V of Morocco's claim of innocence in the matter. Over the course of 1957, the French built an elaborate 700 km electrified fence along the border with Tunisia that became known as the Ligne Morice, after Minister of Defense André Morice. The French spared no expense, with state-of-the-art electronics to detect efforts to cut the fence, numberless land mines, and patrols to attack intruders. Unlike many attempts at fixed fortifications in military history, the Ligne Morice actually proved effective in its goal of starving the FLN of resources from Tunisia.

We will never know exactly how much of this military success we can attribute to the use of torture. While torture was hardly new in the history of colonial warfare, it had novel political repercussions in the War of Algerian Independence. Counterinsurgency warfare depends on intelligence. Those who waged it have tended not to be much concerned with the means of its extraction. Suspects in Algeria would commonly be stripped, beaten, partly drowned, burned with cigarettes, electrocuted (the notorious *gégène*), and more until they provided the information required, or some plausible facsimile thereof. In some cases, such as that in June 1957 of Maurice Audin, a young instructor of mathematics at the University of Algiers, the point seemed to be a sadistic performance of mastery over the captive as a prelude to an extrajudicial execution. Others, such as Larby Ben M'Hidi and Ali Boumendjet, "committed suicide" in French custody under implausible circumstances after extended torture.

Warriors have long practiced rape as a tactic, perhaps not so much out of sexual desire as a wish to send a message of physical mastery to women and men alike. In any patriarchal society, men who cannot protect "their" women from sexual violation by the enemy cannot consider themselves full men. Assuredly, the French military code prohibited rape; but throughout the war in Algeria, rape served both as a tactic of interrogation and a tactic of terror, particularly in the countryside. As women became more important to the FLN as messengers and other operatives, the incidence of rape probably increased. Impregnated women would sometimes be beaten – by the FLN as well as the French – to induce abortions.

All sides in the War of Algerian Independence committed atrocities. The French almost certainly committed more than the FLN, because the French had more force to bring to bear. FLN atrocities included the mutilation of bodies alive and dead, civilians as well as the uniformed. Most of them were committed on Muslims perceived as having collaborated with the French, a policy that continued and even intensified after independence.

At the time, the French did not try as hard as posterity believed to keep torture a secret. Given the scale of military operations and the thousands of conscripts shuttling back and forth across the Mediterranean, the French would have been hard pressed in any event to keep torture a state secret. Senior French commanders seemed content with implausible deniability – since written rules of warfare in Algeria forbade torture, there was no torture. But as early as January 1955, the Catholic intellectual François Mauriac wrote a scathing article in the national weekly *L'Express* detailing and condemning French practices. The torture and murder of the handsome and cherubic Audin, who looked much younger than his twenty-five years of age when he died, helped awaken the consciences of intellectuals of international reputation such as Camus and Jean-Paul Sartre. Through their use of torture, the French handed the FLN a priceless political weapon that in the end helped the nationalists win the war.

No non-state actor, including the Vietminh, made such effective use as the FLN of the postwar international system. The FLN brought the question of Algerian independence to the Bandung Conference held in Indonesia in April 1955. This extraordinary meeting of decolonized and decolonizing imperial domains helped found the "Third World," mostly new states not aligned with either the communist or the liberal/capitalist bloc. FLN operatives in New York relentlessly lobbied delegates to the UN. They kept Algerian independence on the agenda of the General Assembly, at a time when the deliberations of that body did much to shape world opinion on decolonization. The United States, the most important superpower in North Africa after the Suez affair, cared more about stability than the perpetuation of French rule. Few Americans found *pied noir* efforts to paint the FLN as a communist front convincing.

Increasingly friendless internationally, the Hexagon ended its protectorates in Morocco and Tunisia in March 1956, in part to induce the new regimes to cut off support to the FLN. Ironically, France had acquired the Tunisia protectorate in 1881 and the Morocco protectorate in 1912 partly to protect French interests in Algeria. It now gave up these protectorates partly for the same reason. The new states sought a continued relationship with France, even as they discreetly supported the FLN. "Try to understand," Habib Bourguiba, the new prime minister of Tunisia, remarked to a French newspaper in April 1956, "We consider the French as friends. But the Algerians are our brothers. If we are forced to choose, we will be at the side of our brothers."

As the cost of the war in Algeria in blood and treasure continued to mount, the French of the Hexagon began to rethink the status of their non-colony colony. In a September 1957 poll, only 36 percent declared themselves supporters of an "Algerie française." On February 8, 1958, a French pursuit of militants across the border to now-independent Tunisia led to the bombing of the small town of Sakiet Sidi Youseff. The attack killed at least 70 civilians (including some 12 primary school children) and wounded another 148. Encouraged by an outraged Tunisian government, the international news media painted a horrific picture of imperial savagery. French prestige reached a new low, particularly with the Americans. "We are headed for a diplomatic Dien Bien Phu," fretted the governor-general of Algeria, Robert Lacoste.

Yet the political blockage remained. Desperate proposals for reform earned unstable Fourth Republic governments scorn from all sides. These included schemes for regional autonomy, notably for Kabyle areas. Such schemes reminded nationalists of the *politique des races* and threatened settlers with the partition of an Algeria they considered wholly theirs. Worse, serious opposition emerged within the French senior military command in Algeria. Generals in the colonies had revived long-dormant ideas from Lyautey of the colonial military as the repository of an authentic France. On May 13, 1958, and with the encouragement of powerful settlers, senior officers led by Salan and Massu established in Algiers a Committee of Public Safety (Comité de Salut Publique, a term inherited from the Reign of Terror). The committee laid plans to land paratroopers in Paris and take over the National Assembly. For the first time since Napoleon Bonaparte, a military coup in France looked possible.

At this dire moment, Charles de Gaulle, who as a private citizen had cleverly remained on the sidelines on Algerian matters, could now return to power by presenting himself as all things to all people. On June 2, 1958, a panicking National Assembly voted him full powers, to save the republic by redesigning it and agreeing to settle, in ways yet unknown, the whole Algerian question. Two days after he assumed power, de Gaulle embarked on a tour of the major cities of Algeria. He received a tumultuous welcome. Famously, he told a massive crowd in Algiers, comprising mostly but not entirely settlers: "*Je vous ai compris!*" (I have understood you!). The settlers and their allies read this as a ringing endorsement of Algérie française. Indeed, for the time being, de Gaulle continued the war, with its full array of tactics. But his comment soon became more cryptic. Even his famous 1959 quote "L'Algérie de papa est morte" had a less-quoted second clause: "and if we do not understand that we will die with it."

Most historians believe that de Gaulle returned to power with the intent of keeping Algeria French in some form. Certainly, the Plan Constantine of 1959, a massive public spending scheme fueled by the postwar economic boom, encouraged such a belief. France promised to build 200,000 new units of public housing, enough to house some 1 million people. Investment in industry would create some 400,000 new jobs, with provisions for the same pay for equal work in Algeria as in the Hexagon. The state would redistribute some 250,000 ha of agricultural land. The war certainly continued, including a program of *regroupement*, forced rural resettlement that sought to deny support for guerrillas in the countryside under the guise of "modernization." This program ultimately displaced more than 1 million people, sometimes into what critics saw as concentration camps. Old colonial hands might have recognized an unusually coercive version of the *tache d'huile*.

Settler suspicion accelerated with the referendum of September 26, 1958 held throughout the French Union on the constitution for the Fifth Republic. All Algerians – Muslims, Jews, and settlers, as well as men and women – could vote on equal terms whether to approve the constitution (see Illustration 5.2). Settlers were not comforted by de Gaulle's vague assurances of the "necessary evolution" of Algeria "in the French framework" (*dans le cadre français*). Nor were they comforted by the deafening silence in the constitution as to whether *départements* such as those of Algeria could secede from the republic, even though this silence led the FLN to order a boycott of the referendum. The boycott helped produce a lopsided result in Algeria of more than 96 percent in favor of the constitution.

Illustration 5.2 Algerian women campaign for the Fifth Republic constitution, 1958.
Source: United States Library of Congress (no known copyright restrictions), Digital ID: ds 14820//hdl.loc.gov/loc.pnp/ds.14820.

Settlers found even more threatening a speech by de Gaulle on September 16, 1959, in which he asserted that Algeria had a right to self-determination. At Brazzaville back in 1944, he used the English term "self-government." This time, he used the French term "*autodétermination.*" In the spirit of the new constitution, he proposed a referendum involving three choices for Algeria: complete union with the Hexagon, complete independence, or "association." At the same time, De Gaulle's government began to make secret overtures toward the Algerian government in exile, the Gouvernement provisoire de la République Algérienne. So began the end game of the long, agonized process of what Alain-Gérard Slama called the history of a tearing-asunder (*histoire d'une déchirure*) of Algeria and the Hexagon.

In the meantime, a sector of settler opinion in Algeria continued to radicalize. That sector, not unsupported at first among the rest of the settler population, formed the paramilitary Organisation Armée Secrète (OAS) early in February 1961. In April, four sympathetic army generals in Algeria (Raoul Salan, Maurice Challe, Edmond Jouhaud, and André Zeller) plotted a coup to seize control in Algiers, and potentially in Paris. They announced with confidence over Algerian radio on April 22: "There will never be an independent Algeria." But to paraphrase Karl Marx, if the coup plot of 1958 was a tragedy, the coup plot of 1961 was a farce. Hundreds of thousands of conscripts in Algeria had radios as well, and listened attentively to a broadcast from President de Gaulle forbidding them to obey illegal orders from the plotters. Their compatriots in the Hexagon with televisions saw de Gaulle deliver his rebuke in full military uniform. The generals fled or were arrested, and the plot folded almost immediately.

Thereafter, the OAS (probably never comprising more than 3,000 active members) became an overt terrorist organization, both in Algeria and in the Hexagon. They tried several times to assassinate de Gaulle. A bombing directed at the cultural minister André Malraux badly wounded and blinded a four-year-old girl, Delphine Renard. In Algeria, the OAS sought to create chaos as negotiations for independence continued. If order broke down completely, the theory went, the army would have to intervene so forcefully that the FLN would terminate negotiations and Algeria would remain French. Non-human targets included the library at the University of Algiers and hydrocarbon stores for export in Oran. Essentially, urban guerrilla warfare broke out in the cities of Algeria with three protagonists – the FLN, the OAS, and the French army. Caught in the middle were terrorized civilians, of all races and religions. An anti-OAS rally in Paris in October 1961 was suppressed with shocking ferocity by the police – leaving 159 demonstrators dead, some of whose bodies were simply dumped into the Seine. The OAS and its friends in the Hexagon, including the prefect of the Paris police, Maurice Papon, probably did more than the FLN to discredit the cause of the settlers. But the massacre also left the impression that the Fifth Republic was not in complete control of the situation.

Yet negotiations continued, and on March 18, 1962, the French government signed a ninety-page agreement in Évian-les-Bains, near the Swiss border. The Évian accords declared a ceasefire and arranged the exchange of prisoners. France would recognize an independent Algeria. Algerians of European descent would have three years in which to choose Algerian or French citizenship, though those who chose the latter could still live in Algeria as resident foreigners. Likewise, Algerians (notably workers) could continue to migrate to France, though they would do so as foreign nationals. France maintained considerable economic interests in Algeria, notably in the hydrocarbons industries, which in any event could not operate for the time being without foreign expertise. France could maintain its naval base at Mers el Kébir, and, more importantly, its nuclear testing site in Reggane in the Sahara, where France had exploded its first such device in February 1960. The sum total of continued links between independent Algeria and the Hexagon exacerbated divisions among Algerian nationalists and would contribute to a coup in 1965.

The dream of a multicultural, independent Algeria fell apart because of its internal contradictions almost immediately. Independence did not stop the cycle of violence, notably on the part of the OAS, which forbade the settler population to leave. Unsurprisingly, OAS violence begat FLN violence, and vice versa. The European population came to draw the obvious conclusion that its options amounted to, as the expression had it, *la valise ou le cercueil* (the suitcase or the coffin). Some 800,000 settlers left in 1961–2, "repatriated" to a Hexagon many of them had never even visited. Centuries of Jewish life in Algeria came to an end practically overnight, partly as revenge for the Crémieux Decree of 1870. Jews who had accepted "Frenchness" now had to pay the price. While many of the *pieds noirs* bitterly resented their "abandonment" by their compatriots, their economic integration proved rapid in the bustling economy of the Hexagon. In Algeria, the rapid departure of hundreds of thousands of settlers led to urban transformation, as the most desirable quarters of every city acquired postcolonial occupants practically overnight. Over 250,000 Algerians émigrés, refugees mostly to Morocco or Tunisia, returned after the signing of the Évian Accords.

A ghastly fate awaited many *harkis*, a slang term meaning pro-French Muslims. Estimates of the number of *harkis* vary, though at least 150,000 Muslims fought for French Algeria. The UN accepted a figure of 260,000 "pro-French Algerians," certainly more people than ever actively served in the FLN. French soldiers and police were given strict orders not to permit the *harkis* to migrate to the Hexagon with the *pieds noirs*. A postcolonial Hexagon was supposed to mean a white Hexagon. Nevertheless, personal ties of loyalty often prevailed, and some 91,000 *harkis* emigrated in defiance of these orders. Those left behind faced the wrath of the victors. At least 30,000, and according to some estimates as many as 150,000, *harkis* were killed with little to no juridical process, a good many tortured and mutilated. In all, 2,788 European Algerians were killed before independence, though an unknown number became missing and presumed dead not long thereafter. Estimates vary of Muslim Algerians dead over the course of the war, with the most reliable figures between 250,000 and 300,000. The *déchirure* of Algeria and the Hexagon proved a bloody business, from its first days to its last.

5.4   "Decolonization" in West and Central Africa

The French domains in Africa had always comprised an immense amalgam of diverse lands, peoples, and colonial regimes. Decolonization reflected that diversity. No experience caused bloodshed on the scale of Algeria or Indochina. However, an armed revolt in Madagascar in 1947 was repressed with brutal efficiency by 18,000 French troops, mostly Moroccan and Algerian colonials. The French military estimated some 89,000 Malagasy killed in the revolt, which like so many such conflicts was also a civil war. At the other end of the spectrum, most of the indigenous colonial elite in West Africa, including Senghor, initially did not want "decolonization" at all, at least not in the sense of fully independent sovereign successor states. Yet it was in West Africa where the internal contradictions of republican imperialism and French imperial variants of "federalism" literally deconstructed, in falling apart through their internal contradictions.

The complicated configuration of centrifugal and centripetal forces in West and Central Africa made "decolonization" far from a foregone conclusion. Certainly, millions of Africans continued to strain under the colonial yoke. Just as certainly, the Bandung Conference of 1955 helped certify "decolonization" as a global norm that meant self-determined independent states. As we have seen, imperial powers in Africa had drawn borders to suit themselves. But once drawn, colonial elites who became nationalists had a stake in previously demarcated geographic spaces.

Powerful Africans maintained strong ties to the Hexagon. As we saw, the Loi Lamine Guèye of 1946 had guaranteed "citizenship," thereby opening up an avenue for 77 million colonial subjects to make claims of political, social, and economic equality on a "France" of which they were now explicitly some sort of part. Persons from Africa or of African descent maneuvered in the highest circles of power in the Hexagon, including Senghor of Senegal, Gaston Monnerville of Guyane, Aimé Césaire of Martinique, and Félix Houphouët-Boigny of the Côte d'Ivoire. Many influential Africans saw the Hexagon with its wealthy and booming economy as a continued source of aid, trade, investment, and worker remittances. To some extent, the contrarian presidency of de Gaulle made the Hexagon a neutral space between the American and Soviet superpowers.

Even if Africa "decolonized," what would become of its constituent parts? Senghor warned of the "Balkanization" of Africa, a descent into a panoply of small, impoverished states seething with ethnic hatreds. He advocated differentiated layers of sovereignty in a single "French" community, meaning one level at the former colony, a second at the level of a West African confederation, a third at the level of the larger Francophone world. Through layered sovereignty, former colonies would achieve an independence while remaining part of some greater "French" whole. Houphouët-Boigny had founded the Rassemblement Démocratique Africain (RDA) in association with the communists in 1946, to press pan-African claims in the National Assembly. As time went on, however, he became more of an Ivorian nationalist. The relatively prosperous Côte d'Ivoire, he later insisted, would not become the "*vache à lait*" (milk cow) of any West African federation. He came to prefer a "hub and spoke" network of bilateral relations between the former colonies and the metropole.

By the mid-1950s, because of the endless array of conflicting centripetal and centrifugal forces, discontent with the French Union in West Africa had become general. The Loi Lamine Guèye, by then about a decade old, had raised uncomfortable questions in the Hexagon about matters such as uniform labor codes and equal pay for equal work. Understandably, claimants directed their concerns to Paris, as the hub of the Union. With Vietnam gone and the rest of Indochina likely to follow, with France relinquishing its protectorates in Tunisia and Morocco, and with the situation in Algeria deteriorating by the day, French leaders in the Hexagon and beyond longed to stabilize what remained of their would-be liberalizing empire in Africa.

The National Assembly passed the Loi-Cadre of June 26, 1956 with the intent of decentralizing the French Union and thus preserving it.[8]

---

[8] Also known as the Loi-Cadre Defferre, after Minister for Overseas Territories Gaston Defferre.

A unique species of legislation, a *loi-cadre* provides broad outlines of a given policy, which ministerial decrees subsequently fill in. The increasingly factious parliamentary regime of 1956 could scarcely have done otherwise, given the challenges to providing precise legislation on much of anything. In some respects, the former colonies would all become protectorates. The Services d'État (defense, foreign affairs, and finance) would remain in the hands of the Hexagon, in which the National Assembly would remain the key locus of sovereignty. Overseas territories would continue to send representatives to Paris, though still not remotely in proportion to their populations.

Domestically, the *loi-cadre* devolved real power and financial responsibilities to a degree unprecedented in the history of the French empire. Contrary to its original intent, it also provided a political and legal framework for decolonization within a few years. The Services territoriaux, including state-owned land, agriculture, education, prisons, and much else, would be managed and paid for by the territories themselves. In effect, the *loi-cadre* divided the civil service, with those in the Services d'État paid by the Hexagon on a Hexagon wage scale, and others directly by the territories. Territorial assemblies would be elected by universal adult suffrage, some 10 million people in all. Government councils, elected by the assemblies, would share executive power with a governor designated by Paris.

The *loi-cadre* paved the way to decolonization by fostering state-building in each territory. Africans would have to turn to the territorial governments rather than to Paris to make social and financial claims. This decentralization of venue in effect endorsed the nationalist views of Houphouët-Boigny and Ahmed Sékou Touré of Guinea, a co-founder of the RDA who earlier had advocated an anticolonial, pan-African labor movement. Touré had also previously favored federal arrangements, provided they had more anticapitalist leanings than would be favored by Senghor, or for that matter Houphouët-Boigny. Senghor considered the *loi-cadre* a defeat.

According to Titles XI and XII of the 1958 constitution, the French Union would morph into the Communauté française, or French Community. This would comprise the French Republic (the Hexagon and its Overseas Territories), and other entities, which would choose freely to associate with the Community. The exact legal character of "association" awaited definition. The Community would have a single citizenship, though all Community citizens would not ipso facto become citizens of the French Republic. The president of the French Republic would represent the Community as a whole and would chair a Conseil exécutif comprising ministers of the French Republic and the heads of government of Community members.

The constitution did not specify just how the Executive Council would govern Community affairs. As per Article 79, the French Republic would provisionally manage the Community pending the enactment of appropriate legislation. The West African and Equatorial African federations would dissolve, and the now self-governing entities of the Community would no longer send deputies to the National Assembly. A Community Senate would consider measures sent to it by the National Assembly or the other bodies. But it would meet only twice a year, for a period not exceeding one month.

As we have seen, the referendum on the 1958 constitution took place across the entire French Union. This meant that the imperial domains could join the Community only through a positive exercise of popular sovereignty by voting in favor of the constitution. Thereafter, and assuming approval, the constitution offered those domains that were not already *départements* three choices: "complete" integration with the French Republic as Overseas Territories, membership in the Community, or complete independence. Consequently, as in Algeria, de Gaulle had made "decolonization" a legal option. He also made clear its price. Complete independence would mean severing all ties to France in matters of aid and technical assistance. Any territory that voted "no" on the constitution would become just another foreign country.

In August 1958, De Gaulle toured Africa in support of the referendum and the Community. Large and enthusiastic crowds greeted him in Chad, Madagascar, the Côte d'Ivoire, Guinea, and Senegal. From the perspective of today, it is hard to avoid comparisons to the tours made by the young and beautiful Queen Elizabeth II as the British Empire morphed into the Commonwealth of Nations. No one could compete with the British in imperial or post-imperial pageantry. More substantively, the British crown, while symbolically sovereign, was an empty vessel, into which former colonizer and former colonized could pour any economic or cultural arrangements they liked. In the French Republic, however, "the people" were sovereign. But all peoples in the former empire would not be sovereign in the same sense, given the role of the Hexagon in directing Community affairs. One could argue that the provisions for the Community in the constitution simply rephrased the issues of republican empire. What then exactly did the African crowds cheer – continued association with France, independence, or both?

The referendum of September 1958 seemed on the surface to be a stunning success for de Gaulle. Nearly all the former domains voted for the constitutions, many by suspiciously large margins (99.99 percent in the Côte d'Ivoire, 98.28 percent in Chad, 99.18 percent in Upper Volta [today Burkina Faso], 97.55 percent in Senegal). Even Madagascar, the site of a major revolt in 1947, voted 77.64 percent in favor. Only Guinea voted no, also by a suspiciously large margin of 95.22 percent. Sekou Touré completed his ideological journey to the anticolonial Left, and actively campaigned against the constitution, as he put it, "out of dignity." No mean phrasemaker himself, he continued: "We prefer poverty in liberty to riches in slavery." De Gaulle, perhaps by that time already mentally preparing himself to let go of Algeria, was not going to extend himself to hold on to Guinea. He responded laconically: "Adieu, Guinea." After the referendum, the Hexagon immediately withdrew all economic aid, advisers, and technical staff. The pointlessly vindictive Opération Persil, launched in 1960 under the guidance of De Gaulle's point man in Africa, Jacques Foccart, sought to destabilize the postcolonial regime by, among other measures, flooding it with counterfeit currency.

What, then, were to be the new Community arrangements for the rest of sub-Saharan Africa? The success of the referendum proved the downbeat for full legal independence. The idea of West African federalism did not die, at least not right away. As early as December 1958, Senghor and his allies sought to forge a federation comprising Senegal, French Sudan (today Mali), Dahomey (today Benin), and Haute-Volta (today Burkina Faso). The latter two declined to join and participated instead (along with Niger) in an alternative quasi-federal scheme called the Conseil de l'Entente led by Houphouët-Boigny. Togo would join them in 1966. The Conseil established a customs union and called for a vaguely defined common diplomatic presence, a form of association diffuse enough that it still exists today.

Undeterred, Senegal and former French Sudan in June 1959 adopted their own constitution for a Mali Federation, as a collective member of the Community. Yet even this reduced enterprise faced perhaps insurmountable obstacles. Both entities were highly diverse in language and religion. The Senegalese spoke some thirteen languages, the former French Sudanese at least fifteen. Senghor (along with the still-powerful *métis* elite) was Catholic and basically capitalist. Modibo Keïta of French Sudan, though educated at an elite lycée in Dakar, descended from a Muslim royal dynasty that long predated the colonial period. As an adult, Keïta supported a specifically African variant of socialism. Senegalese and Sudanese elites each feared "colonization" by the other. In August 1960, a dispute over the senior leadership of the federation led to an attempted coup on the part of Keita to establish his authority militarily. The collapse of this ill-conceived plan guaranteed the demise of the federation. The structural tension between unity and particularism that characterized so much of postcolonial West African politics established itself at independence.

In the meantime, the newly incarnated Fifth Republic, increasingly preoccupied with its bloody extrication from Algeria, concluded that each Community members could both "associate" and have its own international legal personality and national citizenship. The British had concluded the same in their Commonwealth. With the apparent blessing of the Hexagon, the former African domains rushed to declare themselves republics. In April 1959, a constituent assembly in Madagascar approved a republican constitution. In August 1960, Dahomey, Niger, Haute-Volta, the Côte d'Ivoire, Chad, the Central African Republic, the Republic of the Congo, and Gabon all declared independence. Each would negotiate its own arrangements of association with the former colonial power. Hophouët-Boigny's West Africa of highly differentiated successor states prevailed. The French Community as such became moribund within two years of its birth.

The very term "decolonization" to some extent equates the end of the story of the French empire after 1945 with the whole story. Certainly, powerful people inside and outside the Hexagon worked to find other solutions. And just as certainly, "decolonization," like "colonization," meant different things in different places. As we will see, some former domains would retain close ties, others scarcely any at all. Decolonization would also prove much more a process than an event. Nothing about legal independence precluded considerable French influence in the former colonies, nor for that matter former colonies influencing life and politics in the Hexagon. The Hexagon might relinquish its empire, but its former empire would not always prove so eager to relinquish the Hexagon. In this reciprocal sense, "decolonization" would continue long after Algerian independence in 1962, and indeed continues today.

As the *Babar* series evolved, Jean and his son Laurent de Brunhoff took their elephant and his entourage further and further from their colonial origins. The early sequels continued to draw from interwar musings about the future of the French empire. *Le Voyage de Babar* (1932) meditated on various perils relatable to the interwar period, from the abduction of Babar and Celeste by the operators of a circus to a war with bellicose rhinoceroses. In an imperial reversal, the old lady provided so much help to the wounded of that war that the royal couple invited her to remain with them in the forest. The empire metaphorically absorbed the metropole. In *Babar le roi* (Babar the King, 1933), faithful and hard-working dromedaries built a well-regulated colonial city, Celesteville. Animals populating the new city came to wear various kinds of clothing, each suited to the animal's position in the social order. But as war loomed later in the 1930s, the concerns of the exceptional elephant king became highly familial. During the war, publication ceased altogether.

As the franchise revived and was further internationalized after 1945, it largely steered clear of the tangles of decolonization, at any rate directly. Children in Brazil, Japan, or the United States, after all, scarcely could be expected to care much about how Babar and his kingdom negotiated delicate issues of the postwar empire and its aftermath. Yet the franchise could not change Babar's essential nature – that of a partly assimilated elephant who began his trek to greatness in a green suit. He could interact with the human world, but would never fully join it, still less renounce his clothes or his monarchial position among the animals. Babar and his kingdom, in short, had been changed forever. Could they ever fully decolonize?

In the 1990s and into the new millennium, criticism of Babar and his legacy hardened, particularly in the Anglophone world. It became increasingly difficult to explain away the patently colonial origins of the whole story, and the obvious comparison of colonial subjects to animals. "Should we burn Babar?," asked Herbert Kohl in the intentionally provocative title of a 1995 book. Kohl actually rejected the generic conclusion of Franz Fanon, that the answer to colonial violence was more violence. Even a figurative burning of the beloved elephant, after all, might well do children more harm than good. Rather, because Babar could never really decolonize, he "would best be relegated to the role of collector's item, an item in a museum of stereotypes."[1]

If Babar could never fully decolonize, what of the French empire? Certainly, in any legal sense, the French empire ceased to exist after the ratification of the Fifth Republic constitution in 1958. The peoples of the former imperial domains could choose their future relationship with France or choose not to have any relationship at all. But empire was never wholly about legal definition. "France" and its former empire would continue to shape one another's trajectories, it would seem forever. Each would live on in the other. Migrants from the empire and their descendants would make the Hexagon a multicultural society in new and constantly changing ways.

Beyond the Hexagon, each former domain had its own post-imperial story. Some domains would decline independence altogether and would remain or become French national territory. In accommodating them, *la République une et indivisible* would remind itself that its sovereignty was divisible after all, at any rate up to a point. Various forms of recognizably imperial authority endured in West Africa, with the support of the post-colonial African leadership. In Algeria, the colonial state long survived the departure of the colonizer. Through it all, France and its former colonial subjects would continue to grapple with just what it had all meant. Decolonization continues today in remembering the colonial past.

6.1   The Empire Migrates to the Hexagon

Since the nineteenth century, the Hexagon has remained a "nation of immigrants," even a "melting pot," not unlike the United States. Industrialization over the course of the century drew arrivals from Mediterranean Europe and future Germany. Reconstruction after World War I drew a new wave of immigrants, some 175,000 Arabs and Berbers from Algeria alone between 1922 and 1924. A 1927 naturalization law made it easier for European migrants to become citizens. Indeed, some 7 percent of the French population was foreign-born at the time of the Great Depression. By way of comparison, in 2018, some 9.7 percent of the French population was foreign-born (6.5 million out of a total population of 67 million). Likewise, anti-immigrant sentiment long preceded

---

[1] Herbert Kohl, *Should We Burn Babar?: Essays on Children's Literature and the Power of Stories* (New York: The New Press, 1995), 18.

decolonization. For example, in 1938, with economic recovery from the Depression already underway because of rearmament, a member of the Senate remarked: "If we had not received so many foreigners, we would not have unemployment. The foreigner is taking the bread out of our mouths."

After World War II, the Hexagon drew immigrants from the empire on an unprecedented scale. The high structural unemployment of the late-twentieth and early-twenty-first centuries made it easy to forget the extent of the labor shortage in France after 1945. If physical destruction in the Hexagon did not rival that of Germany or Japan, the Allied invasion of 1944 had caused considerable casualties and damage. Some 600,000 French had lost their lives in the war, and over 550,000 homes lay in ruins, not to mention destroyed factories and other forms of infrastructure. French planners in 1945 estimated that reconstruction would require at least 1.5 million new workers, with some estimates running as high as 5 million.

During what posterity would refer to wistfully as the *Trentes Glorieuses* (the Thirty Glorious Years) of 1945–75, the economy of the Hexagon grew at the blistering average rate of 5 percent per year. The real purchasing power of the average worker's wages grew by about 170 percent between 1950 and 1975, a rate of increase not remotely approached subsequently. Little surprise, then, that colonial subjects, past and present, found the prospect of employment in Europe attractive. Capitalists after 1945 did not fail to notice the prospect of a vast, hardworking, and inexpensive labor pool. In November 1945, just months after World War II ended, the provisional government established the Office national de l'immigration (ONI), charged with regulating immigration from the empire and elsewhere, as well as balancing the interests of the new arrivals with those of Hexagon workers with whom they would compete in the labor market.

Throughout the *Trente Glorieuses*, government policy focused on the need for labor rather than the welfare of workers or even the long-term consequences of their residence in the Hexagon. As late as 1968, only about 18 percent of labor migration even took place through the ONI. Employers tended not to ask questions about legal status in a booming economy. Even undocumented workers could regularize their situation without great difficulty. Organized labor remained ambivalent, eager for new union recruits yet concerned about downward pressure on wages. Immigrant families began to join single men. As a country of the *ius soli*, France confers citizenship on those born on French soil. A single family could thus comprise persons of several legal situations, such as one parent with a work permit, another in France extra-legally, and children who had been born French citizens. *Bidonvilles*, worker encampments that conspicuously replicated colonial poverty, filled the suburbs of major cities.

By 1973, some 7.3 million foreign nationals were working in France, about half of them without proper documentation. Roughly half of all migrants originated in the former empire, the largest contingents from North and West Africa.[2] Immigrants from overseas national territory, of course, did not count as "immigrants" in population statistics at all. As the *Trentes Glorieuses* came to an end with the oil shocks of the 1970s and ensuing "stagflation" (high unemployment coupled with inflation), the Hexagon found itself with a substantial, settled population not of European descent.

By that time, younger and more technocratically oriented leaders sought to move beyond de Gaulle's fixation on French *grandeur* toward solving the problems of the present. Led by Valéry Giscard d'Estaing, elected president in 1974 at the age of forty-eight, the republic defined "immigration" as one such "problem." The number of arrivals from Mediterranean Europe had been in relative decline for some time, as postwar growth rates began to synchronize in countries such as Italy and Spain. It became politically expedient to rebrand "immigrants" as non-Christians, particularly Muslims, from the former empire. "Immigration" also became more a matter of color, with social and police suspicion rising independent of actual legal status. Of course, for example, persons of black African descent labeled "immigrants" could have been born in sub-Saharan Africa, Guyane, the Caribbean, or the Hexagon. "Immigration" and "immigrants" became shorthand for what Anglophones commonly call "race."

Essentially, in all the Center-Left and Center-Right governments that have ruled the Hexagon since de Gaulle, policy on "immigration" has revolved around restricting new immigration and assimilating the "immigrants" already present. The Hexagon brought to bear the full array of state policies toward those ends. An attempt in 1974 to ban immigration altogether proved unfeasible, and had to be modified just a year later. Employers, after all, still needed to fill positions most white French considered beneath them. Then as now, millions of French who claimed to despise "immigrants" relied on their labor. The state, for its part, saw an assimilationist interest in continued immigration to reunite families. It considered men with family responsibilities more likely to fit into French society. In addition to the republican education system, the postwar welfare state used social workers, the health system, and public housing as

---

[2] Perhaps 100,000 Vietnamese moved to France between 1975 and 1990, compared with some 1.3 million to the United States by 2014.

instruments of assimilation. Particularly because of new immigration, the *bidonvilles* never completely disappeared. But many settled families of non-European origin eventually moved into suburban low-rent public housing (known as the HLM, or *habitation à loyer modéré*), as white families prospered and moved out. The suburbs or *banlieues* became the laboratories of French multiculturalism.

The French Republic bans the public gathering of data on race and ethnicity, to the scorn particularly of Anglophone multiculturalists. While this policy certainly presents disadvantages, we should see it in the context of the bitter legacy of World War II, when Vichy had a very racialized interest in the "non-French" living in France. Édouard Herriot's claim back in 1946 that France would become *la colonie de nos colonies* never lost a certain resonance among the French electorate, whatever voters told pollsters. At the very least, the human legacies of republic and empire would meet at flashpoints that would help articulate the French Republic itself in the new millennium.

Islam would prove the most important such flashpoint. Most Muslims in France have origins in North and West Africa. Private polling has identified roughly 9 percent of the French population as Muslim, or nearly 6 million people (compared with slightly over 1 percent in the United States). The same polling identified a perception among the general population of a much higher proportion of Muslims – some 28 percent, a figure few demographers believe is close to accurate. Over many decades of conflict, the secular republic worked out a modus vivendi with Christianity and Judaism, which it has not yet found with Islam.

In September 1989, the authorities suspended three middle school students in the Paris suburb of Creil for refusing to remove their headscarf or hijab. Such an assertion of religious identity, the argument went, had no place in the quintessentially secular space of the schoolroom, even though the secular republic had long permitted yarmulkes and crucifixes. So began a public controversy that has ebbed and flowed, but never really gone away. The hijab (also known as the veil or *toile*) became shorthand for various forms of Islamic clothing marking female modesty and privacy – including the niqab (showing only the eyes) and the burka (covering the whole body). A 1994 law sought to establish rules, permitting "discreet" symbols such as "small" stars of David or crucifixes but banning "ostentatious" symbols such as the hijab. Such a measure could hardly resolve the matter, however, given that it puts teachers among others in the unenviable position of discerning what "small" or "discreet" means or just when a headscarf becomes a hijab.

The defense of secular republicanism descended to gendered self-parody in the summer of 2016, with the controversy over the burkini, a specifically Islamic mode of swimwear covering nearly the entire female body. An unrelated matter inflamed emotions, a terrorist attack in Nice on Bastille Day, July 14, 2016. A truck charged into a crowd, killing 86 people and injuring over 400. As an unhelpful immediate response, the mayors of Cannes and Nice banned the burkini. Prime Minister Manuel Valls then took a public position on the matter: "The burkini is not a new range of swimwear, a fashion. It is the expression of a political project, a counter-society, based notably on the enslavement of women." Police duly began the unsavory task of ordering burkini-clad women to disrobe, leave the beach, or face arrest. The Conseil d'État, which rules on constitutional matters, affirmed the ban as recently as June 2022. Was regulating female attire at the beach really what the struggles for democracy in France since 1789 had been about?

Just as no two empires were alike, no two post-imperial states walked the same path toward multiculturalism. The unchanging city in the original Babar story did not much resemble the postcolonial Hexagon. As in other multicultural liberal democracies, persons of all ethnicities and races in France are making children and families together at ever-increasing rates. Doing so will pose ever greater challenges to strict categorization. Back in 1837, before he renounced a multicultural approach to French rule in Algeria, Alexis de Tocqueville called upon his compatriots "to give up this taste for uniformity that torments us." That taste remained deeply embedded in the French republican tradition – with effects as diverse as forbidding the collection of data on race and the banning of the hijab and the burkini. Under the republican empire, difference had legitimized inequality. The post-imperial republic has struggled to reconcile difference and equality. At times it has sought to do so through the annihilation of difference.

6.2   The DOM-TOM[3] and the Divisibility of the Indivisible Republic

On the face of it, the whole republican tradition in France abhorred anything that threatened to divide sovereign authority. *Fédéralisme*, after all, had been a capital crime during the French Revolution. As we saw in West Africa, post-World War II "federal" schemes mostly turned out to be empire under another name. Yet decolonization left an array of highly diverse bits and pieces that have remained "France." Indeed, even today the sun never sets on the French Republic, in that it is always daytime

---

[3] In 2003, the proper juridical acronym became DROM-COM (Départements ou Régions français d'Outre Mer et Collectivités d'Outre Mer). But DOM-TOM as explained below remains the term in common use.

somewhere on French national territory. The 1958 constitution, by design, did not provide much specificity as to what Article 74 identified as *départements* and *"les territoires d'Outre-Mer de la République"* (Overseas Territories of the Republic). In fact, the article allowed for the subsequent creation of other legal collectivities. Various such entities have evolved over the years, with their own attributes of sovereignty. Just to cite two examples, New Caledonia has its own flag and anthem, tiny Wallis and Futuna its own king. Republican sovereignty proved adaptable to forms of rule other than independence. Opinions will differ as to whether these forms of rule mean that the French Republic remains an empire.

The Départements d'Outre mer (DOM), comprising Martinique, Guadeloupe, Guyane, Réunion, and Mayotte, would appear to have the most straightforward relationship to the Republic – identical in principle to that of any *département* in the Hexagon. Four of these five are *vieilles colonies*, part of "France" since the Ancien Régime. In 1946, Aimé Césaire, then a deputy from Martinique, had lobbied vigorously for departmentalization (and thus full legal equality), explicitly as an alternative to decolonization. By an overwhelming margin, Martiniquais endorsed departmentalization in approving the Constitution of 1958. DOM citizens have always had elected representation in the National Assembly and the Senate, and today in the European Parliament. Decentralization during the presidency of François Mitterrand (1981–95), in the DOM as elsewhere in France, gave regional councils more power and more funding under their control. But the *préfet* (prefect), the point person named by Paris in each DOM, remains a more powerful figure than in the Hexagon, and in effect serves as mediator in conflicts between the local and national governments.

The *département* itself has been the geographic building block of sovereignty in France ever since its creation in 1790. Yet even here, the sovereign republic could accommodate two nontrivial changes in status. In 1974, the National Assembly unilaterally made Saint-Pierre and Miquelon a *département*, to foster economic development and to assert French sovereignty against any potential claims by Canada. However, in response to local discontent over regulation from the Hexagon and concern about fishing rights, the assembly rescinded this law in 1985. Today, the islands remain "France." But in the taxonomy of the European Union (EU), they are part of Les Pays et Territoires d'outre-mer (Lands and Overseas Territories), associated with but not an integral part of the EU. This status serves largely to keep Europeans out of now-depleted fisheries.

Mayotte, on the other hand, a small island between Madagascar and Mozambique, seceded from the Comoros Islands after they voted for independence in 1974. Much wrangling ensured in the following years.

The people of Mayotte appeared in large majority to want to remain French, even though doing so required them to renounce Islamic family law. The Comoros government and the African Union have always considered the secession illegal. Yet self-determination in Mayotte prevailed. Referenda on departmentalization held in 2000 and 2009 produced large majorities in favor (73 percent in 2000, just over 95 percent in 2009). In 2011, Mayotte became the 101st department of France.

The plasticity of the 1958 constitution has led to a variety of political designations among the Territoires d'Outre Mer (TOM). Like the DOM, nationals in the TOM are full French citizens with the same representation in Paris as their compatriots in the Hexagon. A plethora of names overlays a plethora of less and more significant political distinctions. Saint-Pierre and Miquelon, for example, now constitute under French (as opposed to EU) taxonomy a *collectivité territoriale*. Some 121 South Pacific islands make up French Polynesia, with the legal status of *pays d'outre mer au sein de la République française* (literally, overseas lands/region in the bosom of the French Republic). New Caledonia, on the other hand, is known as a *territoire sui generis*, with its own assembly able to pass legislation. New Caledonia also maintains a technically separate currency used throughout the South Pacific, the Communauté financiere du Pacifique (CPF). Few consider it a genuinely autonomous currency, however, given its tie to the euro and guarantee of convertibility by the French government.

President Valéry Giscard d'Estaing allegedly once referred to the DOM-TOM as "*les danseuses de la France*" or "the chorus girls of France," kept for decoration and the pleasure of their patron.[4] While sexist and condescending even by the standards of the 1970s, the remark did raise uncomfortable questions about the exact nature of the relationship between the Hexagon and "Overseas France." Whoever actually originated the remark probably referred to the goal of parity in costly social services in the DOM. But the issues go deeper. To what extent had the Hexagon fully assimilated its distant national territories, and to what extent did the peoples of these diverse lands (some 2.2 million out of a total French population of 67 million in 2020) even want complete assimilation?[5] If the point was not assimilation, was "Overseas France" not simply the French empire with yet another rebranding?

---

[4] During the presidential election campaign of 1981, Giscard fervently denied ever using the expression: www.elysee.fr/valery-giscard-d-estaing/1981/04/01/interview-de-m-valery-giscard-destaing-accordee-au-journal-de-lile-de-la-reunion-sur-le-bilan-de-son-action-en-faveur-des-dom-paris-avril-1981

[5] Of these, about 775,000 people live in Martinique and Guadeloupe, by far the most populous of the DOM-TOM.

The Hexagon had no more bare-knuckled an encounter with its colonies-turned-national-territory than nuclear weapons testing in the South Pacific. The Fourth and Fifth Republics assigned the highest priority to developing an independent nuclear deterrent. The guaranteees of the Évian Accords of 1962 notwithstanding, independent Algeria proved disinclined to permit France to explode nuclear devices on its soil. Beginning in 1963, the euphemistically named Centre d'Expérimentation du Pacifique (CEP), with an outpost in Tureia, began to prepare new testing sites on the atolls of Mururoa and Fangataufa, some 1,250 km southeast of Tahiti. Through years of testing, all nuclear powers irradiated thousands of bystanders near and far. France remained unusual in the intensity and duration of its testing. Along with China, France declined to sign the 1963 treaty banning atmospheric testing. Between 1960 and 1996, when France signed the Comprehensive Test Ban Treaty, it exploded some 210 nuclear devices, 193 of them in French Polynesia. Some forty-one of these tests took place above ground, the last in 1974.

The Hexagon represented nuclear testing to its Polynesian citizens as a well-regulated instrument of economic development. In September 1966, before personally observing the explosion of a nuclear device near Mururoa (see Illustration 6.1), President de Gaulle made a speech to an enthusiastic crowd in Papeete, the capital of French Polynesia. He thanked the Polynesians for hosting the CEP and assured them that "all dispositions have been taken" to assure their safety. "There is moreover," he continued, "if I may say so, recompense. The development that accompanies this center is outstanding. What must follow will be no less so." Nuclear testing indeed brought a construction boom to French Polynesia, and at least 3,000 high-paying jobs directly related to the CEP. However, nearly all of them went to French from the Hexagon.

Testing in the South Pacific also brought substantial environmental perils and, over time, international opprobrium. Some 110,000 islanders are now believed to have been exposed to harmful levels of fallout from above-ground testing. Not everyone believes French assurances of the geological stability of the atolls, leading to concerns about radiation leakage from underground testing. What rankled most internationally, not just among small Pacific Island nations but also in larger Pacific powers such as Australia and New Zealand, was the duration of testing well beyond any demonstrable security need. In 1985, the French intelligence service sank the *Rainbow Warrior*, a ship owned by the international environmental organization Greenpeace, which was on its way to protest a planned explosion in Mururoa. Nuclear testing became a performance of French sovereignty in the Pacific, important enough for President Jacques Chirac to continue the practice until the

Illustration 6.1 President Charles de Gaulle attends a nuclear weapon test in French Polynesia, 1966.
Source: Wikipedia Commons (no known copyright restrictions).

last hydrogen bomb test in January 1996, more than six years after the end of the Cold War.

In the economic realm, the very existence of the DOM-TOM has always illustrated the uneasy relationship between the French empire and French capitalism. Compared with the Hexagon, the DOM-TOM are small, remote, and economically fragile. Most of them are surviving bits and pieces of the mercantile empire of the seventeenth and eighteenth centuries. Only New Caledonia, home to some 10 percent of the world supply of nickel, has a commodity that can be sold profitably on a large scale on world markets. Agriculture in the DOM-TOM faces ferocious competition, because of industrialized production and government subsidies by agricultural superpowers such as the United States, Canada, and Australia. Bananas from Martinique, for example, reach tables throughout the EU only because of subsidies, protection, and high prices. In the DOM-TOM, assimilation certainly "worked" in bending tastes in food consumption toward those of the Hexagon. This shift weakened agricultural production in the DOM-TOM, making them net importers of food. Deals with former West African domains have further crowded out commodities from the DOM-TOM. The French franc and its successor the euro have long been strong currencies on world markets, making exports expensive.

At the macro-level, the economics of the DOM-TOM have inverted the classic colonial relationship, in that they extract resources from the metropole more than the reverse. State transfers constitute a major sector in the DOM-TOM economies. Expenditures of the CEP in the South Pacific constituted one such transfer, as does revenue today from its much smaller successor charged with monitoring radiation, the cumbersomely named Département de suivi des centres d'expérimentaion nucléaires (Department for Monitoring the Centers for Nuclear Experimentation). The European Space Agency (ESA), based in Paris, launches its rockets from the Centre Spatial Guyanais in Guyane. It employs over 9,000 people there directly or indirectly, and accounts for some 30 percent of the Guyane economy.[6] State-sponsored construction of roads, bridges, airports, housing, and communications likewise employs thousands in the DOM-TOM. The postwar expansion of the French state throughout national territory has fostered the growth of a class of civil servants, who often receive a supplement for postings far from the Hexagon. Direct transfers, notably to families and retirees, can account for 20 percent or more of household incomes.

Through the postwar period, tourism constituted the most promising growth area in the private sector. Most of the DOM-TOM exist in tropical or subtropical regions, with uncrowded beaches and spectacular landscapes. In the Hexagon, a growing middle class and increasingly affordable air travel across the *Trente glorieuses* and beyond meant an expanding clientele. Multinational corporations such as the Club Méditeranée (or Club Med) grew skilled at marketing an exoticized, yet controlled and familiar vacation experience in far-flung places. French Polynesia drew 1,472 tourists in 1959, 161,000 in 1986. The rapid growth of cruise ship tourism in the new millennium, while controversial on environmental grounds, further expanded markets, particularly in the Caribbean.

Yet in the DOM-TOM, as elsewhere, tourism proved an unsteady and decidedly differentiated avenue of economic development. Excluding local handicrafts and specialties in cuisine, most of what tourists consume has been imported, along with the materials to build the tourist infrastructure itself. Profits are largely exported. Certainly, tourism created jobs, though not nearly enough to provide adequate employment for large, fast-growing, and young populations. Most of the senior

---

[6] Even the Americans, for decades the leaders in space exploration, launched the James Webb telescope from Guyane on December 25, 2021 aboard an ESA rocket.

and well-paid management positions have gone to recent and temporary migrants from the Hexagon. As with agricultural exports, use of the French franc, CPF franc, and the euro have long made DOM-TOM tourist destinations expensive by world standards, limiting their appeal beyond Europe and Japan. Even in Polynesia into the 1990s, state transfers from nuclear testing mattered far more than tourism in supporting local economies.

"Neocolonialism," like "neoliberalism," has more often been employed as a rhetorical weapon than as a worthwhile analytical tool. But neither term lacks meaning in interpreting the DOM-TOM, its economies, and the resulting social tensions. The role of public subsidies makes the DOM-TOM more dependent on the state as French national territories than they ever were as colonies. Most of the 5,800 persons living in Saint-Pierre and Miquelon, for example, live as wards of the French state in one way or another. World markets, not to mention the abolition of slavery, made irrelevant the colonial economies in commodities such as sugar and coffee. Even niche commodities such as indigo and vanilla could be produced far more cheaply synthetically. Subsistence agriculture long ago ceased to be an option for large populations and would in any event embarrass so "modern" a nation as France.

The state-driven, service-based economies that replaced the colonial economies have made living standards in many DOM-TOM higher than in neighboring independent countries. But incomes overall remain far lower than in the Hexagon, and unevenly distributed by race. Guyane, to name one example, has the highest per capita gross domestic product in South America, largely because of the ESA. Yet in general, low-wage persons of color work in service sectors for high-paid white persons such as rocket scientists. The protectionism and subsidies for bananas in Martinique serve a minute but remarkably resilient and self-reproducing caste of descendants of the colonial planters, the Béké. Despite constituting less than 1 percent of the Martinique population, the Béké largely dominate production and distribution across the island. Béké influence perpetuated the use of a chlordecone, a carcinogenic pesticide, for decades after the United States banned it. Backed as in colonial days by powerful patrons in Paris, the Béké have perpetuated a small Caribbean version of what Algérie française might have looked like had the dreams of the wealthiest *pieds noirs* come true.

Tensions notwithstanding, assimilation has succeeded to some degree in the politics of the DOM-TOM. The people of Saint-Pierre and Miquelon engineered *de-départementalization*, but have never expressed much interest in becoming Canadian, let alone independent. The peoples of the French Caribbean and Réunion, beset by inequalities rooted in race and class, have proved restive. But in form and content, their protests have remained decidedly "French" – demonstrations and particularly strikes. The Union Générale des Travailleurs Guadeloupéens (General Union of Guadeloupean Workers, or UGTG), for example, claims some 18 percent of Guadeloupean workers as members, more than twice the level of union membership in the Hexagon. Straddling the public and private sectors, UGTG labor actions have been able to bring normal business and governmental activities to a standstill to a degree that Hexagon unions may well envy. But its origins in the 1970s among independence activists have been quietly shelved, in favor of striking better bargains with business and the state. Language issues have become increasingly politicized in a French Caribbean variant of multiculturalism. Activists have attached particular importance to the use of Creole dialects in public speech and public transactions.

But like their compatriots in the Hexagon, the French of the DOM-TOM have sought justice through the state more than in opposition to it. As one islander, a middle-school teacher, put it in 2005: "It's not that I don't believe in independence for Guadeloupe. It's that I don't believe in independence! It doesn't exist – anywhere! You're always dependent on something." He himself drew inspiration from his nèg mawon (maroon or escaped enslaved) ancestors. Like them, he saw Guadeloupeans as having established their own society. They could do business with the neocolonial notables around them and attack them politically through strikes and demonstrations. But "independence" remained a personal and group affair, and to some degree a state of mind. For the DOM-TOM, however hard it may be to live with the French state, it seems harder still to imagine living without it.

Certainly, New Caledonia became the most politically complicated of the DOM-TOM, for deep historical reasons. In many ways, New Caledonia proved more a settler colony than Algeria had ever been, though many settlers did not come from Europe. As we saw, the indigenous Kanak (Melanesian) suffered a demographic collapse in the nineteenth century. As the population gradually recovered, the Kanak found themselves still the largest single demographic group, but a minority. New white settlers came during periods of boom in nickel mining. The relatively robust and diversified economy of New Caledonia has also attracted settlers from the South Pacific, including about half of the population of Wallis and Futuna in the 1970s. Today, New Caledonia has a population of some 272,000 people, roughly 42 percent Kanak, 24 percent of European origin, 11 percent Polynesian, and 23 percent other (mixed 11 percent, plus other groups such as Indonesian and Vietnamese).

Had there been a consensus in favor of independence, the Hexagon doubtless would have granted it long ago. Therein lay the problem. Kanaks have generally favored independence, while Europeans, Polynesians, and others have generally opposed it. The economic effects of fluctuating nickel prices exacerbated social tensions. By the 1980s, radical Kanaks lost patience with constitutional means, and embarked on a campaign of direct action, including the taking of hostages and killing police and Kanak "collaborators." French governments responded with political campaigns to diffuse discontent, through the Matignon Accords (1988) and the Nouméa Accord (1998). The first agreement established a de facto federation – a European- and Polynesian-led south, and a Kanak-led north. The second encouraged New Caledonians to choose whether to cooperate within this structure, evolve toward either a continued unique status in the French Republic, or achieve independence.

The Nouméa agreement called for no fewer than three referenda on independence, in 2018, 2020, and 2021. The first two trended somewhat toward independence, though neither produced a majority. The 2018 referendum returned a 43.4 percent vote for independence, with 81 percent turnout; the 2020 referendum produced a 45.7 percent vote for independence with an 86 percent turnout. The 2021 referendum, which was supposed to settle the matter definitively, produced a very different result – only 3.5 percent in favor of independence with a much-reduced 44 percent turnout. Kanak activists had favored a postponement because of the coronavirus pandemic. The government in Paris refused, in part to avoid confluence with the French presidential election of April 2022. In response, the Kanak activists urged a boycott of the referendum, which at least partly explains the reduced turnout as well as the lopsided result.

Still, part of the crushing "no" result can also be explained by a government campaign to highlight the economic consequences of French withdrawal, with more than a hint that an independent New Caledonia would be much more dependent on China. If so, the campaign produced the desired result. "France is more beautiful," crowed President Emmanuel Macron in December 2021, "because New Caledonia has decided to stay part of it." It remains to be seen whether Kanak activists will return to violence to bring about what would be minority indigenous rule.

6.3   *Françafrique*

As we saw, many powerful West Africans did not even desire "decolonization" as conventionally understood. The quick failure of the Mali Federation by 1960 meant that Houphouët's vision would prevail, with each former colony making its own postcolonial arrangements with the

Hexagon. Political independence in West and Equatorial Africa coincided with the consolidation of the executive-dominated Fifth Republic designed by de Gaulle. Policy on Africa became a *domaine réservé* (reserved or personal domain) of the president – something more reminiscent of the Ancien Régime than liberal democracy in the second half of the twentieth century. Special advisers to the president on Africa had an office in the Elysée Palace rivaled in splendor only by that of the president himself, the symbolism lost on no one. Contemporaries bandied about a remarkably imperial term to describe West and Central Africa – as the *pré carré* (best translated here as the "front yard" or privileged space) of the Hexagon. Houphouët coined a term to describe the entirety of postcolonial relationships – *Françafrique*. He did not mean it, at any rate consciously, as the byword for unwholesome symbiosis and corruption that it later became.

In the Hexagon, the main architect of *Françafrique*, Jacques Foccart (1913–97), served de Gaulle as a loyal and ruthless retainer. The son of planters from Guadeloupe, Foccart joined the general in London in the first days of the Free French. Influential from the 1950s to the 1990s, Foccart held a variety of titles, including counselor for the French Union and secretary general of the French Community for African and Malagasy affairs. But Foccart's influence far exceeded any formal title. Known as "Monsieur Afrique," he served as the personal emissary of the president, beyond the authority of any ministry. More generally, Foccart exercised power in postcolonial Africa through his *reseaux*, personal networks straddling the Hexagon and its former domains.

Foccart shared his friend Houphouët's preference for bilateral arrangements, which with Foccart multiplied into a complex web of bilateral arrangements with himself at the center. Foccart enjoyed wide discretion in the employment of French intelligence and military assets to intervene in favor of one party or another in the endless tangles of postcolonial domestic politics. Intervention could include assassination for those who resisted *Françafrique*, particularly if they could be portrayed as tainted by communism. For example, most observers admit today that in 1960 the French intelligence services administered a fatal dose of thallium to the drink of Félix Moumié of Cameroon. Foccart's *réseaux* made it practically impossible to distinguish where the state in the Hexagon left off and that in the former colony began. No one did more to make the term *Françafrique* synonymous with neo-colonialism.

Beyond the individualized court politics played by Foccart, the French state distributed a considerable amount of aid to its former African domains. Exact amounts of aid are surprisingly difficult to determine, in the postcolonial French empire as elsewhere. Aid was distributed through various ministries, which facilitated the role of Foccart as the puller of strings behind the scenes. In addition, accounting in foreign aid is not intrinsically apolitical. How should we count "aid" that flowed directly back to the Hexagon, whether in the form of capital equipment purchased in Europe, repatriated salaries of aid workers, or Paris apartments and Côte d'Azur villas purchased with aid siphoned off by African notables?

Further, how also to factor in aid to which France contributed but distributed through international organizations such as the UN, the World Bank, or the EU and its predecessors? However calculated, direct aid from the French state to its former domains in sub-Saharan Africa at the height of the *Trentes glorieuses* constituted a substantial political investment – some 1.3 billion francs per year between 1963 and 1971, a value of nearly €2 billion per year today.[7] Sums that may seem small on Wall Street can buy real influence in sub-Saharan Africa.

In 1959, de Gaulle established the Ministère de la Coopération distinct from both the Foreign Ministry and the ministry responsible for the DOM-TOM. *Coopération*, like *Françafrique*, became a broad, postcolonial neologism. Prime Minister Georges Pompidou described its origins baldly in 1964: "The policy of cooperation follows from the expansionist policies of nineteenth-century Europe, when vast colonial empires were created or extended, and Europe made its economic and political influence felt over an enormous area." Initially, *coopération* involved assistance to the new states to assure the basic functions of governance – essentially French civil servants training their indigenous replacements. For example, French officials served governments in Madagascar into the early 1970s. After the ministry for *coopération* was absorbed by the Foreign Ministry in 1999, France continued to send teachers, agricultural experts, and many other skilled workers to its former domains in Africa. *Coopérants* can still work abroad as form of national service. In its way, *coopération* has continued the *mission civilisatrice*.

It would be a mistake to imagine *Françafrique* as wholly the personal creation of Foccart. *Françafrique* has been a discourse, not to say a vortex, that drew in French politicians of many political stripes, African leaders, and private persons in business in Europe and Africa. While Foccart himself appeared to care more about power than money, the same could not be said of his confederates and successors. The personal networks of *Françafrique* structurally confused public and private interests. Power in the new states lent itself to whole genres of subcontracting

---

[7] Calculated from Gérard Bossuat, "French Development Aid and Co-operation under de Gaulle," *Contemporary European History* 12, No. 4 (2003): 443.

that bred corruption – such as private deals on leases, import and export licenses, and simple bribes in cash or in kind.

Some African leaders acquired stunning personal fortunes, though stories of financial atrocities, like other kinds of atrocities, tended to get better with the telling. Estimates of Houphouët's worth at the time of his death in 1993 ran as high as $11 billion, though it is hard to see how anyone could have stolen quite so much from so poor a country as the Côte d'Ivoire. But no one doubted that Houphouët died an immensely wealthy man. Posterity has struggled to understand just how someone who had devoted almost his whole career to public service could honestly have acquired even a tithe of the amounts attributed to him. Houphouët surely could never have amassed whatever fortune he possessed without help from his former colonial masters.

Economists and political scientists write of a "resource curse," in which abundant natural resources make the postcolonial state a patronage machine in ways that inhibit long-term economic growth, not to mention good governance. Gabon, of former French Equatorial Africa, has been blessed and cursed with vast deposits of oil and uranium. So involved was Foccart in the affairs of Gabon that some called it "Foccartland." The first president of independent Gabon, Gabriél Léon M'ba, having survived a coup attempt in 1964 thanks to French intervention, died of natural causes in 1967. His vice president, Albert-Bernard Bongo, succeeded him, having been personally vetted by President de Gaulle as M'ba's condition worsened. Bongo converted to Islam in 1973 and took the first name of Omar. Quasi-democratic institutions emerged in Gabon, notably a legislature, as a machine well-lubricated by patronage from the top. Bongo's son Ali succeeded him upon his death and remains president of Gabon, despite his own continued medical challenges. Bongo family assets are so clandestine and dispersed that no one outside the family knows their exact worth. But the elder Bongo was believed to have been worth $1–2 billion at his death. A 2007 United States Senate investigation concluded that Ali Bongo had some $130 million on deposit at Citibank alone, most of which had been siphoned off public funds.

Omar Bongo is alleged once to have stated that "Gabon without France is like a car with no driver, France without Gabon is like a car with no fuel." This last can be taken literally, given the search in France from the 1970s forward for hydrocarbons not from the Middle East and North Africa, as well as the need for uranium for the French nuclear power industry and nuclear weaponry. In the 1990s, Gabonese and French officials, public and private, became embroiled in a massive scandal involving Elf-Aquitaine, an oil company in which the French state held a majority stake until 1996. Money flowed back and forth among Elf, Gabonese notables, and French politicians, who used Elf funds of highly dubious legality as campaign funds. Indeed, we must see Elf for many years before the scandal as a de facto instrument of French policy in Africa.

Scandals arising from *Françafrique* routinely reached the highest political circles. President Giscard d'Estaing counted among his friends Jean Bédel Bokassa, president of the Central African Republic (formerly the colony of Ubangi-Shari). Bokassa proclaimed himself emperor of a Central African Empire in 1977, and ruled a domain not recognized internationally until his deposition with French support in 1979. In 1973, Bokassa made a personal gift of diamonds to Giscard, then minister of justice, valued at some $10,000 in the most generous estimates. While probably not the largest shady gift in the history of *Françafrique*, let alone the history of French imperialism, it was quite illegal under French law. Giscard never provided a satisfactory explanation of the episode, which contributed to his defeat in the presidential election of 1981 by François Mitterrand. However, the Socialist president made his son, Jean-Christophe Mitterrand, his adviser on African affairs, following in the footsteps of Foccart. He apparently did not have Foccart's political gravitas, however, and earned the nickname "Papamadit" (papa-told-me), a name befitting an errand boy for the President of the Republic. Mitterrand the Younger later came under a series of indictments for illegal arms peddling, illegal influence peddling, and tax evasion.

Less overtly sordid but probably more influential has been the Communauté financière en Afrique (CFA), which issues its own currency, the CFA franc. The currency is used in fourteen African countries, twelve of them former French colonies.[8] Originally standing for Colonies françaises en Afrique, the French established the CFA franc immediately after World War II. Essentially, the CFA guaranteed convertibility at a fixed rate between the French franc and the CFA franc, guaranteed in turn by the Banque de France. In return, CFA countries have had to deposit 50 percent of their foreign reserves with the Banque de France, and agree, in effect, to the Hexagon controlling the value of their currency, and thus their interest rates. Today, the CFA has a peg to the euro, guaranteed by the European Central Bank and backed still by a theoretically unlimited line of credit from the French state.

---

[8] Technically, there are two such currencies, the CFA Ouest Africain (West African franc, based mostly in former French West Africa) and the CFA Afrique centrale (Central African franc, based mostly in former French Equatorial Africa), linked to two regional central banks. However, the two CFA francs are pegged at parity.

From its origins, the CFA franc has been a two-edge sword. Long-term investment and economic development, the argument goes, depend on a stable and convertible currency. Guinea, which as we saw abjured all French aid in 1958 by voting "no" on the constitution of the Fifth Republic, had chronic exchange rate problems, not all of them of Foccart's making. Through much of the postcolonial era, CFA countries (particularly the Côte d'Ivoire and Senegal) have enjoyed generally higher and more consistent growth rates than their sub-Saharan Africa peers. Indeed, Guinea-Bissau and Equatorial Guinea eventually joined the CFA zone even though they had not been French colonies.

On the other hand, membership in the CFA zone has always carried with it a degree of economic dependence and a nontrivial circumscription of national sovereignty. The peg first to the franc and then the euro tended to protect European consumers from exchange rate fluctuations in notoriously volatile markets in the commodities exported by CFA countries. The peg also encouraged the purchase of finished goods from Europe, and thus discouraged the development of value-added industries in Africa. In January 1994, the French unilaterally imposed a 50 percent devaluation of the CFA franc, in part to protect their own creditworthiness. While this aided CFA exports, it substantially increased inflation in CFA countries, leading to strikes and demonstrations. But the word of the Hexagon proved law, as in colonial days.

More recently, however, the "decolonization" of the CFA has continued through Africa and the Hexagon gradually going their separate ways. In 2019, the Economic Community of West African States (ECOWAS), together with the French government, announced plans to replace the West African CFA franc with a new currency called the Eco. Anglophone countries such as Ghana, Gambia, and Nigeria would join. Members would no longer be required to keep foreign exchange reserves on deposit with the Banque de France. While the French treasury would technically still guarantee convertibility, the real power in French monetary affairs today lies with the European Central Bank. If the Hexagon has looked more toward Europe, sub-Saharan Africa has looked more toward regional trade, and trade with China. Even so, the idea of an African currency pegged to a strong European currency remains controversial.

Military force always provided the ultimate backstop of *Françafrique*, particularly in cases where the kind of clandestine skulduggery pioneered by Foccart proved insufficient. Defeats in Indochina and Algeria have encouraged observers, particularly in the Anglophone world, to underestimate postcolonial French military power. France remains the only Western European power with a capacity for sustained air and ground operations abroad. It maintains a number of bases beyond French national territory, in former colonies such as Djibouti, the Côte d'Ivoire, Gabon, and Senegal. The French military has taken part in dozens of missions since 1960, from protecting a base at Bizerte in independent Tunisia (1961), to supporting friendly regimes in Chad (1969–71, 1978–80, 1983, 1986, 2006, 2008, 2014). French forces also came to the aid of regimes in Togo (1986), Cameroon (1990), Burkina-Faso (1998), and the Côte d'Ivoire (2002). Nor did the French limit themselves to their former empire, with interventions in the former Belgian Congo (Zaire, today the Democratic Republic of the Congo) in 1978 and 1993.

At an ideological level, *Françafrique* came to restate the contradictions of republican empire. French universalism called for democratization. But French influence in postcolonial Africa catered to the realist position of France as a Great Power, and to African collaborators who could perpetuate and extend that influence. Through interventions in Rwanda in the 1990s and the ongoing intervention in the Sahel, *Françafrique* literally deconstructed, falling apart of its internal contradictions.

In a speech on June 20, 1990 at a summit in France with African leaders from thirty-seven countries, President Mitterrand sought to reinvent *Françafrique* for the post-Cold War era by reasserting republican universalism. France would continue to help Africa, but that help would be more lukewarm (*tiède*) toward those countries that remained authoritarian. It would reserve its enthusiasm for "those that take, with courage, the step toward democratization." The explicit link between aid and democratization, the theory went, would define a specifically French sphere of influence in Africa in the the post-Cold War world.

In Rwanda, rebranded *Françafrique* sowed the wind and reaped the whirlwind, making the Hexagon a partner in genocide. Rwanda, in fact, had never been part of the formal French empire. Part of German East Africa before World War I, it had become, alongside Burundi, a Belgian mandate under the League of Nations. As their own version of the *politique des races*, the Belgians had based rule in Rwanda and Burundi on turning a class difference into a toxic ethnic difference. They delegated considerable power to the Tutsi, traditional herders and thus relatively wealthy. Tutsi constituted perhaps 15 percent of the population in the mandatory period. Sedentary farmers, the Hutu, constituted a large and poorer majority. Identity cards developed in the 1930s listed the bearer's ethnicity. Rwanda became a UN trusteeship in 1945 and an independent state in 1961. Tutsi and Hutu lived in both Rwanda and Burundi, both of which preserved the colonial system of ethnic identification after independence.

In Rwanda, deep-seated tensions between Tutsi and Hutu impeded the development of a stable regime. After independence, a Hutu-led undemocratic republic had replaced a Tutsi-led undemocratic monarchy. Tutsi who considered themselves politically and economically dispossessed created rebel military units operating out of Burundi and Uganda. The most prominent proved the Front Patriotique Rwandais (FPR), led by Paul Kagame. The FPR initiated a civil war, beginning in October 1990.

Up to that time, France had not been deeply involved in Rwandan affairs, at least not by the traditional standards of *Françafrique*. Mitterrand's announced policy of 1990 provided an opportunity to extend French influence. As FPR incursions began, the Rwandan president Juvénal Habyarimana appealed for military aid from Zaire, Belgium, and France. Jean-Christophe Mitterrand wrote to his father in a memo of October 16, 1990 that France should respond favorably: "This aid will permit France forcefully to ask for respect for human rights and a rapid democratic opening, once calm has returned."[9] It proved convenient to forget that Habyarimana was a Hutu military man who had first come to power in a 1973 coup, and not to think too deeply about just how supplying him with more lethal weaponry would foster his democratic instincts. Rather, aiding Habyarimana provided occasion to "defend" a piece of Francophone Africa from insurgents supported by Anglophone Ugandans. The Rwandan leader routinely referred to "Ugandan-Tutsi" insurgents. In supporting Habyarimana, France in effect chose the Hutu side in the revived Rwandan civil war.

Its problematic origins notwithstanding, the French military and diplomatic initiative appeared to make progress in the next few years. Indeed, under the leadership of the Organization of African Unity, the FPR and the Rwandan government signed the Arusha accords in August 1993, which would have established power sharing and democratization, and provided for the return of Tutsi refugees. A multilateral peacekeeping force under the auspices of the UN would oversee implementation of the accords. Along the way, however, Habyarimana's regime had become increasingly dependent on French military aid. French policy, in turn, became increasingly identified with the fortunes of that regime, which made it necessary to overlook the radicalization of Hutu factions within the government that saw any agreement with the FPR as an existential threat. The drone of official, anti-Tutsi propaganda, notably by radio, increased steadily throughout the country.

On April 6, 1994, a plane carrying Habyarimana and the Burundi president Cyprien Ntaryamira was shot down near the airport in Kigali, the Rwandan capital. The responsible party remains unknown, though

---

[9] Quoted in Commission de Recherche sur les archives françaises relatives au Rwanda et au génocide des Tutsi, *La France, Le Rwanda et le génocide des Tutsi (1990–1994)* (Paris: Armand Colin, 2021), 64.

suspicion has trended toward Hutu radicals in the Habyarimana government. Certainly, radicals assumed control of the interim regime, and ignited a firestorm of ethnic hatred with few precedents. Within hours, and with official instigation by radio, massacres began of Tutsi in Rwanda. The presidential guard played a leading initial role. Known pro-Tutsi political figures were killed immediately. Hutus who had lived alongside Tutsi neighbors for decades suddenly turned to murdering them with farm implements. For thousands of women, rape preceded murder. By consensus estimates, between 800,000 and 1,000,000 Tutsi died in the following three months of genocide, about two-thirds of the entire Tutsi population then living in Rwanda[10] Certainly, Hutus died as well, notably in areas taken over in the FPR offensive that ultimately changed the regime in Rwanda and ended the genocide. Estimates run from 25,000 to 80,000 Hutus killed. But there was never a systematic Tutsi countercampaign of genocide against what after all remained a majority Hutu population.

World media paid little attention to the Rwanda genocide right away, for reasons ranging from the physical risks facing journalists to a more general disinterest in intra-African strife. The genocide was also partly eclipsed by the final defeat of apartheid in South Africa and the inauguration of Nelson Mandela as president on May 10, 1994. President Mitterrand himself visited South Africa in July 1994 and offered effusive praise of the post-apartheid regime as a partner in future cooperation. Even genocide in nearby Rwanda could not derail the Mitterrand imaginary in reinventing and expanding *Françafrique*.

French policy in Rwanda reached its nadir in Opération Turquoise, from June to August 1994. As the killing began in April, initial French military efforts focused on the evacuation of French nationals. More controversially, the French immediately evacuated the powerful widow of the deceased president, Agathe Kanziga Habyarimana, and their inner circle. This affirmed the French connection to the besieged Hutu regime as the FPR advanced on Kigali. Serious discussion ensued within the French government about intervening militarily to keep the murderous Hutu regime in power.

As the genocide continued and became more generally known, the French sought a more active role, ostensibly to stop the killing and revive the process that produced the Arusha accords. The UN Security Council authorized French intervention under Resolution 912,

---

[10] Oman Shahabudin McDoom provides a methodologically serious but controversial estimate of about 500,000 Tutsi deaths: "Contested Counting: Toward a Rigorous Estimate of the Death Toll in the Rwandan Genocide," *Journal of Genocide Research* 22 (2020): 91–2.

pending the formation of a more robust multinational force. The French landed some 2,500 personnel in Rwanda, along with helicopters, mortars, and military aircraft. As the Hutu government crumbled before the FPR advance, the French forces established a "safe zone" for refugees in southwestern Rwanda. To be sure, some Tutsi refugees found their way to protection there; but many perpetrators and not a few organizers of the genocide found protection as well. The French made no effort to identify those responsible for the killing before they withdrew in late August. Indeed, the Zone Turquoise provided a corridor for perpetrators to escape to Zaire. Massacres of Tutsi even continued in the zone. The French gave up supporting the Hutu regime in Kigali only when the FPR victory compelled them to do so.

At best, the French intervention in Rwanda after 1990 showed what France would do when faced with a choice between humanitarian universalism and backing a friendly regime. However genuine the convictions of the French government on democratizing Africa, it chose the Hutu government of Habyarimana as its ally, genocidal tendencies and all. "Defending" Francophone Africa meant basically accepting the Hutu interpretation of the RPF as a hostile, foreign, Anglophone-backed force. The French military created a safe zone for murderers, and in the end earned international opprobrium for having done so. If any additional evidence of the repudiation of French policy were needed, Francophone Rwanda joined the British-led Commonwealth of Nations in 2009.

Mitterrand's successors, one after another, have distanced themselves from the very concept of *Françafrique*, in favor of multilateral relationships among states that would consider themselves equals. "The future of Africa," President François Hollande told the National Assembly of Senegal in October 2012, "will rest on Africans' increased capacity to handle by themselves the crisis that the continent is going through." Even the term *mission civilisatrice* came to be considered racist, though the more palatable postcolonial term "state building" implied many of the same ends. A special interest in the former colonies of West Africa has endured through successive presidential regimes. Partly in response to the debacle in Rwanda, the French have been more careful to operate in a multilateral framework, even when they provided the preponderant forces.

After the attacks of September 11, 2001, the American-led invasions of Afghanistan and Iraq drove militant Islamists toward Africa. The collapse of the regime of Muammar Gaddafi in Libya in October 2011 provided a boon to paramilitaries throughout Africa, as his formidable armory was privatized virtually overnight. Under UN auspices and with international support, France took a leading role fighting militant Islam in the Sahel, a vast transnational border region between the

Sahara and the jungle. Doing so meant supporting African regimes as de facto clients of France, indeed increasing their dependence on the Hexagon for their own survival. Throughout the Sahel, and particularly in Mali, France mostly sought stability, to keep militant Islam at bay. In so doing, it also sought to discourage migration to Europe by making Africa more hospitable to Africans.

The ethnic and linguistic diversity of Mali always posed a challenge to stable postcolonial governance. Military coups, the most recent in May 2021, have punctuated periodic attempt at democratization. The single largest ethnic group, the Bambara, make up only about one-third of the population. French remains the language of state, because of its relative political neutrality. Mali, one of the poorer countries in the world per capita, has as its only major natural resources about enough gold and other minerals to support a small postcolonial elite based in the cities.

In January 2012, rebellious Tuareg (Berbers) joined forces with the African offshoot of Al-Qaeda. By January 2013, this alliance ruled most of northern and eastern Mali (including Timbuktu) and began to close in on the capital of Bamako. The success of the insurgency led to yet another military coup. The interim regime appealed to the former colonizer, as the one power capable of making sufficient support available in time. Opération Serval, supported by a UN Security Council resolution, sent some 4,000 French military personnel to Mali, with small amounts of mostly logistical support from European and American allies. Nearly 3,000 African troops subsequently joined them, under independent command organized by ECOWAS. Tribes and warlords continued to change sides opportunistically, enough to shift the fortunes of one side or another. By the fall of 2012, the rebel forces had been driven back, and the major towns and cities retaken by the Malian government and its allies.

But rescuing Bamako did not defeat the Islamic insurgency in Mali, let alone across the thousands of miles of the Sahel. In 2014, Opération Serval morphed into Opération Barkhane, an ongoing anti-insurgency campaign. France allied with five former colonies straddling the Sahel, all of them at risk – Burkina Faso, Chad, Mali, Mauritania, and Niger. Here, too, European and American allies provided small amounts of logistical support. Some 5,100 French military personal fought in Opération Barkhane at its peak. Counterinsurgency warfare is the direct descendant of colonial warfare. Small numbers of troops operate across vast spaces and focus more on the destruction of the enemy than on the conquest of territory. Air power, both jet aircraft and helicopters, remains critical. The loyalties of civilians can be difficult to discern, and they have frequently been unintentional or intentional targets by both sides.

Illustration 6.2 The *mission civilisatrice* lives on: French soldiers and civilian seek stability in southern Mali, March 2016.
Source: Wikipedia Commons (no known copyright restrictions), File: Opération Barkhane.jpg.

Like colonial warfare, counterinsurgency warfare is about attrition, perhaps even more political than military. The Sahel became one more front in the seemingly endless "war on terror," and in its way sought to continue the *mission civilisatrice* (see Illustration 6.2).

Like American involvement in Afghanistan, patience in the Hexagon waned with what looked like permanent stalemate. With the new interim military regime in Mali expressing no interest in democratization, President Emmanuel Macron announced in a press conference on June 10, 2021: "We cannot secure areas that are falling back into lawlessness [*anomie*] because states decide not to shoulder their responsibilities. It is impossible, or else it is a task with no end." ECOWAS imposed sanctions on the military regime in Bamako in January 2022. In November 2022, Macron announced the official end of Operation Barkhane. The French would leave Mali and confine their presence throughout the Sahel mostly to training African troops. In January 2023, the military leaders of Burkina Faso requested that the French withdraw some 400 military personnel there. But the French fight against militant Islam in Africa would continue, on a smaller scale and based in two other former colonies, Chad and particularly Niger.

For its part, the new military regime in Bamako resented what it described as French "neocolonial" meddling, which included mentioning the delicate subject of elections. The regime found a less judgmental partner in the Wagner Group, a shadowy Russian private company with close ties to President Vladimir Putin and known to supply mercenaries. Implausible denials from Bamako notwithstanding, what *The Economist* called a "goons for gold" scheme brought some 1,000 mostly Russian mercenaries to Mali by 2022.[11] Atrocity stories emerged right away, including mass executions of suspected Islamists, some by burning alive. Burkina Faso was widely believed to be following suit in early 2023. Few observers doubt that the Putin regime has ambitions of replacing *Françafrique* with a more ruthless *Russafrique*.

By the third decade of the new millennium, "*Françafrique*," like "neocolonial," had become an epithet, deployed liberally in virtually any case of disagreement between the former colonizer and the former colonized. This did not mean, however, that either term wholly lacks meaning. Like colonial arrangements, postcolonial arrangements require partnerships. For African elites, *Françafrique* has offered an alternative to the dislocations of decolonization, and for quite a few leaders personal enrichment. French businesses likewise could reap imperial-scale profits, underpinned by a currency that structurally favored their interests. Nor were the ethical issues of *Françafrique* wholly economic. To be sure, the ethics of French involvement in Mali and the Sahel differed greatly from those in Rwanda. The latter showed *Françafrique* at its ugliest. In the Sahel, no one doubted that Islamic terrorists posed a genuine threat to France, or that the peoples of the Sahel did not deserve to have a ferocious version of sharia imposed on them against their will. But the French did not intervene in the Sahel to open the door to Russian mercenaries. Whatever else may be said of it, the long-lived traces of *Françafrique* have shown how difficult it has been for the former African colonies to live without the French, as well as with them.

6.4   Algeria after the French

The tumultuous demonstrations across Algeria on Independence Day, July 5, 1962, temporarily overlaid deep divisions in the body politic. Opinions will differ as to the responsibility of the French in creating those divisions over 130 years of colonial rule. As we saw, the fate of the settler population had been settled by the scorched-earth policy of the OAS in refusing to accept defeat and by nationalist violence and

---

[11] *The Economist* (2022). "Wagner, Worse Than It Sounds," January 15.

counterviolence. But plenty of other fault lines remained, based in policies, ethnicities, religion, personalities, and much else. The FLN had always cut a more coherent figure in the corridors of the UN and in the world media than on the ground in Algeria. Still, postcolonial Algeria faced independence with formidable assets – immense prestige in the Third World as a left-leaning new nation that had defeated the French yet owed nothing to the Communist bloc, as well as vast natural resources in the form of hydrocarbons.

Yet few outside the ruling elite would argue that postcolonial Algeria has realized many of the hopes of 1962. The explanatory narrative here does not claim exclusivity, though it maintains that the French empire lived on in Algeria through the inheritance and refinement of the colonial state. It perhaps is not a coincidence that most of the numerous actors in postcolonial Algerian politics are known by French acronyms. In more than a half-century since independence, these actors have competed for power in bafflingly complex and sometimes deadly ways. For all the tumult, however, a ruling oligarchy has gone from strength to strength. In this oligarchy, the state, the military, and the hydrocarbons industry comprise essentially the same people. In its tactics and even its objectives, what Algerians call *le pouvoir* (the power) has provided uncomfortable reminders of colonial rule, now minus the colonizer.

Slippage along fault lines among Algerian nationalists would result in a coup within three years of independence. There had long been tension among FLN leaders, either in exile or in prison before independence, and military commanders of the Armée de liberation nationale (ALN), who operated mostly out of Tunisia. Since the interwar years, some nationalists sought a more "socialist" independent Algeria while others did not. Nonsocialists comprised both liberals and religiously oriented Muslims, some of whom considered socialists godless infidels. But in many cases, if the personal remained political, the political remained personal. In the tumultuous first years after independence, Ahmed Ben Bella of the FLN and Houri Boumédiènne of the ALN joined forces, to the exclusion of more socialist elements, notably those led by Mohamed Boudiaf, whom they chased into exile in Morocco.

As president of the council of ministers, Ben Bella cut a fine figure internationally, as a leader of *tiers mondisme* ("Third Worldism," a search for an independent socialist, postcolonial path). How many people at the time, after all, could stand before photographers in the same year next to the American president John F. Kennedy, the Egyptian president Gamal Abdel Nasser, the Cuban president Fidel Castro, and the revolutionary-at-large Che Guevara? Yet Ben Bella never really ruled over the FLN, let alone over the military, which became increasingly suspicious of any competing figures it saw as having authoritarian instincts. As Ben Bella planned an Afro-Asian conference in Algiers for June 1965, a successor to the Bandung Conference ten years earlier, a bloodless military coup placed him under house arrest and made Boumédiènne the president of a self-styled Conseil de la Révolution.

Less ideological, more capable at juggling factions, and probably more ruthless than Ben Bella, Boumédiènne put in place the basic model of politics and economic development that has ruled Algeria ever since. The state, supported by hydrocarbon revenues, became the primary allocator of capital through nationalized industries. The largest of these, Sonatrach, a cumbersome acronym for an even more cumbersome name,[12] controls the hydrocarbon reserves. Throughout the history of independent Algeria, hydrocarbon revenues have held the entire economy hostage to the vicissitudes of world prices. For example, Sonatrach earned some $60 billion in 2014, $20 billion in pandemic-afflicted 2020, and $34.5 billion in 2021. It expected to earn $50 billion in 2022, because of the disruptions in world markets caused by the Russian invasion of Ukraine. Public finances have had corresponding peaks and troughs. Through ferocious austerity, Algeria reduced a massive foreign debt in the 1990s, and subsequently used substantial foreign exchange reserves as a partial buffer in times of low prices.

Algeria was not the only postcolonial country in which the independent state simply inherited the extractive role of the colonial state. This model made the state a gigantic and inefficient patronage machine. Economists consider independent Algeria to be a textbook example of the "resource curse," in which natural resources serve as a barrier to good governance and good economics. *Le pouvoir* created plenty of jobs for those closest to it. Various "bread and circuses" policies directed toward other Algerians delivered subsidized housing, subsidized food (much of it imported as agriculture declined), and even Chevrolets built under license from General Motors, fueled by subsidized gasoline. As in the late-colonial period, the population grew at a gallop, over 3 percent per year through the 1970s and beyond. This made Algeria a very young country, with very unequal opportunities. Official figures for unemployment in Algeria stood at nearly 12.7 percent in 2021, with youth unemployment more than double the overall rate. Sceptics consider the real rates much higher. Few Algerians starve, but millions of young people particularly in volatile cities have struggled to occupy themselves.

In *The Ancien Regime and the French Revolution* (1856), Alexis de Tocqueville observed that a corrupt regime is most vulnerable not when it is

---

[12] Societé Nationale pour la Recherche, la Production, le Transport, la Transformation, et la Commercialisation des Hydrocarbures.

most repressive, but when it tries to reform. Reform undercuts repressive instruments of rule before reformers can replace them. In the late-1980s, Chadli Bin Djedid of the army and Mouloud Hamrouche of the more technocratic tendencies of the FLN made a sincere attempt to open the Algerian polity and economy. As president, Chadli introduced a constitution in 1989 that paved the way for diverse political parties and more authentic elections.[13] For some years previously, Hamrouche had worked to reform the economy, not so much to "liberalize" or "privatize" the state sector as to make it more accountable to markets and open it to competition. A more open economy, the theory went, would eventually reduce the massive bill for consumer subsidies, and improve employment and living standards.

While most Algerians might have detested the existing political and economic system as a whole, most had a stake in their piece of it, whether a job, public housing, cheap gasoline, or subsidized bread. *Le pouvoir* might want a more contented body politic, but not at the expense of its own position. Market accountability would inevitably mean lost jobs in state industry. Reduced subsidies would disproportionately affect poorer Algerians. Millions of unemployed young people might do better eventually, but probably not right away. At the same time, utopians from Trotskyists to Islamists pressed for much more radical change than anything envisaged by Chadli and Hamrouche.

Long-simmering discontent, particularly among young men, coupled with the consolidation of the Islamic Republic in Iran, the victory of the mujahideen of Afghanistan over the Soviets, and outrage over the 1991 American-led victory in the First Gulf War to give new impetus to politicized Islam. In February 1989, the *le pouvoir* legalized the Front Islamique de Salut (FIS, or Islamic Salvation Front), partly as a matter of liberalization, partly to co-opt some of its leaders. To some extent, however, the FIS became a religious counterpart of the FLN in the colonial period, an umbrella group for a wide range of activists. Unlike the FLN, however, the FIS could operate legally. In municipal elections in June 1990, the FIS drew no less than 54.3 percent of the vote, the FLN 28.1 percent.

Undeterred, the regime went forward with legislative elections that began in December 1991, and like those in France would take place in two rounds. In the first round, the FIS won 188 of 430 seats outright, meaning that the candidates won more than 50 percent of the vote. It seemed likely to win most of the 198 seats that would go to a second round. On January 11, 1992, at the insistence of a cadre of senior

---

[13] Like "Napoleon," and "Toussaint," Chadli Bin Djedid was commonly referred to by his first name.

military officers, Chadli resigned in favor of a self-styled Haut Comité d'État (HCE, or High Committee of State). The second round of elections was cancelled, and a state of emergency declared on February 9, 1992. The FIS was banned.

The HCE then invited Mohamed Boudiaf, then approaching his third decade of exile in Morocco, to return to politics as president. But if *le pouvoir* expected a pliant mouthpiece, they picked the wrong man. Boudiaf took measures to begin fighting corruption and ordered the release of thousands of people arrested as FIS sympathizers. He also began making speeches on such delicate topics as "re-founding the state." Lest anyone miss his target audience, he spoke in the Algerian dialect of Maghreb Arabic. During one such speech, on June 29, an Islamist suspiciously placed in Boudiaf's own bodyguard assassinated him. His murder provided the downbeat for civil war.

We will probably never know how many Algerians died in the ensuing years of internal conflict. Opinions even differ as to when that conflict began and ended. Most estimates run between 100,000 and 200,000 dead by 2002. Violence was rising before the assassination of Boudiaf in 1992 and continued at lower levels after a government amnesty in 2000. If the state even kept comprehensive figures on how many died, it is unlikely to release them. The diffuse nature of the violence also makes precision difficult. Two broad forces tried to annihilate each other – *le pouvoir*, and an Islamist-led force of insurgents whose motivations ranged from religious fervor to personal avarice. The vast majority of the Algerian people simply got caught, murderously, in the middle. The French word *normal* entered everyday Algerian speech in a new, ironic sense, to describe their perilous existence.

Le pouvoir inherited the resilience as well as the brutality of the colonial state. The military remained organized, and the hydrocarbon revenues continued to flow. The Islamists, for their part, never really cohered, or found a single charismatic leader like the Ayatollah Khomeini in Iran. It is debatable, therefore, that the actual overthrow of the regime was ever likely. However, the war tore at the fabric of Algerian society. The banning of the FIS meant the removal of a host of local officials elected in June 1990. Doing so meant a temporary withdrawal of state authority, and a vacuum at the local level that was filled by strongmen of any shade of ideological opinion, or none at all. Conspiracy theories abounded, notably of *le pouvoir* commissioning violence then branded as "Islamic" to engineer public reaction. Islamists, for their part, used techniques of terror made notorious in coming years by Al-Qaeda and the Islamic State. Yet another French phrase entered Algerian common parlance – *qui tue qui*? (who is killing whom?).

Many episodes of violence recalled some of the most grim days of the war of independence, such as the gunning down of six police in the Casbah in February 1992, or the bombing of the Algiers airport in August 1992, which killed 9 people and injured 125. In March 1996, the murder and beheading of seven Catholic monks, all French nationals, after their abduction from a monastery at Tibhirine in the Atlas Mountains drew international attention. In August 1997, a massacre at Sidi Moussa, some 20 km southeast of Algiers, resulted in the death of somewhere between 98 and 300 men, women, and children. Rapes, beheadings, and the eviscerations and burning of bodies live and dead provided some of the worst reminders of past strife. According to one estimate, more than 1,000 Algerians were killed in just the first two weeks of Ramadan in 1997. Some well-known people were targeted for execution, such as the *raï* singer Cheb Hasni and Nabila Djahnine, an architect who headed a women's organization called Thighri n'metout (The Cry of Women). Many more of the dead, however, were simply everyday people who happened to be in the wrong place at the wrong time.

In response, the government showed just how well it had understood counterinsurgency warfare as waged by the former colonizer. The Département du renseignement et de la sécurité (the Department of Intelligence and Security) was the direct heir of the French intelligence services, and during the civil war accelerated the use of colonial methods – mass arrest, torture, and "disappearances." An unknown number of Algerians, presumably of varying levels of culpability, fell into its net. The failure of the police or the army to intervene in massacres when logistically they could have done so fed conspiracy theories. As the war dragged on, *le pouvoir* permitted and even armed "self-defense groups," which sometimes had their own agendas. A society with such endemic violence created almost unlimited opportunities for the settling of personal scores.

There are two main ways to win a war of ideologically based insurgency – exterminating the insurgents or dividing them, co-opting some, killing others, marginalizing the rest. *Le pouvoir* in Algeria chose the second course. A "people's war" in the manner of China under Mao or Vietnam under Ho was never an option in Algeria in the 1990s. Most Algerians, whatever their views on *le pouvoir,* wanted *normal* to mean something besides simmering carnage. The Algeria civil war ended as a process rather than an event. Its underlying causes still exist.

In April 1999, Abdelaziz Bouteflika was elected president in a managed election as the consensus candidate of *le pouvoir*. A protégé of Boumédiènne and one of the architects of the 1965 coup, Bouteflika had long experience as an operator in Algerian politics. He promised "peace," or at any rate the further diminution of civil war. Sweeping amnesty provisions covered perpetrators on all sides. Islamists willing to cooperate, rumor had it, could enjoy a lucrative stake in the fast-growing mobile phone industry. Bouteflika proved the figure who divided Algerians the least as the civil war wound down. Because of the lasting impact of that war and a massive show of police force at the outset, the "Arab Spring" of the early 2010s produced barely a ripple in Algeria. Bouteflika, seriously debilitated by a stroke in 2013, would continue to serve until April 2019, when he resigned in a wave of popular protest. In its fundamentals, however, and for better or worse, postcolonial Algeria had returned to its status quo ante bellum.

Beyond the structures of the postcolonial state, plenty of reminders of the colonial period exist in Algeria today. Postal trucks are painted in exactly the same colors as those of the Hexagon, and the acronym for the national railway system differs from its French counterpart by only one letter.[14] More substantively, despite decades of "Arabization," French persists as a language of publication and speech, particularly among the middle class. At independence, writer Kateb Yacine referred to the French language as Algerians' *butin de guerre*, war booty taken from the colonizer. A 2008 study found that about one-third of Algerians could read, speak, and write in French, with doubtless a much higher percentage in the cities. French even acquired a new respectability as a language of dissent, particularly among young writers well aware of the large (and uncensored) market throughout the Francophone world. It has proved easier to take Algeria out of "France" than to take "France" out of Algeria.

6.5   Conclusion

A "conclusion" seems to fit this chapter better than this book, because the history of the French empire has not ended. Millions of its children now live in the Hexagon, and quite a few bits and pieces of that empire remain ruled directly from Paris. The symbiotic arrangements, however insalubrious, of *Françafrique* have surely weakened in the new millennium. But France remains more than just another ex-colonial power in Africa. France and its former empire continue to shape each other's destinies.

Memory, whether of individuals or national communities, is a creative process, paradoxically based in forgetting as well as remembering. Further, memory involves the creation of narratives that in turn articulate

---

[14] Société Nationale des Transports Ferroviaires (Algeria, SNTF); Société Nationale des Chemins de Fer (French, SNCF).

identities. Decolonization certainly had its own idealized narrative. Oppressed peoples over time achieved national consciousness. Guided by that consciousness, they eventually grew strong enough to see off their oppressors. In the case of the French empire, the generic decolonization narrative suited not just the former colonized, but the former colonizer. For the colonized, the decolonization narrative made nationalists the heroes of the piece, however oppressive the postcolonial regimes they led. The narrative also made it possible for nationalists to hide their own often bitter divisions. For the French, the narrative of decolonization suggested that the "authentic" France had always been the European Hexagon. Imperialism had been one big misadventure, if to some a romantic one, that had always cost more in blood and treasure than it yielded in national profit or prestige. Always below the surface and sometimes above it, the decolonization narrative reminded white French that they populated the somehow more "authentic" France of the Hexagon. Forgetting empire could mean forgetting color and remembering whiteness in the real, multicultural, post-imperial France.

Simply put, the generic decolonization narrative does not tell us everything we need to know about the history of the French empire. Like any empire, the French empire was a murky and frequently sordid business, from the Ancien Régime to the present. Even at its most idealistic, the French empire existed to serve the interests of the Hexagon. Imperial contracting once recognizable as such was always asymmetrical, usually profoundly so. From the mercantile empire of North America and the Caribbean to the Eco and the French presence in the Sahel in the twenty-first century, imperialism was never possible without substantial cooperation from indigenous elites. Powerful people on both sides of imperial contracting always had a stake in the French presence. To the extent that the history of empire is about placing blame, no one pretends that posterity should partition blame equally between colonizer and colonized. The decolonization narrative describes imperialism clearly, but through leaving out important parts of the story.

Indeed, the immense grey zone including colonial oppression and resistance has shaped the analytical rather than the moralistic tone of this book. Attention here has focused more on contextualizing ethical and moral questions than on providing answers to them. Foremost among these questions may be how to right the historical wrongs of French colonialism. Answers in public discourse today include (but are not limited to) reparations, apologies, and "truth commissions." Ironically, no one did more than the French to monetize the righting of historic wrongs, with their insistence on an unprecedented regime of reparations from Germany after World War I. That experience did not bode well for anyone.

How would one begin to monetize the wrongs of empire? What amount of money could right the wrongs of slavery? And exactly who would owe what to whom? Do the descendants of African chiefs owe reparations because of the millions of enslaved they sold to Europeans over centuries? Or what of the billions that postcolonial leaders stole from their own people through their privileged relationships with the French?

One theory of reparations sees them as intrinsically utopian. The wrong of imperialism would be righted, in other words, when the inequalities attributable to imperialism no longer exist. Many people of many shades of opinion have trouble even imagining what such a time would look like. Apologies are scarcely less controversial. To some, apologies constitute an official recognition and acceptance of responsibility for the crimes of history. Others counter, simply put, that apology is talk and talk is cheap. Apology, however theatrical, cannot substitute for restitution. Some counter that an apology itself opens avenues for legal redress. To others, that is precisely the problem.

In the fraught politics of liberal democracies in the new millennium, the ethical questions of empire and post-empire have caused considerable controversy, in France as elsewhere. In February 2005, the National Assembly passed Loi No. 2005-158, which in its original version required public education to "recognize in particular the positive role [*rôle positif*] of the French presence abroad," specifically in North Africa. The law had its origins in the complex politics of the political Right, notably the continued influence of the *pieds noirs* and their children in the Hexagon, and perhaps a belated and oblique attack of conscience over the *harkis*. Predictably enough, the law provoked a firestorm, both in the Hexagon and among postcolonial and anticolonial leaders such as Abdelaziz Bouteflika in Algeria and Aimé Césaire in Martinique. Even though his own minister of defense had introduced the law, President Chirac came to oppose it, somewhat disingenuously on the principle that France should not have the teaching of its history legislated. Of course, one could reasonably ask just what republican history teachers in France had been doing since 1871 if not teaching republican values through history as required by the representatives of the people. Such a position, of course, enabled the president and his ministers to conceal their own views on the matter. The offending passage was suppressed in the final version, in favor of a highly ambiguous instruction that the French presence abroad be taught according to "the place it deserves" (*la place qu'elle mérite*).

The Truth and Reconciliation Commission established in post-apartheid South Africa in 1995 greatly influenced the negotiation of memory throughout the postcolonial world. The commission established a platform wherein perpetrators would publicly confess their misdeeds, and most of the time receive an amnesty in exchange. The commission did not create but certainly fostered an international culture of confession, based on the notion that the path to reconciliation began with exposing the facts and the acceptance of responsibility. Culpability could certainly be bequeathed to posterity. While stopping short of apologies as such, French presidents have embraced the theatrics of admitting all manner of colonial wrongs in which they could have played no personal role because they were too young.

In a speech in Constantine on December 5, 2007, President Nicolas Sarkozy admitted that "the colonial system is by nature unjust, and the colonial system could not survive other than as an enterprise of servitude and exploitation." In a speech on March 16, 2016 commemorating the signing of the Évian Accords, President François Hollande lamented the shameful abandonment of the *harkis*, and pledged greatly enhanced access to the archival record of the war in Algeria. On September 13, 2018, Emmanuel Macron confessed, at last, to the complicity of the French state in the murder of Maurice Audin, which happened in 1957, two decades before Macron's birth. As a presidential candidate in 2017, Macron had called colonialism a "crime against humanity," and had been roundly criticized for doing so by his opponents. Tempers among the electorate had cooled enough for him to win handily anyway.

Reports commissioned by the French state and written by highly prominent panels of scholars have come to constitute their own genre of postcolonial writing. Part exposé and part policy document, these reports share the juridical goal of discovery, of bringing into the public light of day the facts of colonialism and postcolonialism as a prelude to reconciliation. Such reports proliferated in 2021. One such report sought to reveal the extent of the damage caused by French nuclear testing in the South Pacific, and to make viable an existing compensation program.[15] A report on Algeria led by historian Benjamin Stora, himself of Algerian Jewish origin, addressed fraught questions of memory.[16] A team led by Vincent Duclert, an academic and high functionary in the Ministry of Education, investigated the complicity of France in the Rwandan genocide.[17]

---

[15] Moetai Brotherson, Député, Assemblée Nationale, "Rapport fait au nom de la commission de la défense nationale et des forces armées sur la proposition de loi (no. 3966) visant à la prise en charge et à la réparation des conséquences des essais nucléaires français," June 9, 2021.

[16] Benjamin Stora, "Les Questions mémorielles portant sur la colonisation et la guerre d'Algérie" (presidential commission), January 2021.

[17] Commission de recherche sur les archives français relatives au Rwanda et au génocide des Tutsi, *La France Le Rwanda et le génocide des Tutsi*.

Such reports differ from each other in tone and in prescriptions. French Polynesia, of course, remains national territory, and remedies there are matters of domestic law. Any report on Algeria or Rwanda would have to stride across multiple domestic and foreign political minefields. It is difficult to see how any report on such volatile subjects could satisfy everyone. But all these reports sought at least a prelude to closure, to the past becoming the past. Whether investigating a cover-up of radiation poisoning, the whereabouts of disappeared corpses on both sides of the war in Algeria, or just what transpired in the Zone Turquoise of Rwanda, the underlying assumption is that the truth can assist the liberation of oppressed and oppressors. Once this happens, the theory goes, the past can become the past and former colonizers and colonized can begin together to build a better world.

Yet dysfunctional postcolonial habits have proved hard to break. Once in power, Macron's publicly stated views on the colonial past became less repentant. In October 2021, he asked rhetorically in an interview with the newspaper *Le Monde*: "Was there an Algerian nation before French colonization? That is the question."[18] Historians can debate questions that heads of state may wish to avoid. Not content to leave bad enough alone, Macron referred to a "tired politico-military system" in Algeria. While the more serious and immediate issue was a reduction in the number of French visas given to Algerians, President Abdelmadjid Tebboune withdrew the Algerian ambassador, and announced that his return would be "conditioned on complete respect [*respect total*] of the Algerian state." Eventually, of course, the ambassador returned.

France and Algeria seem permanently implicated in each other's destinies. One result of Macron's second visit to Algeria, in August 2022, was the formation of yet another commission, this one comprising both French and Algerian historians, to investigate the colonial past. This was one of several conciliatory gestures, which included a visit by Macron to a disco in Oran to hear *raï* music, about as popular in France as it is in Algeria. Perhaps the heightened need throughout the EU for Algerian hydrocarbons in the wake of the Russian invasion of Ukraine beginning in February 2022 was simply a coincidence; perhaps not.

Clichés can become clichés for a reason. One such comes from William Faulkner's novel *Requiem for a Nun* (1951): "The past is never dead. It is not even past." This book has argued that the French empire is not wholly a matter of history because important aspects of it live on today.

---

[18] www.lemonde.fr/international/article/2021/10/10/algerie-le-president-tebboune-exige-de-la-france-le-respect-total-de-l-etat-algerien-apres-les-propos-d-emmanuel-macron_6097839_3210.html.

The present cannot, by definition, achieve closure. As elsewhere, efforts to achieve closure on the history of the French empire have been more popular in the Hexagon than in its former imperial domains. In the former colonies, the ability to blame the French for almost anything no matter how historically distant is far too valuable a political tool to lay down lightly. Postcolonial leaders from Dessalines at the dawn of the nineteenth century, to the junta claiming to rule Mali today, to the current president of Algeria have understood this very well. Further, there is enough truth in all such claims for anyone to appreciate their political utility. For this reason and many others, France and its former and present overseas domains will continue to shape each other's historical trajectories as far into the future as anyone can see.

Bibliography of Secondary Sources

Agéron, Charles-Robert. *Genèse de l'Algérie algérienne* (Paris: Éditions Bouchène, 2005).

Agéron, Charles-Robert. *Modern Algeria: A History from 1830 to the Present*, Michael Brett, trans. (Trenton, NJ: Africa World Press, 1991 [translated from 9th French edition, 1990]).

Agmon, Danna. *A Colonial Affair: Commerce, Conversion, and Scandal in French India* (Ithaca, NY: Cornell University Press, 2017).

Aldrich, Robert and Connell, John. *France's Overseas Frontier: Départements et Territoires d'Outre-Mer* (New York: Cambridge University Press, 1992).

Aldrich, Robert. *Greater France: A History of French Overseas Expansion* (Houndmills: Palgrave, 1996).

Aldrich, Robert. *Colonialism and Homosexuality* (London: Routledge, 2003).

Aldrich, Robert and McCreery, Cindy, eds. *Crowns and Colonies: European Monarchies and Overseas Empires* (Manchester: Manchester University Press, 2016).

Aldrich, Robert and McCreery, Cindy, eds. *The French Presence in the South Pacific, 1842–1940* (Houndmills: Macmillan, 1990).

Andrew, Christopher M. and Kanya-Forstner, Alexander Sydney. "The French 'Colonial Party': Its Composition, Aims, and Influence, 1885–1914," *The Historical Journal* 14 (1971): 99–128.

Anonymous. "Démographie de l'A.O.F," *Présence Africaine* 15 (1953): 687–82.

Baer, Werner. "The Promoting and the Financing of the Suez Canal," *Business History Review* 30 (1956): 361–81.

Bahar, Matthew R. *Storm of the Sea: Indians and Empires in the Atlantic's Age of Sail* (New York: Oxford Universitiy Press, 2019).

Barbançon, Louis-José. *L'Archipel de fourçats: histoire du bagne de Nouvelle-Calédonie* (Lille: Presses Universitaires du Septentrion, 2003).

Barrows, Leland Conley. "The Merchants and General Faidherbe: Aspects of French Expansion in Senegal in the 1850's," *Revue française d'histoire d'outre-mer* 61 (1974): 236–83.

Barrows, Leland Conley. "Faidherbe and Senegal: A Critical Discussion," *African Studies Review* 19 (1976): 95–117.

Bernard, Odile, Locard, Élizabeth, and Marbotte, Pierre. *Le Chemin de fer du Yunnan: une adventure française en Chine* (Bordeaux: Elytis, 2016).

Bertrand, Christophe, Herbelin, Caroline, and Klein, Jean-François. *Indochine: Des territoires et des hommes, 1856–1956* (Paris: Gallimard/Musée de l'Armée, 2013).

Betts, Raymond F. *Assimilation and Association in French Colonial Theory: 1890–1914* (New York: Columbia University Press, 1961).

Binoche-Guedra, Jacques. "La Représentation parlementaire coloniale (1871–1940)," *Revue Historique* 280 (1988): 521–35.

Bonilla, Yarimar. *Non-Sovereign Futures: French Caribbean Politics in the Wake of Disenchantment* (Chicago: University of Chicago Press, 2015).

Borrel, Thomas, Boukari-Yabara, Amzat, Collombat, Benoît, and Deltombe, Thomas, eds. *L'Empire qui ne veut pas mourir: une histoire de la Françafrique* (Paris: Seuil, 2021).

Bossuat, Gérard. "French Development Aid and Co-operation under de Gaulle," *Contemporary European History* 12 (2003): 431–56.

Bouche, Denise. "Les écoles françaises au Soudan à l'époque de la conquête, 1884–1900," *Cahiers d'Études Africaines* 6 (1966): 228–67.

Bouchène, Abderrahmane, Peyroulou, Jean-Pierre, Tengour, Ounassa Siari, and Thénault, Sylvie, eds. *Histoire de l'Algérie à la période coloniale, 1830–1962* (Paris: Éditions La Découverte, 2012).

Branche, Raphaëlle. *La Torture et l'armeé pendant la guerre d'Algérie, 1954–1962* (Paris: Gallimard, 2001).

Branche, Raphaëlle. *Prisonniers du FLN* (Paris: Payot, 2014).

Brauner, Christina. "To Be the Key for Two Coffers: A West African Embassy to France (1670/1)," *IFRA-Nigeria E-Papers Series*, No. 30 (2013), 1–26. www.academia.edu/3618036/To_Be_the_Key_for_Two_Coffers_A_West_African_Embassy_to_France_1670_1_.

Brett, Michael. "Legislating for Inequality in Algeria: The Sénatus-Consulte of 14 July 1865," *Bulletin of the School of Oriental and African Studies* 51 (1988): 440–61.

Brocheaux, Pierre and Hémery, Daniel. *Indochina: An Ambiguous Colonization, 1858–1954*, Li Lan Dill-Klein, trans. (Berkeley and Los Angeles: University of California Press, 2009 [originally published in French in 1995]).

Brower, Benjamin Claude. *A Desert Named Peace: The Violence of the French Empire in the Algerian Sahara, 1844–1902* (New York: Columbia University Press, 2009).

Buchez, Anne. "La Fin de la presence française en Syrie: de la crise de mai 1945 au depart des dernières troupes étrangères," *Relations Internationales* 122 (2005): 17–32.

Bullard, Alice. *Exile to Paradise: Savagery and Civilization in Paris and the South Pacific, 1790–1900* (Stanford, CA: Stanford University Press, 2000).

Burbank, Jane, and Cooper, Frederick. *Empires in World History: Power and the Politics of Difference* (Princeton, NJ: Princeton University Press, 2010).

Burnard, Trevor and Garrigus, John. *The Plantation Machine: Atlantic Capitalism in French Saint-Domingue and British Jamaica* (Philadelphia: University of Pennsylvania Press, 2016).

Butler, Shirley Oakes. "Owning Antarctica: Cooperation and Jurisdiction at the South Pole," *Journal of International Affairs* 31 (1977): 35–51.

Byrne, Jeffrey James. *Mecca of Revolution: Algeria, Decolonization, and the Third World Order* (New York: Oxford University Press, 2016).

Campbell, Gwyn. "Gold Mining and the French Takeover of Madagascar, 1883–1914," *African Economic History* 17 (1988): 99–126.

Candar, Gilles. "La Gauche colonial en France socialistes et radicaux (1885–1905)," *Mille neuf cent: Revue d'histoire intellectuelle* No. 27 (2009): 37–56.

Cantier, Jacques and Jennings, Eric, eds. *L'Empire coloniale sous Vichy* (Paris: Odile Jacob, 2004).

Carroll, Christina. "Imperial Ideologies in the Second Empire: The Mexican Expedition and the Royaume Arabe," *French Historical Studies* 42 (2019): 67–100.

Castaldo, André. "Les 'Questions ridicules': la nature juridique des esclaves de culture aux Antilles," *Bulletin de la Société d'Histoire de la Guadeloupe*, No. 157 (2010): 55–144.

Chafer, Tony. *The End of Empire in French West Africa: France's Successful Decolonization* (Oxford: Berg, 2002).

Chafer, Tony, Cumming, Gordon D., and van der Velde, Roel. "France's Intervention in Mali and the Sahel: A Historical Institutionalist Perspective," *Journal of Strategic Studies* 43 (2020): 482–507.

Clancy-Smith, Julia, ed. *North Africa, Islam and the Mediterranean World: From the Almoravids to the Algerian War* (London: Frank Cass, 2001).

Cohen, William B. *Rulers of Empire: The French Colonial Service in Africa* (Stanford, CA: Hoover Institution Press, 1971).

Cole, Jennifer. *Forget Colonialism?: Sacrifice and the Art of Memory in Madagascar* (Berkeley: University of California Press, 2001).

Cole, Joshua. *Lethal Provocation: The Constantine Murders and the Politics of French Algeria* (Ithaca, NY: Cornell University Press, 2019).

Collins, James B. *The State in Early Modern France* (Cambridge: Cambridge University Press, 1995).

Commission de Recherche sur les archives françaises relatives au Rwanda et au génocide des Tutsi. *La France, Le Rwanda et le génocide des Tutsi (1990–1994)* (Paris: Armand Colin, 2021).

Conklin, Alice L. *A Mission to Civilize: The Republican Idea of Empire in France and West Africa, 185–1930* (Stanford, CA: Stanford University Press, 1997).

Connell, John and Aldrich, Robert. *The Ends of Empire: The Last Colonies Revisited*, 2nd ed. (London: Palgrave Macmillan, 2020).

Connelly, Matthew J. *A Diplomatic Revolution: Algeria's Fight for Independence and the Origins of the Post-Cold War Era* (New York: Oxford University Press, 2002).

Cooke, Nola, "Early Nineteenth-Century Vietnamese Catholics and Others in the Pages of the *Annales de la propagation de la Foi*," *Journal of Southeast Asian Studies* 35 (2004): 261–85.

Cooper, Frederick. *Citizenship between Empire and Nation: Remaking France and French Africa, 1945–1960* (Princeton: Princeton University Press, 2014).

Cooper, Frederick and Stoler, Ann L. "Introduction: Tensions of Empire: Colonial Control and Visions of Rule," *American Ethnologist* 16, No. 4 (1989): 609–621.

Coquery-Vidrovitch, Catherine. *Le Congo au temps des grandes concessionnaires, 1898–1930* (Paris: Mouton & Co., 1972).

Coursier, Alain. *Faidhere, 1818–1889: du Sénégal à l'Armée du Nord* (Paris: Talladier, 1989).

Cunningham, Michele. *Mexico and the Foreign Policy of Napoleon III* (Houndmills: Palgrave, 2001).

Daughton, James P. *An Empire Divided: Religion, Republicanism, and the Making of French Colonialism, 1880–1914* (New York: Oxford University Press, 2006).

Daughton, James P. *In the Forest of No Joy: The Congo-Océan Railroad and the Tragedy of French Colonialism* (New York: W.W. Norton & Company, 2021).

Davis, Diana K. *Resurrecting the Granary of Rome: Environmental History and French Colonial Expansion in North Africa* (Athens, OH: Ohio University Press, 2007).

Desan, Suzanne, Hunt, Lynn, and Nelson, William Max, eds. *The French Revolution in Global Perspective* (Ithaca, NY: Cornell University Press, 2013).

Devillers, Philippe and Lacouture, Jean. *End of a War: Indochina, 1954* (New York: Frederick A. Praeger, 1969 [originally published in French in 1959]).

Dubois, Laurent. *Avengers of the New World: The Story of the Haitian Revolution* (Cambridge, MA: Belknap Press, 2004).

Dunstan, Sarah C. *Race, Rights and Reform: Black Activism in the French Empire and the United States from World War I to the Cold War* (Cambridge: Cambridge University Press, 2021).

Duyker, Edward. *Dumont d'Urville: Explorer and Polymath* (Honolulu: University of Hawai'i Press, 2014).

Eccles, William J. *The French in North America*, revised ed. (East Lansing, MI: Michigan State University Press, 1998).

Echenberg, Myron. *Colonial Conscripts: The Tirailleurs Sénégalais in French West Africa, 1857–1960* (Portsmouth: Heinemann, 1991).

Einaudi, Jean-Luc. *Octobre 1961: un massacre à Paris* (Paris: Fayard, 2001).

Erforth, Benedikt. "Multilateralism as a Tool: Exploring French Military Cooperation in the Sahel," *Journal of Strategic Studies* 43 (2020): 560–82.

Finch, Michael P. M. *A Progressive Occupation?: The Gallieni-Lyautey Method and Colonial Pacification in Tonkin and Madagascar, 1885–1900* (Oxford: Oxford University Press, 2013).

Fischer, David Hackett. *Champlain's Dream* (New York: Simon & Schuster, 2008).

Fogarty, Richard S. *Race and War in France: Colonial Subjects in the French Army, 1914–1918* (Baltimore, MD: Johns Hopkins University Press, 2008).

Fogarty, Richard. "The French Empire," in Robert Gerwarth and Erez Manela, eds., *Empires at War, 1911–1923* (Oxford: Oxford University Press, 2014), 109–129.

Forrest, Alan. *The Death of the French Atlantic: Trade, War, and Slavery in the Age of Revolution* (New York: Oxford University Press, 2020).

Forster, Colin. *France and Botany Bay: The Lure of a Penal Colony* (Melbourne: Melbourne University Press, 1996).

Förster, Stig, Mommsen, Wolfgang J., and Robinson, Ronald, eds. *Bismarck, Europe, and Africa: The Berlin Africa Conference of 1884–1885 and the Onset of Partition* (Oxford: Oxford University Press, 1988).

Foster, Elizabeth A. *Faith in Empire: Religion, Politics, and Colonial Rule in French Senegal, 1880–1940* (Stanford, CA: Stanford University Press, 2013).

Fradera, Josep M. "L'esclavage et la logique constitutionelle des empires," *Annales. Histoire, Sciences Sociales* 63 (2008): 533–60.

Frémaux, Jacques. *Les Colonies dans la grande guerre: combats et épreuves des peoples d'outre-mer* (Paris: Soteca, 14–18 Éditions, 2006).

Fuglestad, Finn. *Slave Traders by Invitation: West Africa's Slave Coast in the Precolonial Era* (Oxford: Oxford University Press, 2018).

Fuligni, Bruno. "Le Retour de Blaise Diagne," *Humanisme* 3 (2014): 80–85.

Gasse, Michel. *Tahiti 1914: le vent de guerre* (Lardy: À la frontière, 2009).

Gastaut, Yvan. *L'Immigration et l'opinion en France sous la Ve République* (Paris: Éditions du Seuil, 2000).

Gelvin, James L. *Divided Loyalties: Nationalism and Mass Politics in Syria at the Close of Empire* (Berkeley: University of California Press, 1998).

Gershovich, Moshe. *French Military Rule in Morocco Colonialism and Its Consequences* (London: Frank Cass, 1999).

Girollet, Anne. "La Politique colonial de la IIe République : un assimilationnisme modéré," *Revue française d'histoire d'outre-mer* 85 (1998): 71–83.

Goebel, Michael. *Anti-Imperial Metropolis: Interwar Paris and the Seeds of Third World Nationalism* (New York: Cambridge University Press, 2015).

Greer, Allan. *The People of New France* (Toronto: University of Toronto Press, 1997).

Guignard, Didier. "Conservatoire ou révolutionnaire? Le sénatus-consulte de 1863 appliqué au régime foncier d'Algérie," *Revue d'Histoire du XIXe Siècle* 41 (2010): 81–95.

Gunn, Geoffrey C. "'Mort pour la France': Coercion and Co-option of 'Indochinese' Worker-Soldiers in World War One," *Social Scientist* 42 (2014): 63–84.

Gunn, Geoffrey C. *Ho Chi Minh in Hong Kong: Anticolonial Networks, Extradition and the Rule of Law* (Cambridge: Cambridge University Press, 2021).

Hamilton, Andrew. "God in Samoa and the Introduction of Catholicism," in Phyllis Herda, Michael Reilly, and David Hilliard, eds. *Vision and Reality in Pacific Religion: Essays in Honour of Neil Gunson* (Christchurch: Macmillian Brown Centre for Pacific Studies, 2005), 87–105.

Harris, Richard Colebrook. *The Seigneurial System in Early Canada* (Madison, WI: University of Wisconsin Press, 1966).

Harrison, Nicholas. *Our Civilizing Mission: The Lessons of Colonial Education* (Liverpool: Liverpool University Press, 2019).

Headrick, Rita. *Colonialism, Health and Illness in French Equatorial Africa, 1885–1935* (Atlanta, GA: African Studies Association Press, 1994).

Heffernan, Michael J. "The Parisian Poor and the Colonization of Algeria During the Second Republic," *French History* 3 (1989): 377–403.

Hollister, C. Warren. *Medieval Europe: A Short History*, 7th ed. (New York: McGraw Hill, 1994), 188.

House, Jim and Macmaster, Neil. *Paris 1961: Algerians, State Terror, and Memory* (New York: Oxford University Press, 2006).

Hulot, Fréderic, et al. *Les Chemins de fer de la France d'Outre-mer*, 2 vols. [vol. 1 by Frédéric Hulot (vol. 2 by Pascal Bejui, Luc Raynaud, and Jean-Pierre Verger-Larrouy)] (Chanac: La Régordane, 1992).

Jacquin, Philippe. *Les Indiens blancs: Français et Indiens en Amérique du Nord (XVIe su XVIIIe siecle)* (Paris: Payot, 1987).

Jennings, Eric T. *Vichy in the Tropics: Pétain's National Revolution in Madagascar, Guadeloupe, and Indochina, 1940–1944* (Stanford, CA: Stanford University Press, 2001).

Jennings, Eric T. *Imperial Heights: Dalat and the Making and Undoing of French Indochina* (Berkeley: University of California Press, 2011).

Jennings, Eric T. *Free French Africa in World War II: The African Resistance* (New York: Cambridge University Press, 2015).

Jennings, Eric T. *Escape from Vichy: The Refugee Exodus to the French Caribbean* (Cambridge, MA: Harvard University Press, 2018).

Johnson, G. Wesley, Jr. *The Emergence of Black Politics in Senegal: The Struggle for Power in the Four Communes, 1900–1920* (Stanford, CA: Stanford University Press, 1971).

Jones, Hilary. *The Métis of Senegal: Urban Life and Politics in French West Africa* (Bloomington, IN: Indiana University Press, 2013).

Kanya-Forstner, Alexander Sydney. *The Conquest of the Western Sudan: A Study in French Military Imperialism* (Cambridge: Cambridge University Press, 1969).

Karabell, Zachary. *Parting the Desert: The Creation of the Suez Canal* (New York: Alfred A. Knopf, 2003).

Keith, Charles. *Catholic Vietnam: A Church from Empire to Nation* (Berkeley: University of California Press, 2012).

Khoury, Philip S. *Syria and the French Mandate: The Politics of Arab Nationalism* (Princeton: Princeton University Press, 1987).

Klein, Martin A. *Slavery and Colonial Rule in French West Africa* (Cambridge: Cambridge University Press, 1998).

Kohl, Herbert. *Should We Burn Babar?: Essays on Children's Literature and the Power of Stories* (New York: The New Press, 1995).

Koller, Christia, "The Recruitment of Colonial Troops in Africa and Asia and their Deployment in Europe during the First World War," *Immigrants & Minorities* 26 (2008): 111–33.

Lacouture, Jean. *Ho Chi Minh: A Political Biography*, Peter Wiles, trans. (New York: Random House, 1968 [originally published in French in 1967]).

Larcher, Silyane. "L'Égalité divisée: la race au cœur de la ségrégation juridique entre citoyens de la métropole et citoyens des 'veilles colonies' après 1848," *Le Mouvement Social* 3 (2015): 137–58.

Law, Robin. *The Slave Coast of West Africa, 1550–1750: The Impact of the Atlantic Slave Trade on an African Society* (Oxford: Clarendon Press, 1991).

Law, Robin. "The Slave Trade in Seventeenth-Century Allada: A Revision," *African Economic History* 22 (1994): 59–92.

Le Cour Grandmaison, Olivier. *De l'indigénat: Anatomie d'un "monstre" juridique: le droit colonial en Algérie et dans l'Empire français* (Paris: Zones, 2010).

Lecocq, Baz. "Mali: This Is Only the Beginning," *Georgetown Journal of International Affairs* 14 (2013): 59–69.

Légier, Henri Jacques. "Institutions municipales et politique coloniale : les communes de Sénégal," *Revue française d'histoire d'outre-mer* 55 (1968): 414–64.

Levallois, Michel. *Ishmaÿl Urbain, 1812–1884: une autre conquête de l'Algérie* (Paris: Maisonneuve et Larose, 2001).

Lewis, Mary Dewhurst. *Divided Rule: Sovereignty and Empire in French Tunisia, 1881–1938* (Berkeley: University of California Press, 2014).

Lorcin, Patricia M. E., ed. *Algeria and France, 1800–2000: Identity, Memory, Nostalgia* (Syracuse: Syracuse University Press, 2006).

Lorcin, Patricia M. E. *Imperial Identities: Stereotyping, Prejudice and Race in Colonial Algeria* (London: I.B. Tauris, 1995).

Lorin, Amaury. *Paul Doumer, gouverneur général de l'Indochine, 1897–1902* (Paris: L'Harmattan, 2004).

Loualich, Fatiha. "Les esclaves noirs à Alger (fin du XVIIIᵉ-début XIXᵉ siècle: de l'esclave à l'affranchi, vers une relation d'allégeance," *Mélanges de l'École française de Rome* 115 (2003): 513–522.

Lunn, Joe. *Memoirs of the Maelstrom: A Senegalese Oral History of the First World War* (Portsmouth: Heinemann, 1999).

McDoom, Omar Shahubudin. *The Path to Genocide in Rwanda: Security, Opportunity, and Authority in an Ethnocratic State* (New York: Cambridge University Press, 2020).

McDoom, Omar Shahubudin. "Contested Counting: Toward a Rigorous Estimate of the Death Toll in the Rwandan Genocide," *Journal of Genocide Research* 22, No. 1 (2020): 83–93.

McDougall, James. *A History of Algeria* (Cambridge: Cambridge University Press, 2017).

McShea, Bronwen. *Apostles of Empire: The Jesuits of New France* (Lincoln, NE: University of Nebraska Press, 2019).

Malye, François and Stora, Benjamin. *François Mitterrand et la guerre d'Algérie* (Paris: Calmann-Lévy, 2010).

Mann, Gregory. "What was the Indigénat?: The 'Empire of Law' in French West Africa," *Journal of African History* 50 (2009): 331–53.

Marr, David G. *Vietnamese Anticolonialism, 1885–1925* (Berkeley: University of California Press, 1971).

Marshall, D. Bruce. *The French Colonial Myth and Constitution-Making in the Fourth Republic* (New Haven, CT: Yale University Press, 1973).

Matot, Bertrand. *Fort Bayard: quand la France vendait son opium* (Paris: Éditions François Bourin, 2013).

Mélia, Jean. *L'Algérie et la guerre, 1914–1918* (Paris: Plon, 1918).

Merleau, Marc. *Des Pionniers en extrême-orient: Histoire de la Banque de l'Indochine (1875–1975)* (Paris: Fayard, 1990).

Meyer, Jean, Tarrade, Jean, Rey-Goldzeiguer, Annie, and Thobie, Jacques. *Histoire de la France coloniale des origines à 1914* (Paris: Armand Colin, 1991).

Michel, Marc. *Les Africains et la Grande Guerre: l'appel à l'Afrique, 1914–1918* (Paris: Karthala, 2003).

Mintz, Sidney. *Sweetness and Power: The Place of Sugar in Modern History* (New York: Viking Penguin, 1985).

Morton, Patricia A. *Hybrid Modernities: Architecture and Representation at the 1931 Colonial Exposition, Paris* (Cambridge, MA: MIT Press, 2000).

Murray-Miller, Gavin. "A Conflicted Sense of Nationality: Napoleon III's Arab Kingdom and the Paradoxes of French Multiculturalism," *French Colonial History* 15 (2014): 1–38.

Mussard, Christine. "Réinventer la commune?: genèse de la commune mixte, une structure administrative inédite dans l'Algérie coloniale," *Histoire@ Politique*, 3 (2015): 93–108.

Nélias, Thierry. *Algérie la conquête, 1830–1870: comment tout a commencé* (Paris: Vuibert, 2022).

New York Times (2003). "Cécile de Brunhoff, 99, Creator of Babar," April 8. www.nytimes.com/2003/04/08/books/cecile-de-brunhoff-99-creator-of-babar .html.

Noirel, Gérard. *The French Melting Pot: Immigration, Citizenship, and National Identity*, Geoffroy de Laforcade, trans. (Minneapolis, MN: University of Minnesota Press, 1996 [originally published in French in 1988]).

Ozavci, Ozan. *Dangerous Gifts: Imperialism, Security, and Civil Wars in the Levant, 1798–1864* (Oxford: Oxford University Press, 2021).

Peabody, Sue. "'A Dangerous Zeal': Catholic Missions to Slaves in the French Antilles," *French Historical Studies* 25 (2002): 53–90.

Péan, Pierre. *L'Homme de l'ombre: éléments d'enquête autour de Jacques Foccart, l'homme le plus mystérieux et le plus puissant de la Ve République* (Paris: Fayard, 1990).

Pedersen, Susan. *The Guardians: The League of Nations and the Crisis of Empire* (New York: Oxford University Press, 2015).

Pigeaud, Fanny and Sylla, Ndongo Samba. *L'Arme invisible de la Françafrique: une histoire du franc CFA* (Paris: La Découverte, 2018).

Piquet, Caroline. *La Compagnie du canal de Suez: une concession française en Égypte (1888–1956)* (Paris: Presses de l'Université Paris-Sorbonne, 2008).

Piton, Florent. *Le Génocide des Tutsi de Rwanda* (Paris: La Découverte, 2018).

Pitts, Jennifer. *A Turn to Empire: The Rise of Imperial Liberalism in Britain and France* (Princeton: Princeton University Press, 2005).

Podruchny, Carolyn. *Making the Voyageur World: Travelers and Traders in the North American Fur Trade* (Lincoln, NE: University of Nebraska Press, 2006).

Porch, Douglas. *The Conquest of Morocco* (New York: Alfred A. Knopf, 1983).

Porch, Douglas. "Bugeaud, Gallieni, Lyautey: The Development of French Colonial Warfare," in Peter Paret, ed., *Makers of Modern Strategy: From Machiavelli to the Nuclear Age* (Princeton: Princeton University Press, 1986), 376–407.

Porch, Douglas. *The French Secret Services from the Dreyfus Affair to the Gulf War* (New York: Farrar Straus and Giroux, 1995).

Porch, Douglas. *Counterinsurgency: Exposing the Myths of the New Way of War* (New York: Cambridge University Press, 2013).

Price, Roger. *The French Second Empire: An Anatomy of Political Power* (Cambridge: Cambridge University Press, 2004).

Prochaska, David. *Making Algeria French: Colonialism in Bône 1870–1920* (Cambridge: Cambridge University Press, 1990).

Provence, Michael. *The Great Syrian Revolt and the Rise of Arab Nationalism* (Austin, TX: University of Texas Press, 2005).

Rahal, Malika. *Algérie 1962: une historie populaire* (Paris: La Découverte, 2022).

Ramsey, Jacob. "Extortion and Exploitation in the Nguyễn Campaign against Catholicism in 1830s–1840s Vietnam," *Journal of Southeast Asian Studies* 35 (2004): 311–328.

Randrianja, Solofo. *Société et luttes anticoloniales à Madagascar de 1896 à 1946* (Paris: Karthala, 2001).

Randrianja, Solofo and Ellis, Stephen. *Madagascar: A Short History* (Chicago: University of Chicago Press, 2009).

Reudy, John. *Land Policy in Colonial Algeria: The Origins of the Rural Public Domain* (Los Angeles: Near Eastern Center, University of California, 1967).

Rey-Goldzeiguer, Annie. *Aux Origines de la guerre d'Algérie, 1940–1945: de Mers-el-Kébir aux massacres du nord-constantinois* (Paris: Éditions la Decouverte, 2002).

Rid, Thomas. "Razzia: A Turning Point in Modern Strategy," *Terrorism and Political Violence*, 21 (2009): 617–35.

Roberts, Richard. *Two Worlds of Cotton: Colonialism and the Regional Economy of French Soudan, 1800–1946* (Stanford, CA: Stanford University Press, 1996).

Rousseau, Jean-François. "An Imperial Railway Failure: The Indochina-Yunnan Railway, 1898–1941," *Journal of Transport History* 35 (2014): 1–17.

Saada, Emmanuelle. *Empire's Children: Race, Filiation, and Citizenship in the French Colonies*, Arthur Goldhammer, trans. (Chicago: University of Chicago Press, 2012 [original published in French in 2007]).

Sanchez, Jean-Lucien. "Les 'Incorrigibles' du bagne colonial de Guyane: genèse et application d'une catégorie pénale," *Genèses*, No. 91 (2013): 71–95.

Saul, Samir. "Politique nationale du pétrole, sociétés nationales et 'pétrole franc'," *Revue Historique*, No. 638 (2006): 355–88.

Schmidt, Nelly. *Victor Schœlcher et l'abolition de l'esclavage* (Paris: Fayard, 1994).

Scott, James C. *Weapons of the Weak: Everyday Forms of Peasant Resistance* (New Haven, CT: Yale University Press, 1985).

Scott, Joan Wallach. *Only Paradoxes to Offer: French Feminists and the Rights of Man* (Cambridge, MA: Harvard University Press, 1997).

Sèbe, Berny. *Heroic Imperialists in Africa: The Promotion of British and French Colonial Heroes, 1870–1939* (Manchester: Manchester University Press, 2013).

Sessions, Jennifer E. *By Plow and Sword: France and the Conquest of Algeria* (Ithaca, NY: Cornell University Press, 2011).

Sessions, Jennifer E. "Colonizing Revolutionary Politics: Algeria and the French Revolution of 1848," *French Politics, Culture & Society* 33 (2015): 75–100.

Shawcross, Edward. *France, Mexico and Informal Empire in Latin America, 1820–1867* (London: Palgrave Macmillan, 2018).

Shaxson, Nicholas. *Poisoned Wells: The Dirty Politics of African Oil* (New York: Palgrave, 2007).

Singer, Barnett. "Lyautey: An Interpretation of the Man and French Imperialism," *Journal of Contemporary History* 26 (1991): 131–57.

Slama, Alain-Gérard. *La Guerre d'Algérie: histoire d'une déchirure* (Paris: Gallimard, 1996).

Slobodkin, Yan. *An Empire of Hunger: A History of Famine and French Colonialism, 1867–1945* (Ithaca, NY: Cornell University Press, 2023).

Smith, Leonard V., Audoin-Rouzeau, Stéphane and Becker, Annette. *France and the Great War, 1914–1918* (Cambridge: Cambridge University Press, 2003).

Smith, Leonard V. *Sovereignty at the Paris Peace Conference of 1919* (Oxford: Oxford University Press, 2018).

Sondhaus, Lawrence. *The Great War at Sea: A Naval History of the First World War* (Cambridge: Cambridge University Press, 2014).

Spet, Lt. Col. Stéphane. "Operation Serval: Analyzing the French Strategy against Jihadists in Mali," *ASPJ Africa & Francophonie* (3rd Quarter 2015): 66–79. www.airuniversity.af.edu/Portals/10/ASPJ_French/journals_E/Volume-06_Issue-3/spet_e.pdf.

Spieler, Miranda. *Empire and Underworld: Captivity in French Guiana* (Cambridge, MA: Harvard University Press, 2012).

Spieler, Miranda. "Slave Flight, Slave Torture, and the State: Nineteenth-Century French Guiana," *French Politics, Culture, & Society* 33 (2015): 55–74.

Stora, Benjamin and Daoud, Sakya. *Ferhat Abbas: un utopie algérienne* (Paris: Denoël, 1995).

Stora, Benjamin. *Histoire de l'Algérie coloniale, 1830–1954*, 2nd ed. (Paris: La Découverte, 2004).

Stovall, Tyler. "The Color Line behind the Lines: Racial Violence in France during the Great War," *American Historical Review* 103 (1998): 737–69.

Stovall, Tyler. *Transnational France: The Modern History of a Universal Nation* (Boulder, CO: Westview Press, 2015).

Stovall, Tyler. *White Freedom: The Racial History of an Idea* (Princeton: Princeton University Press, 2021).

Strauss-Schom, Alan. *The Shadow Emperor: A Biography of Napoléon III* (New York: St. Martin's Press, 2018).

The Economist (2022). "Wagner, Worse Than It Sounds," January 15. www.economist.com/middle-east-and-africa/2022/01/15/small-bands-of-mercenaries-extend-russias-reach-in-africa.

Thobie, Jacquess, Meynier, Gilbert, Coquery-Vidrovitch, Catherine, and Agéron, Charles Robert. *Histoire de la France coloniale, 1914–1990* (Paris: Armand Colin, 1990).

Thomas, Martin, ed. *The French Colonial Mind*, 2 vols. (Omaha, NE: University of Nebraska Press, 2011).

Thompson, Elizabeth F. *Colonial Citizens: Republican Rights, Paternal Privilege, and Gender in French Syria and Lebanon* (New York: Columbia University Press, 2000).

Thompson, Elizabeth F. *How the West Stole Democracy from the Arabs: The Syria Arab Congress of 1920 and the Destruction of Its Historic Liberal-Islamic Alliance* (New York: Atlantic Monthly Press, 2020).

Thornton, John K. *A Cultural History of the Atlantic World, 1250–1820* (New York: Cambridge University Press, 2012).

Tocqueville, Alexis de. *Writings on Empire and Slavery*, Jennifer Pitts, ed. and trans. (Baltimore, MD: Johns Hopkins University Press, 2003).

Todd, David. *A Velvet Empire: French Informal Empire in the Nineteenth Century* (Princeton, NJ: Princeton University Press, 2021).

Tombs, Robert. "How Bloody Was the Semaine Sanglant of 1871: A Revision," *The Historical Journal* 55 (2012): 679–704.

Tønnesson, Stein. *Vietnam 1946: How the War Began* (Berkeley: University of California Press, 2010).

Toth, Stephen A. *Beyond Papillon: The French Overseas Penal Colonies, 1854–1952* (Omaha, NE: University of Nebraska Press, 2006).

Trang, Phan T. H. "Paul Doumer: aux origins d'un grand projet, le chemin de fer transindochinois," *Histoire, économie & société* 30 (2011): 114–40.

Tronchon, Jacques. *L'Insurrection malgache de 1947: essay d'interprétation historique* (Paris: François Maspero, 1974).

Vaillant, Janet G. *Black, French, and African: A Life of Léopold Sédar Senghor* (Cambridge, MA: Harvard University Press, 1990).

Velmet, Aro. *Pasteur's Empire: Bacteriology and Politics in France, Its Colonies, and the World* (New York: Oxford University Press, 2020).

Verschave, François-Xavier. *La Françafrique: le plus long scandale de la république* (Paris: Éditions Stock, 1998).

Verschave, François-Xavier. *Noir Silence: Qui arrêtera la Fraçafrique?* (Paris: Les Arènes, 2000).

Wanquet, Claude. *La France et la première abolition de l'esclavage: le cas des colonies orientales, Île de France (Maurice) et La Réunion* (Paris: Karthala, 1998).

Weber, Jacques. *Pondichéry et les comptoirs de l'Inde après Dupleix: la démocratie au pays des castes* (Paris: Éditions Denoël, 1996).

Weil, Patrick. *How to Be French: Nationality in the Making since 1789*, Catherine Power, trans. (Durham, NC: Duke University Press, 2008 [originally published in French in 2002]).

Weinstein, Brian. *Éboué* (New York: Oxford University Press, 1972).

Weiss, Gillian. *Captives and Corsairs: France and Slavery in the Early Modern Mediterranean* (Stanford, CA: Stanford University Press, 2011).

White, Owen. *Children of the French Empire: Miscegenation and Colonial Society in French West Africa, 1895–1960* (Oxford: Clarendon Press, 1999).

White, Owen and Daughton, James P., eds. *In God's Empire: French Missionaries and the Modern World* (New York: Oxford University Press, 2012).

White, Richard. *The Middle Ground: Indians, Empires, and Republics in the Great Lakes Region, 1650–1815*, Twentieth Anniversary Edition (New York: Cambridge University Press, 2011 [originally published 1991]).

White, Sam. *A Cold Welcome: The Little Ice Age and Europe's Encounter with North America* (Cambridge, MA: Harvard University Press, 2017).

Wilder, Gary. *The French Imperial Nation-State: Negritude and Colonial Humanism between the World Wars* (Chicago, IL: University of Chicago Press, 2005).

Wilder, Gary. *Freedom Time: Negritude, Decolonization, and the Future of the World* (Durham, NC: Duke University Press, 2015).

Wong, John Yue-wo. *Deadly Dreams: Opium, Imperialism, and the Arrow War (1856–1860) in China* (Cambridge: Cambridge University Press, 1998).

Wood, Laurie M. *Archipelago of Justice: Law in France's Early Modern Empire* (New Haven, CT: Yale University Press, 2020).

Wood, Peter H. "LaSalle: Discovery of a Lost Explorer," *American Historical Review* 89 (1984): 294–323.

Wright, Gordon. *France in Modern Times*, 5th ed. (New York: W.W. Norton, 1995).

Wyrtzen, Jonathan. *Morocco: Colonial Intervention and the Politics of Identity* (Ithaca, NY: Cornell University Press, 2015).

Xu, Guoqi. *Strangers on the Western Front: Chinese Workers in the Great War* (Cambridge, MA: Harvard University Press, 2011).

Zimmerman, Sarah J. *Militarizing Marriage: West African Soldiers' Conjugal Traditions in the Modern French Empire* (Athens, OH: Ohio University Press, 2020).

Index

Printed in Great Britain
by Amazon

26818361R00139